Richard Bean

PLAYS THREE

HARVEST
IN THE CLUB
THE ENGLISH GAME
UP ON ROOF

OBERON BOOKS
LONDON

This collection first published in 2009 by Oberon Books Ltd
521 Caledonian Road, London N7 9RH
Tel: 020 7607 3637 / Fax: 020 7607 3629
e-mail: info@oberonbooks.com
www.oberonbooks.com

Harvest first published in 2005
In The Club first published in 2007; second edition (revised), 2008
The English Game first published in 2008

Richard Bean is hereby identified as author of these plays in accordance with section 77 of the Copyright, Designs and Patents Act 1988. The author has asserted his moral rights.

A catalogue record for this book is available from the British Library.

ISBN: 978-1-84002-913-0

Cover image by Mark Simmonds

Printed in Great Britain by CPI Antony Rowe, Chippenham.

Contents

Introduction

I used to share a flat with Richard Bean. During that happy period I noticed a number of things about him.

There was his inflexibility in the matter of which brand of teabags to buy. There was the apparent psychological imperative always to be part-way through some elaborate DIY project. There was the ever-present possibility of a brilliantly funny remark at any moment. Perhaps the most striking thing about my former flatmate, however, was how very difficult it was to predict what his opinion would be on any given issue. Think how rare that is. During his routine shouting at the radio or TV news I realised that Richard thinks about things with very few preconceptions. He follows the logic of the matter and lets it take him where it goes, rather than where he wants to get to. This can make him awkward to argue with, since lazy thinking and ill-considered opinion are the rational tools in general use.

I mention this partly as a general observation but partly too by way of explaining how he came to write his mid-career masterpiece, *Harvest*, a play for the hyper-metropolitan Royal Court theatre with a farmer as its hero – and not even an organic farmer at that. It's almost like a dare and I've come to understand that this slight suggestion of confrontation is part of Richard's process. He's not comfortable with the current orthodoxy and incapable of keeping quiet about it.

One of the things Richard does supremely well in his work is the passage of time. Few modern playwrights take the passing decades so confidently in their stride. *Harvest* covers virtually the whole of a preternaturally extended lifespan and takes us through personal, social and political evolutions in a fascinating and moving way. It makes us think about farming and food in ways which most of us won't have considered – properly and without ignorant sentimentality – whilst, at the same time, telling an endlessly involving family saga and introducing us to a series of wonderfully realised and unforgettable characters. I think it's among the best two or three new plays of the last ten years. And of course, and this hardly needs saying, it's also sensationally funny.

In the Club was the product of a very particular commission. Richard was asked to write a farce against the setting of the politics of the European Union. That may sound like the winner of a competition to come up with the least promising comic premise imaginable but, in fact, the complications of sex and the complications of Euro horse-trading turn out to resonate very nicely together. The Bean angle seems to suggest that questions of national politics and questions of sexual relations have more in common than generally acknowledged; that Turkey's desire for European accession and my eagerness to go to bed with you are analogous and involve the same kinds of negotiation.

The play features a bluntly outspoken Yorkshireman who keeps coming out with awkward and uncomfortable remarks about corruption and shady deals which the smoother, more political elements prefer to skate over – no doubt a character plucked entirely from the air.

Typically, the play manages to be moving even in the midst of its most absurd flights of farce. There's always a beating heart in Richard's work, even at his apparently bluffest.

The third play in this volume has been thirty years or more in the preparation. My first meeting with Richard was on a cricket field near Oldham. We were introduced as people who were bound to get on so, of course, it took months before we could even be civil. Since that day, sometime in the mid 1980s, we've played for the same team Sunday after Sunday, summer after summer, hamstring injury after knee strain. What is it with cricket and the theatre? It's not just the famous lovers of the game; the Becketts, the Pinters, the Hares. There's also a whole network of teams featuring actors, writers and directors fighting it out on playing fields around London to the accompaniment of conspicuously well projected appealing. Perhaps it's something to do with the way the game nurses individual performance in an ensemble context. Or perhaps it's simply the excuse to sit about talking entertaining rubbish. Of course, everyone's always saying, 'you should write a play about this.' And *The English Game* is that play.

It's also the third of Richard's plays to feature the word 'England' or its cognates in the title. He's much concerned with Englishness, our author. He thinks it's still a legitimate subject for enquiry rather than a slightly embarrassing relic from a pre-post-modern world. Although the play darkens towards the end and begins to confront some of our most pressing societal problems, it contains a sun-filled tribute to a certain kind of week-end as well as a superb range of characters; most of them based pretty closely on people I know and one of them, in fact, on me. We're all there – only funnier.

Up on Roof is a sort of homecoming play. It was a commission from Hull Truck and is based on a historic incident in Hull Prison. When I saw the play produced in Hull, I felt as though I'd been transported to an earlier time when audiences felt they owned the stage, the play and the theatre. Every local reference or gag was greeted with show-stopping ovations and I saw several people who didn't look as though they were likely to survive the titanic paroxysms of laughter shaking them to their roots.

It's typical of Richard's work in that it's hysterically funny, well researched, thought provoking and ultimately tender. Of course, you may not look for those qualities in a play. Better look elsewhere.

Christopher Campbell
Deputy Literary Manager
National Theatre

HARVEST

Characters

ALBERT

WILLIAM

MAM

PARKER

MAUDIE

LORD PRIMROSE AGAR

STEFAN

LAURA

WARCLIFFE

ATS OFFICER

ALAN

TITCH

VET

BLUE

DANNY

YOUNG AGAR

Harvest was first performed at The Royal Court Jerwood Theatre Downstairs, Sloane Square, London on 2 September 2005, with the following cast:

MAM/ATS OFFICER   Sharon Bower

LAURA   Siân Brooke

WARCLIFFE/LEWIS   Mike Burnside

WILLIAM   Matthew Dunster

ALBERT/ALAN   Gareth Farr

DANNY   Craig Gazey

MAUDIE   Jane Hazlegrove

TITCH   Adrian Hood

VET   Clare Lams

PARKER/BLUE   Paul Popplewell

STEFAN   Jochum Ten Haaf

LORD PRIMROSE AGAR/YOUNG AGAR   Dickon Tyrrell

Director Wilson Milam
Designer Dick Bird
Lighting Designer Paul Keogan
Sound Designer Gareth Fry

1914 THE STALLION MAN

(*1914 August. Mid-morning. The big farmhouse table is set running from stage left to stage right. Enter WILLIAM. He is nineteen, and handsome with refined features. He is dusty from the harvest, and wears sacking around his legs which has become wet. He runs upstairs, and once in his room takes a letter from his trousers, reads it and then hides it. He runs downstairs. As he is half way down the stairs ALBERT enters. He is eighteen, WILLIAM's brother, and broader with rougher features. He is also dusty, with the same sacking on the legs. ALBERT looks at WILLIAM suspiciously. ALBERT quenches his thirst from a jug of water. He is rough and functional in his manners.*)

WILLIAM: 'ot.

ALBERT: Aye.

   (*Pause. WILLIAM quenches his thirst using a cup.*)

   Where d'yer go on yer 'lowance?

WILLIAM: Mind yer own.

ALBERT: Spittle Garth meadow?

WILLIAM: Mebbe. Mebbe not.

   (*Pause. WILLIAM pours some stew from a pot, cuts some bread, sits and begins to eat.*)

ALBERT: He found out worr it was.

WILLIAM: Aye?

ALBERT: Aye.

   (*ALBERT runs wet hands through his hair, and spits noisily into the sink. He ladles himself some stew, cuts some bread, sits and starts to eat. WILLIAM looks to ALBERT for further enlightenment but gets none.*)

WILLIAM: What worr it?

ALBERT: A vixen.

WILLIAM: Aye?

ALBERT: Aye.

WILLIAM: I said it worr a fox all along. I said to him, I said 'that's the work of either one of two beasts. A fox or a Bengal Tiger.'

ALBERT: Aye?

WILLIAM: Aye. D'he kill it?

ALBERT: Aye.

15

WILLIAM: Good.

(*Pause.*)

ALBERT: They say the Kaiser's gorr a withered arm.

WILLIAM: 'They say'.

ALBERT: His left arm. He can't even shek hands with it.

WILLIAM: No-one sheks wi' the left hand. Norr even Kings.

ALBERT: They've given him a little cane to carry. So he's gorr an excuse not to have to use it. Bastard.

(*Pause. They eat.*)

WILLIAM: The problem we've gorr is that we both wanna go. But we can't both go. Worr I'm saying is we have to find a way of deciding who's gooin. Me or you.

ALBERT: Dad's dead.

WILLIAM: I had noticed.

ALBERT: I'm the youngest. Eldest son gets the farm. You get the farm, so you stay. All around here it's the youngest what is gooin. Sid's gooin.

WILLIAM: Mad Sid or Little Sid?

ALBERT: They wouldn't have Mad Sid.

WILLIAM: What's wrong with Mad Sid?

ALBERT: Teeth.

WILLIAM: Aye, he's got terrible teeth. I didn't know they was choosey. So Little Sid's gooin is he?

ALBERT: Aye. He's learning hissen some French. For the girls. They eat a lot of red meat don't they, French girls. They say it meks 'em alles ready for loving.

WILLIAM: Little Sid's an expert on French women is he? Every day he drives a cart from Driffield to Beverley and back again. When he gets adventurous, when he wakes up in the morning and thinks he's Captain Fucking Cook, he goes as far as Hull.

(*Pause.*)

ALBERT: We could have a fight.

WILLIAM: You'd win. Look, you're good with the 'osses. Most things I do, Mam can do, but she don't like the 'osses over much.

ALBERT: They're onny 'osses, you don't have to like 'em. You like Brandy.

WILLIAM: Brandy's a beautiful good natured 'oss. I an't gorr a problem with her. It's the others.

ALBERT: So what yer saying? I stay and work the farm cos I'm good with 'osses and keep it gooin so you can go off to France and have yer fun and when you come back yer can tek it over again beein as you's the awldest.

WILLIAM: Yer mek it sound like summat scheming. I don't see the justice in me missing out on gooin ovverseas just cos I'm twelve month aulder 'an you.

(*Pause.*)

ALBERT: Worrabout your project?

WILLIAM: This war'll all be ovver well afore the spring and spring is the right time for me project.

ALBERT: Why won't yer tell no-one worr it is?

WILLIAM: Cos it's a bloody secret project.

ALBERT: Go on, tell us.

WILLIAM: No, I'm not telling yer.

ALBERT: It's pigs innit?

WILLIAM: Who towld yer?

ALBERT: Mam. I don't like pigs.

WILLIAM: Pigs is onny mathematics. Yer not saying 'I don't like pigs', yer saying 'I don't like mathematics'.

(*Pause.*)

ALBERT: As I see it, we both wanna go, so – [we both go and –]

WILLIAM: – We're gooin round the houses here!

(*Pause.*)

Did yer book the stallion man?

ALBERT: Aye. He's on his way through to Langtoft. He's staying there tonight. Should be here soon.

WILLIAM: Where'd he stay last night?

ALBERT: Rudston.

WILLIAM: Different bed every night eh. You'd like that would yer?

ALBERT: Aye. They say the stallion man has fun in about equal measure to that stallion of his. They say he's fathered –

WILLIAM: – 'They say'. Who are these they?

ALBERT: You should see his clothes. He's all rigged out for the music hall. Breeches, yellow waistcoat, bowler hat. Like a bloody Lord. Cane with a brass knob on the end.

WILLIAM: Aye, well we all know what that's for.

ALBERT: (*Laughing.*) Aye.

WILLIAM: He's a nobody. He's gorr a big 'oss and the gift of the gab. Any fool could be a stallion man. You could be a stallion man.

ALBERT: Oh now – [come on it ain't that easy.]

WILLIAM: – Get yersen a big 'oss and a fancy hat. You're good with 'osses. Then you'd get yer travel. Different bed every night.

ALBERT: To be a proper stallion man you godda have summat…I dunno…summat –

WILLIAM: – indefinable.

ALBERT: Aye.

WILLIAM: Personality.

ALBERT: Aye.

WILLIAM: Well you an't got that.

(*Pause.*)

Will Brandy stand for that stallion of his?

ALBERT: Aye, she's 'ot. Should be a beautiful 'oss out of our Brandy and that big Percheron of his. Pedigree.

(*ALBERT finishes his stew and licks the plate. He then lights his pipe. WILLIAM finishes his stew, cuts himself a piece of bread and wipes his plate with the bread and eats it.*)

Bit fancy.

WILLIAM: I'm courting ain't I.

ALBERT: Aye, you've been behaving summat a long way off the regular all harvest.

WILLIAM: That'll be the courting.

ALBERT: (*After a decent draw on his pipe.*) I 'ad me eye on Maudie.

WILLIAM: We bin through this afore.

ALBERT: I thought you might go for that sister of hers.

WILLIAM: I like Maudie. Kate's a bit of an 'andful. Why don't you have a try at Kate?

ALBERT: (*Knowing he's no chance.*) Oh aye.

(*WILLIAM lights a cigarette.*)

If you're courting Maudie, you'd berrer stay, and I'll go.

WILLIAM: We've onny just started courting.

ALBERT: (*Standing.*) I'm not courting no-one at all. That's all I'm saying. You are. And I'm the youngest. Everywhere round here it's the youngest what is gooin.

(*Enter MAM carrying a dead chicken by the legs. She sticks it in a copper boiler, still holding it by the legs, and starts to count to thirty in her head.*)

WILLIAM: Stew was grand Mam, ta.

ALBERT: Why yer killed that hen?

WILLIAM: Not right, Mam, eating chicken. What are we? The royal family?

MAM: She's stopped laying.

WILLIAM: Tough but fair.

MAM: Gerrin' an egg out of her is like winter waiting for spring.

(*Horses hooves are heard in the fold yard. ALBERT stands and opens the door.*)

WILLIAM: There's yer stallion man.

MAM: I'm not having him in the house. Not with them 'come to bed' eyes of his. (*Laughs.*)

(*To ALBERT.*) Will your Brandy stand for that stallion?

ALBERT: Aye, she's 'ot.

(*ALBERT leaves closing the door behind him.*)

MAM: What have I been hearing about you William Harrison?

WILLIAM: I built me own spacecraft and went off to the moon. There in't nowt much up there burr a load of brambles. I filled up fifteen Kilner jars. Yer can mek yer bramble jelly now. Mek sure yer wash the dust off fost. Might be electrical.

MAM: You're walking out with Maudie.

WILLIAM: That's so typical of round here, yer mek the effort of gerrin to the moon and back, without suffering a scratch, and no-one's bloody interested.

MAM: Language!

(*MAM pulls the chicken out of the pan and immediately starts plucking the chicken.*)

I don't approve of you and Maudie.

WILLIAM: Oh right then, I'll call it off.

MAM: Yer using Maudie to get to that sister of her's. I know you. It's Kate yer got yer eye on. I know men. I'm never wrong.

WILLIAM: Yer wrong this time.

MAM: Have yer sorted out which one of yer's gooin?

WILLIAM: As it stands we're both gooin.

MAM: Tut! That can't be, yer know that.

WILLIAM: Try telling him that.

(Enter ALBERT followed by Company Quartermaster SERGEANT PARKER. PARKER is a man in his thirties in army uniform.)

ALBERT: It in't the stallion man. It's the army.

(PARKER shakes hands with everyone.)

PARKER: Company Quartermaster Sergeant Parker. Beautiful day, ma'am.

MAM: Yer requisitioning?

PARKER: You've heard have you?

MAM: Aye.

PARKER: I'll just talk you through the powers bestowed on me –

MAM: – We know yer powers. Just gerr on with it.

PARKER: *(Laughs.)* I like doing business in Yorkshire. At the end of the day, when all's said and done, there's a lot of time saved, you know what I mean. Have you got your harvest in?

WILLIAM: The corn, aye.

PARKER: What are you, here?

WILLIAM: Corn, barley, we're using peas as a break. Sheep. Chickens. We gorr eight Holsteins an'all.

PARKER: Holsteins?

WILLIAM: Cows.

PARKER: You were getting a bit technical with me there, with your 'Holsteins'. 'Cows', I've heard of. *(Laughs.)* I'm from Befnal Green, we fink milk was born in a bo"le. *(Laughs.)* Nice up this way. Wouldn't mind –

MAM: – It's August.

PARKER: Yes, I can imagine.

WILLIAM: Are you gonna tek the cows?

PARKER: We're an army, not a dairy. (*Laughs.*) What do you have in the way of horses?

WILLIAM: Six.

ALBERT: One of them's lame.

(*WILLIAM glances at ALBERT. PARKER notices this.*)

PARKER: Sorry, ma'am, would you have a drink of water for a not-so-young man fighting the Germans. (*Laughs.*) It's a hot one.

MAM: Lemonade? I med it mesen.

PARKER: Ooh! Smashing. We need a hundred and sixty thousand horses by next Tuesday. So far I've got seven. (*Laughs.*) And I've already come out in a rash. (*Laughs.*) (*MAM gives him a glass of lemonade. He takes a long swig.*) Marvellous. Have you two lads enlisted? My colleague, Major Caddick, is at the corn exchange in Driffield from eight tomorrow morning.

WILLIAM: We know. We'll be there.

PARKER: Ooh! Keen! Don't get to thinking it's automatic. There's a medical you know.

MAM: Onny one of 'em's gooin. Me husband's bin dead ower ten year.

PARKER: The youngest then, that's the form.

ALBERT: That's me.

PARKER: Anyhow, I'm not men, I'm horses. Can all your horses draw pole wagons?

WILLIAM: Aye.

PARKER: Lovely.

ALBERT: It don't tek long to train an 'oss up to draw a pole wagon.

PARKER: Maybe, but we're a bit pushed for time at the moment what with the Kaiser strolling through Belgium.

MAM: What d'yer do if yer tek any of our 'osses?

PARKER: You'll get a ticket. Every ticket's got a picture of the King on it.

(*PARKER takes out his ticket book and flicks it.*)

So you've got six horses.

WILLIAM: We need at least a pair to keep going, for the ploughing.

PARKER: We're not going to take them all, don't worry. The army needs feeding same as everyone.

ALBERT: We gorr a mare that's 'ot, she's gerrin serviced this afti. We've booked and paid for the stallion man. She's onny used for breeding. She's not been schooled to draw a pole wagon.

PARKER: And she'll be the lame one is she?

ALBERT: Aye.

Pause.

PARKER: Look son, it's not an easy job this. I try and do it with a smile and a laugh, but at the end of the day you're looking at the government. Your old mum, excuse me ma'am, gave me lemonade not water. She understands who I am, and what I can do. I can take whatever I like, and all I have to do is give you a ticket. I can take your cows, your pigs, your chickens, your pole wagons, your salt and pepper pots, (*Laughs.*) your doors, your wallpaper, your walls. So don't start getting clever with me son, because it's not even lunchtime yet and I've got a full book of tickets. Your brother here said 'all' your horses can draw a pole wagon. All. Let's go have a look at the beauties, eh. (*ALBERT and PARKER leave, closing the door behind him.*)

MAM: He'll leave us a pair.

WILLIAM: Aye, Bess and that auld bastard Punch.

MAM: He'll tek one look at Brandy and that'll be that.

WILLIAM: Aye.

MAM: D'yer hear him? He said the form is – it's the youngest what goes. You're the eldest. By rights it's you what should be staying.

WILLIAM: Aye, well mebbe I'm tired of doin what's right.

MAM: Why'd'yer wanna go?

WILLIAM: Mother, I've exhausted these fields. I'm a man and I ant never done nowt. Seen nowt, done nowt, been nowhere. Me whole life's been these eighty acres of chalk and clay.

MAM: Yer got yer pigs.

WILLIAM: The pigs is onny an idea.

MAM: This farm needs ideas.

WILLIAM: There int nowt clever about pigs. It's nowt but mathematics.

MAM: Nowt difficult for you mebbe.

WILLIAM: I'll be back afore the spring when all that starts up. (*Horses hooves are heard in the fold yard. WILLIAM goes over to the window and holds back the nets.*)

MAM: What's he tekkin?

WILLIAM: Venus. He's tekkin the harness an'all. (*WILLIAM lets the nets drop back.*)

MAM: What's this with Maudie? Yer should be walking out with that sister of hers. I was hoping Albert might tek a fancy to Maudie. She's right for him, Maudie She's plain.

WILLIAM: I'll tell her when I see her. Mam. I like Maudie. I find Maudie calm. I find Kate alarming. Self-admiring.

MAM: Aye, that's why you're right for each other. (*Horses hooves are heard, and a horse's neighing. WILLIAM goes over to the window and looks through the nets.*) Saturn?

WILLIAM: Aye. (*WILLIAM lets the nets drop again.*)

MAM: Aye, well, they're a pair. Don't tek this the wrong way. I don't want neither of yer to go but you love, you've got Eskritt blood. Albert's gorr his father's. Don't go to the army now, let Albert go, and you can leave here when he gets back if yer must.

WILLIAM: If Dad were alive we'd both be gooin.

MAM: If you were truly courting Maudie you wunt want to be going. You're the eldest, no-one would blame you staying, you wunt get white feathered. Mebbe yer think gooin away will give yer that summat extra, the uniform, the glory, your absence. That summat extra to sway Katie.

WILLIAM: It in't Katie what interests me! It's Maudie. I love Maudie!

MAM: Yer love her?

WILLIAM: Aye.

MAM: Well, well, I never.

(*WILL moves over and sits at the table. He seems annoyed with the table for some reason.*)

WILLIAM: Why do we have the table like this?

MAM: Like what?

WILLIAM: Running this way. It feels all wrong.

MAM: It's alles been there. I'm used to it.

WILLIAM: Aye, but what I'm saying is it'd be better if we turned it round. If someone's at the sink, and someone wants to get past, it's impossible. The table's in the way. And look, there's a shadow. I'm casting a shadow.

MAM: Sit t'other side then.

WILLIAM: That wouldn't feel right though would it.

(*Horses hooves are heard in the fold yard.*)

MAM: Shurrup wi' yer nonesense and go tell me what 'oss that is.

(*WILLIAM goes over to the window.*)

WILLIAM: Ha! You'll never believe it, he's tekkin Punch. Ha, ha! Never mind cows he can't know nowt about 'osses neither. Ah, well, s'pose they could eat the auld bugger.

MAM: What's that? Three.

WILLIAM: Aye. He's gorra leave us a pair. So he can only tek one more.

(*Extended silence. WILLIAM stays watching at the window.*)

MAM: Yer might get killed. Have you thought about that?

WILLIAM: There's an angel for farmers.

MAM: That's yer dad's talk. And he's dead.

(*Horses hooves are heard on the yard. WILLIAM looks over to his mother and says nothing, but lets the net curtain fall back into place. His mother goes over, pushes the curtain to one side.*)

MAM: Lord God Almighty! She's a beautiful 'oss. That'll kill our Albert. They'll need hossmen. Mebbe Albert can go with her.

(*Enter ALBERT. His eyes are watering. ALBERT sits, and puts his head in his hands.*)

WILLIAM: Is he done? He's leaving us a pair is he?

(*ALBERT doesn't answer. Enter PARKER.*)

PARKER: All done. Everything tickety boo.

(*He starts writing out tickets on the kitchen table. Still standing. He glances at* ALBERT.)

I've taken four horses ma'am and four sets of harness. I've left you a good pair for your ploughing.

(*He stamps the ticket. When he finishes a ticket he stamps it with a government stamp.*)

Shire mare. Venus.

(*He stamps the ticket.*)

Shire mare. Saturn.

(*He stamps the ticket.*)

(*Doubtful.*) Clydesdale gelding. Punch. He's a bit old. Alright is he?

WILLIAM: Punch? Aye, he's a smashing 'oss. He'll win the war for yer.

PARKER: (*Doubtful.*) Lovely. Right.

(PARKER *stamps the ticket.*)

Percheron mare. She's a beauty. Kaw! Have you ever showed her?

WILLIAM: Aye. She's won a couple.

PARKER: Not surprised. Lovely looking horse. What d'yer call her? He wouldn't tell me.

WILLIAM: Brandy.

PARKER: Brandy? Lovely! It's that dapple grey isn't it. (*Laughs.*)

(ALBERT *starts sobbing.*)

If I had a penny for every shilling I'd put on a grey, I'd be laughing. (*Laughs.*)

MAM: You're laughing anyhow.

PARKER: Indeed.

(PARKER *stamps the ticket.* ALBERT *is now crying. No-one attends to him.*)

After this war is won, if she comes back, you can tear up the tickets, if she don't come back, them'll be worth something. Good day to you ma'am.

(PARKER *gives the tickets to* MAM. *They all listen to* ALBERT *crying.*)

If it's any use to you, seeing as how one of your lads has to stay on the farm – and I can say this because I know war Mrs Harrison, I was in South Africa and I saw a few things

25

that I can only describe as impolite – on behalf of Major
Caddick, God and the King, in that order – that lad of
yours there is a fine strapping lad, but he's no use to us.
(*PARKER exits closing the door behind him. ALBERT continues his
sobbing. MAM looks over to WILLIAM who looks away.*)
(*To black.*)

1934 ADAM AND EVE

(*1934. March. Early evening, and not yet dark. The farmhouse kitchen. Enter MAUDIE, she is carrying a freshly killed rabbit. She hangs the rabbit on a nail from a beam and swiftly pulls down on the rabbit's fur and skins it completely in one go. She unhooks the rabbit and begins to prepare it. Enter ALBERT with a shotgun. He goes to the gun cabinet to get more cartridges.*)

MAUDIE: Wet.

ALBERT: Aye.

MAUDIE: It's been fair siling down all day. How many more have yer lost then?

ALBERT: Tither.

MAUDIE: What were you doing? Sleeping? That's more than one fox then. You don't lose three lambs to the one fox.

ALBERT: Aye.

MAUDIE: Yer wanna tek William up there with you. He'd be alright in the hut.

ALBERT: I don't want him up theere with me.

MAUDIE: He's gorra good eye. He can handle a rifle, he's had the training. You can't hit a barn door at ten paces.

ALBERT: I don't want his rifle and I don't want his company. (*Beat.*) Did he do it? What he said he was gonna do?

MAUDIE: Aye.

ALBERT: Oh bugger. Has the squire bin round?

MAUDIE: Not yet.

(*Enter WILLIAM. He is in a wheelchair which is a comfy chair set on a bogie of pram wheels. He has lost both legs. He has with him stashed in his chair a pad of paper, a book, and a newspaper, a scarf, a hat. The chair is more a 'station' than a chair. He smokes a pipe.*)

ALBERT: What you bin doing?

WILLIAM: Chasing rabbits.

ALBERT: I've heard what you done. Did anyone see yer?

WILLIAM: Aye. It'll be all round Yorkshire bi now. Bin losing lambs?

ALBERT: Aye.

MAUDIE: There's no use offering, he don't want yer company.

AGAR: Ah!

ALBERT: This new German fellah looks like a bit of a rum un.

AGAR: (*Mimes putting ingredients into a mixing bowl and mixing them.*) Socialism. Nationalism. Sentimentality. (*He makes the sound of an explosion.*)

MAUDIE: Aye, well war's always good for cereal prices.

ALBERT: Onny time we int swamped by imports eh!

WILLIAM: That hunt of yours in't doing much good round Kilham top.

AGAR: Losing lambs eh?

ALBERT: I'll spend the night in the hut again with the gun.

AGAR: It's a wonderful thing for a man isn't it. A night in a hut.

ALBERT: Aye. I bin up there all day.

AGAR: What did you say?

ALBERT: I've been up there all day sir. In the hut.

(*AGAR frowns, puzzled, finishes his whiskey, and claps his hands.*)

(*To WILLIAM.*) What have you done with my dairy herd?

WILLIAM: I took 'em all to Scarborough for the day out. You shoulda seen their little faces. None of them had ever seen the ocean.

AGAR: Where are they?

WILLIAM: Where's our rent for the field?

(*WILLIAM picks out a diary from the side of the chair and reads from it.*)

October, no rent, spoke to Sammy Ellwood, he ses, 'I'll talk to the young squire.' November, no rent, spoke to Sammy, 'I'll talk to the young squire'. December, no rent. Rode up to the house, asked to speak to the young squire, tawld he was in London meeting his publishers. February, no rent, spoke to Sammy Ellwood, he said to me – 'fuck off you'.

AGAR: I'll have a word with Mr Ellwood.

WILLIAM: Five months rent. Five shillings. Pay up and I'll tell yer where I've put yer cows.

(*AGAR counts out five shillings. He makes to give the money to WILLIAM.*)

Maudie's in charge of money.

(*MAUDIE takes it, counts it, and nods approval to WILLIAM.*)
Yer cows are at Fimber. Rogersons. I don't understand yer
mentality. Yer've got forty thousand acres across Yorkshire
but yer choose to rent a field from us. It in't cos yer need to
rent, it's cos yer want the field. If yer had a scheme to tek
our best grazing and not pay us and thereby bust us it ain't
gonna work. Yer grandad lost Kilham Wold Farm in a bet,
fair and square, it's all legal, I seen the mandate in writing.

AGAR: My grandfather had a character flaw.

WILLIAM: He was a drunk and a gambler. And worst of all a
loser.

ALBERT: We're not for sale sir. We're doing alright. We gerr a
monthly milk cheque. I'm thinking very long term.
(*AGAR stands and makes to go.*)

AGAR: You don't have a son.
(*Pause.*)
Did you buy anything today in Beverley? At the farm sale?

ALBERT: A cake crusher.

AGAR: I thought I'd seen you there. You looked right
through me.
(*Standing.*) Pappachakwoquai! Innuit for 'may your
ancestors walk beside you'. Goodnight Mrs Harrison.

MAUDIE: Goodnight sir.

WILLIAM: If this farm were still in the estate, what would you
be doing on it?

AGAR: Pigs.
(*AGAR and ALBERT leave. ALBERT closes the door behind him.*)

MAUDIE: You had no right to talk to him like that! Ever since
you come back from abroad you bin as lippy as I don't
know what.

WILLIAM: Abroad? I dint go on the grand tour you know.
(*Enter ALBERT.*)

MAUDIE: (*To ALBERT.*) What the bloody hell's this about
Beverley?

ALBERT: I went to a farm sale.

MAUDIE: You told me you were up on the tops! You lied to me
Albert Harrison!

ALBERT: I went to Beverley to a farm sale to try and pick up a cake crusher.

MAUDIE: We've already gorr a cake crusher!

ALBERT: It's on its last legs.

MAUDIE: I found yer a second hand cake crusher onny a minute down the road.

ALBERT: It's onny Beverley I an't bin to bloody London.

MAUDIE: Stop cursing in my kitchen! So you went to Beverley to gerr a cake crusher?

ALBERT: Aye.

WILLIAM: So did you get one then?

ALBERT: Aye. I gorr a couple.

MAUDIE: Two!?

WILLIAM: Why d'yer buy two?

ALBERT: It was a bargain. The second one.

MAUDIE: Why dint yer just buy the second one then?

ALBERT: I'd already bought the fost one.

WILLIAM: That's three bloody cake crushers we got now!

MAUDIE: We've onny got twennie five head of cattle! We've hardly need of one cake crusher!

WILLIAM: If you buy the cake crusher down the road we'll have four!

MAUDIE: There's farm sales every week by the end of the month we could have a dozen cake crushers!

WILLIAM: Start a cake crusher museum.

ALBERT: (*He bangs the gun on the table.*) We needed a cake crusher! I went to Beverley and got one.

(*Pause.*)

WILLIAM: Two.

(*MAUDIE laughs.*)

Don't gerr him mardy, he's gorra gun in his hand.

MAUDIE: You're up to summat!

ALBERT: (*To MAUDIE.*) You! Leave us a minute.

MAUDIE: No! If it's farm talk I'm having some of it.

ALBERT: It's not farm talk! It's brothers! You're my wife! Leave us be for a while.

WILLIAM: Go on love, go and give yer chickens a bollocking.

MAUDIE: Aye, I will, might gerr a bit of respect.

(She slams the door behind her. ALBERT struggles and fiddles. WILLIAM lets him struggle.)

WILLIAM: Some women, I've heard, do what yer tell 'em without any fuss.

(Pause.)

ALBERT: I've done some wrong, some evil. Don't tell Maudie will yer?

WILLIAM: You bin to see a tart in Beverley?

ALBERT: No. I dint go straight to the farm sale. I went up to the hospital.

WILLIAM: Yer what?

ALBERT: Aye. I climbed ovver the 'ospital fence, went through the gardens. I knew where to go cos that's where Katie had her little Laura. There was a side door open and I went in and it's just after dinner time and I teks me hat off, and smiles at the mothers like I'm a dad, and I just have to gerrout cos I can feel me face just burning up, and I'm in a corridor and there's a side room and I can see there's a bain in theere and the mother's asleep. Little lass, couldn't be more than sixteen, bonny but summat common about her. Mebbe she wan't wed and that's why she were in that room, I dunno. I have a look see if the bain is a boy. He is. I pick him up and he dunt cry or owt. I walk out.

WILLIAM: Get yersen a drink.

(ALBERT stands and pours himself a whiskey, then sits.)

Don't worry about me.

ALBERT: Aye. Sorry.

(ALBERT stands and pours a drink for WILLIAM. Then sits and drinks.)

Never been one for this stuff. It's alright. I picked the bain out the cot…and headed straight out across the gardens with 'im. I gorr half way across and there's this nurse, a sister I think, bit aulder, sitting on a bench and she stands and ses 'hello'. Just like that. 'Hello'. And I ses 'how do?' – and she ses 'd'yer want me to tek that bain off yer hands?' and I ses 'Aye.' and I gives her the little bugger and she looks at me and it was like them auld eyes of hers is looking deep down into my soul, and me face is burning up again, and I climb the fence and I run to the hoss and I'm away.

(*ALBERT drinks.*)

I can see why some folk can get accustomed to this stuff.

(*He tops up his drink, and drinks again.*)

He was a fine, dark looking boy, despite his mother. I think he woulda ended up being a good, big lad. Aye, well. I don't think she was a country lass though. She'd be Beverley or Hull mebbe.

WILLIAM: Yer picked a bain up, walked ten yards, and give it to a nurse.

ALBERT: The Good Lord's seen everything.

WILLIAM: Yer intent was badly wrong, but at the end of the day, when all's said and done, the world is the same today, as it was yesterday.

ALBERT: Fastest way of losing this land is having no-one to work it.

WILLIAM: That's beyond argument.

ALBERT: That's what the squire was talking about. 'You ain't gorr a son.' Did yer heard him?

WILLIAM: They cut me legs off Albert, not me ears.

ALBERT: There int no more Harrisons.

WILLIAM: There's Laura.

ALBERT: (*As if it's been said before.*) She's not an Harrison.

WILLIAM: She's our niece. She's fifteen now and is still showing a liking for the life. She's up from Hull every holiday. (*Beat.*) Are yer still doing it?

ALBERT: There dunt seem no reason no more. She bin fifteen years wi me and she ant bin nowhere near carrying. I think the Lord has seen fit to punish me for my sinning as a young man.

WILLIAM: Maudie might be barren.

ALBERT: I can feel the sin within me. The Lord gave me Maudie, when by rights she was yourn. I'm in the same position as Adam's brother.

WILLIAM: Adam who?

ALBERT: Adam and Eve.

WILLIAM: He didn't have a brother.

ALBERT: That's me point. Mebbe he did, but if the brother din't have a son he wouldn't gerr in the story, d'yer see? We need a son. Do yer understand worr I'm saying?

WILLIAM: I do.

ALBERT: Sometimes I wish Grandad Harrison hadn't med that wager with the Squire. He's med a rod for the back of every Harrison following him. You know worr I'm asking don't yer?

WILLIAM: Aye.

(*ALBERT stands and picks up the shotgun.*)

ALBERT: Yer loved her once. I'm off up the tops.

WILLIAM: Tek the rifle.

(*ALBERT swaps the shotgun for the rifle.*)

You won't have spoken to Maudie then?

ALBERT: No. I thought I'd leave that one to you.

(*ALBERT leaves taking the rifle. WILLIAM sits and thinks. There is the hint of a smile. Enter MAUDIE.*)

MAUDIE: Ha! He's tekken the rifle then eh?

WILLIAM: Aye.

MAUDIE: How much did you drink in the end?

WILLIAM: The fox'll be safe purr it that way.

MAUDIE: What are you looking at?

WILLIAM: You.

MAUDIE: You're terrible you.

WILLIAM: Aye. You make me terrible.

MAUDIE: Shh!

WILLIAM: I like lambing time. Every year I like lambing more and more.

MAUDIE: He might not be gone.

(*She checks by looking through the window.*)

WILLIAM: Do you like lambing?

(*She kisses him on the top of the head.*)

MAUDIE: It's me favourite time of the whole year.

(*To black.*)

1944 THE NAZI

(*1944. April. Afternoon, still light, but beginning to fade. The nets are covered with blackout curtains, open. A wireless sits on the sideboard. LAURA sits up in bed. She is aged about twenty-five and dressed in farm gear.*)

LAURA: Do all Germans fuck like that?

(*STEFAN sits up. He is a young German of about twenty-five.*)

STEFAN: Only the Luftwaffe.

(*They kiss. They both begin to dress. She in overalls and he in Prisoner of War issue overalls with a big yellow circle on the back.*)

Laura, I want to sleep here tonight. In this bed.

LAURA: Don't be daft!

STEFAN: I will go back to the camp, sign in, and sneak out when it is dark.

LAURA: They'll shoot yer.

STEFAN: In two years now they have shot no-one.

LAURA: Worr I mean't is – Uncle Albert'll shoot yer.

STEFAN: Why doesn't he like me Laura?

LAURA: You're German, and we're at war with Germany.

STEFAN: Ah, I see. Is that it do you think?

(*STEFAN snuggles up to her.*)

LAURA: He wun't shoot yer just cos yer German, but a German fucking his niece in his house – then he'd not go looking for any other excuses. Everything's black and white for Uncle Albert. He never liked me mam, so he dunt like me. Uncle Will likes yer.

STEFAN: You smell of paraffin. Nothing, even if I live to be a hundred and ten will smell more beautiful than paraffin.

LAURA: Who in their right mind would wanna live to an hundred and ten?

STEFAN: Anyone who is a hundred and nine.

(*They go downstairs.*)

LAURA: My great Uncle Tom lived to one hundred and seven.

STEFAN: So that's true then?! Uncle Will told me he won the farm in a bet. He wagered the squire that he would live longer than the squire's dog?

LAURA: They had a legal mandate drawn up. The dog was a puppy and Great Uncle Tom was ninety-four.

(*They kiss. He undoes her top. The drone of a low flying aircraft approaching. STEFAN dives under the table.*)

STEFAN: Heinkel…H E. One eleven. Laura!

(*LAURA goes to the doorway. She undoes her top and shows her brassiered bust to the aircraft as it roars overhead. She laughs.*)

LAURA: He's waving! Ha, ha!

(*STEFAN from under the table.*)

STEFAN: Don't wave back! He'll either bomb us or land. Get under the table!

(*LAURA crawls under the table. They kiss.*)

LAURA: You can't stay the night, Steffie.

STEFAN: I am crazy for you. Like a bat in a dairy.

LAURA: (*Laughs.*) Like a bat in a dairy? (*Laughs.*) What?

STEFAN: Confused, lost in love. Like a bat in a dairy.

(*They kiss.*)

Why do they have the table here?

LAURA: It's a kitchen table. In England the English put their kitchen tables in the kitchen.

STEFAN: No, I mean it would obviously be better if it ran at ninety degrees to the window then the light from the window would run down the length of the table.

LAURA: God you're lovely! Say something else like that. I love it. Makes me want you again.

STEFAN: All I'm saying is that logically such a big table should be a utility and not an obstruction. If anyone is standing at the sink then a whole section of the room is technically closed off.

LAURA: It's always been here, as long as I can remember. Come on.

(*LAURA goes for his trousers and starts to unbutton his flies. They break as WILLIAM enters in a wheelchair.*)

WILLIAM: Haende Hoch!

STEFAN: (*Through embarrassed laughter.*) Good afternoon. Mr Harrison.

WILLIAM: Anyone we know?

LAURA: We were hiding from the bomber.

WILLIAM: Since when has hiding involved jumping up and
down and flashing yer tits? I suppose yer under the table
cos there's the whole committee standing around down
Spittle Garth meadow. Where yer normally go.
(*Looks exchanged between STEFAN and LAURA.*)
I an't told no-one. That's where we used to go, in me hey
day. Aye. Lovely. Grass. Get the sun on yer back.

STEFAN: I'm sorry Mr Harrison.

(*WILLIAM lights his pipe.*)

WILLIAM: Don't you dare say sorry sunshine. You're the best
bloody thing ever happened round here. I wish you'd bin
shot down in nineteen twenny two.

STEFAN: Thank you. I like the work.

WILLIAM: British airmen in prisoner of war camps in Germany
spend all their time digging tunnels and dressing up in
women's clothing. I often ask myself 'why dunt our Stefan
try and escape?'.

STEFAN: I am very happy here.

WILLIAM: Fed and watered, and the best looking lass in
Yorkshire running around and knackering you out every
time yer on yer 'lowance. Happy? Yer should be bloody
delirious.

STEFAN: I like farming.

WILLIAM: Farming's alright if yer just wanna gerra bit involved
but it's commitment that this farm needs.

LAURA: (*To STEFAN.*) It's an old Harrison saying. Egg and bacon
breakfast. The chickens are involved but the pigs are
committed.

STEFAN: I spoke to the Colonel about the huts.

WILLIAM: Aye.

STEFAN: He said you must know something that he doesn't.
About the war being nearly over.

WILLIAM: What's he think all these Yanks are doing legging
it up and down our hills? Training for Hide and Seek?
They'll soon be running up the beaches of Belgium. The
Yanks have done it again. Turned up just in time to pick
up all the dead men's caps. I'll buy the huts off the army if

the price is right and I'll even dismantle them mesen cos Albert won't have owt to do with it.

LAURA: How will you do that Uncle?

WILLIAM: When I say me I mean him.

STEFAN: You mean I'd dismantle, and...mantle those sheds all on my own?

WILLIAM: Mantle's not a word I know about.

LAURA: Erect.

STEFAN: Erect?

WILLIAM: Aye. Erect.

STEFAN: They are very big sheds. It's not straightforward. It would be a lot of work.

WILLIAM: I'd be paying yer then.

STEFAN: What do you want them for?

WILLIAM: Me secret project.

LAURA: Pigs.

STEFAN: Our huts are very cold in winter.

WILLIAM: I'll double line 'em on the inside.

LAURA: (*To STEF.*) You'll double line 'em on the inside.

STEFAN: Not with wood. They chew on wood. Pigs.

WILLIAM: I'll find summat that in't wood, that they don't like chewing on and I'll double line 'em with that.

LAURA: (*To STEF.*) You'll double line 'em with that.

WILLIAM: Anyhow, pigs is a secret project. Now listen up you two – it's gerrin ugly down there.

LAURA: Is that the War Rag committee then?

WILLIAM: Aye.

LAURA: Are they gonna take the farm off us Uncle?

WILLIAM: Norr if I can help it.

(*To STEFAN.*) I want you out the way. Any suggestion that we're not working the skin off yer back is gonna go again us.

(*To LAURA.*) You're family. You stay in here. You're another soul they'll be mekking homeless if they boot us off the land.

(*WILLIAM takes the shotgun and the rifle out of the cabinet and gives them both to STEFAN.*)

(*To STEFAN.*) Get these guns out of Albert's sight. Go up on
the tops, bag us a couple of rabbits. What's the marrer?

STEFAN: You're giving me a gun.

LAURA: He's a Nazi.

WILLIAM: If he's a Nazi I'm Jesse Owens. Go on. Off yer go.
(*STEFAN looks at LAURA and leaves. LAURA looks at WILLIAM,
gets a nod, and follows him out. We see STEFAN and LAURA
kissing outside. LAURA comes back in.*)

LAURA: Is that the squire then? The one in that funny coat.

WILLIAM: Aye.

LAURA: I can't believe they sent him to prison for writing that
book.

WILLIAM: He med a fool of a few monied folk along the way.

LAURA: If they believed them stories more fool them. You
gorra be stupid to believe that someone with no training
could separate siamese twins.

WILLIAM: He didn't separate them, they both died.

LAURA: He never did claim they lived.

WILLIAM: That's the trick though innit! Having 'em live. Any
idiot can separate siamese twins. D'yer love Stefan?
(*LAURA starts to cry.*)
Aye, it's a wonderful joyous thing is love. It's had me in it's
snare in the past. Bout five times in all.

LAURA: Who?

WILLIAM: Yer mam.

LAURA: Me mam!?

WILLIAM: I was a kid and she never even noticed. I was crazy
for her.

LAURA: Like a bat in a dairy? It's a German saying.

WILLIAM: That's a good un. It's all radar innit, bats. In a dairy,
with all that metal about. Play havoc, wunt it. Aye. Like
a bat in a dairy for your mam I was, and never did owt
about it.

LAURA: Who else? You said five.

WILLIAM: (*Singing.*) 'Three madamoiselles from Armenteers,
who hadn't been fucked for forty years. Inky pinky parlez-
vous!'

LAURA: Uncle!

WILLIAM: And there's another woman I can't talk about.

LAURA: Maudie?

WILLIAM: That'd be telling. You could marry Stefan you know. Some prisoners stayed on last time round. Henry Brown?

LAURA: What, him what has his hair growing through his cap?

WILLIAM: Heinrich. We'd give Stefan a job here. You're not an Harrison, and he's a fucking Hohenstaufer, burr it's the nearest we're gonna get.

LAURA: How much of what you're saying is because Uncle Albert and Auntie Maudie don't have any children?

WILLIAM: That's the whole of it.

LAURA: Where would we live?

WILLIAM: My room's gonna be free soon. When I move into the barn.

LAURA: I couldn't live here. Not with Uncle Albert.

WILLIAM: He wunt be my first choice either. That'd be Greta Garbo but – [fat chance of that...]

LAURA: – Uncle Albert dunt like me and he dunt like Stefan!

WILLIAM: For a long time now I ant had much of a say in how things are done round here. But today the world is gonna change.

LAURA: They can't mek us plough up Spittle Garth can they?

WILLIAM: They took our 'osses last time. Knocked on the door, drank me mam's lemonade, and walked off with the hosses.

LAURA: But that grass is our hay for the winter. We can't get cattle cake.

WILLIAM: We'll have to slaughter half the herd. God knows what that'll do to Albert. People he dunt care for, burr if it stinks, shits everywhere and can't feed itsen then it pulls on his heart summat terrible.

(*Enter MAUDIE carrying an enamel bowl which has had corn in it. She slams this down on the top.*)

MAUDIE: I've never heard so much cursing! Aud Nick hissen'd be blushing.

WILLIAM: I've heard you curse.

MAUDIE: (*Laughs.*) Onny at you. Is that pot on? He's threatening to shoot the cows in front of the committee. If he dunt shoot the cows he'll shoot the bloody committee.

WILLIAM: Stop cursing.

MAUDIE: Am I? Bloody hell. Yer see, he's got me started.

WILLIAM: The guns are out the house.

LAURA: Stefan's gorr 'em both. Up on the tops.

MAUDIE: Oh good, that's a relief. We're gonna lose the farm Will. I can't gerr him to budge.

WILLIAM: He'll see sense. We got no choice.

MAUDIE: All he's gorra do is plough that bloody field!

(*Enter ALBERT.*)

WILLIAM: Where are they?

ALBERT: Gassing. Sitting in the young squire's car writin' summat up.

(*To LAURA.*) You'd best mek yersen scarce lass.

MAUDIE: She's my sister's girl. She's family.

ALBERT: There was a time when what a man said in his own house was listened to!

MAUDIE: Yer not in your own house, yer in my kitchen!

(*LAURA distributes teas.*)

ALBERT: That committee is judge, jury and bloody hangman! I tell yer, if any soldier sets foot on this land I'll shoot 'em.

WILLIAM: What with?

(*ALBERT looks to the gun cabinet.*)

I've give the guns to Stefan. Tawld him to bag some rabbits.

ALBERT: It's tekken me thirty fuckin' year to build that herd up. If I plough that grass, I can't feed 'em through the winter. And they bloody well know that.

(*Knock on the door.*)

I'm in the khazi.

(*ALBERT leaves to the loo. LAURA opens the front door. Enter AGAR, followed by WARCLIFFE. AGAR is now thirty-three years old. He is a picture of gloom. WARCLIFFE is a scruffy, stocky Yorkshire farmer of indeterminate age.*)

MAUDIE: Boots!

(*They both stop and take their boots off.*)

LAURA: Would you like tea?

WARCLIFFE: We won't be ovver long.

MAUDIE: Why'd'yer tek yer boots off then?

WARCLIFFE: Milk, one sugar please love. Have yer got sugar?

MAUDIE: Mebbe! If we had sugar, you'd wanna know why we had sugar! This war's just an excuse so you can go nosing around. No! We an't gorr any sugar! Burr I might be lying! Well?!

WARCLIFFE: Milk, no sugar, please. Where's –

MAUDIE: Washing his hands.

Silence.

LAURA: (*To AGAR.*) I've read your book. I think it's brilliant.

AGAR: I made it all up. I never went to the Arctic. I spent three years in the reading room of the British Museum. Near…a radiator.

LAURA: That doesn't stop it being brilliant. When Ingachook has to dig his father's grave, I thought that were great.

AGAR: Many thanks. Are you a Harrison?

MAUDIE: Her mother's Kate, my sister. From Hull.

(*A toilet flush. Enter ALBERT. WARCLIFFE looks to AGAR. AGAR nods. WARCLIFFE reads.*)

WARCLIFFE: (*Reading.*) As the local Chairman of the War Agricultural Committee –

MAUDIE: (*To WARCLIFFE.*) – If you're the Chairman why are you letting him tell yer what to do?

WARCLIFFE: Lord Agar int telling me what to do.

MAUDIE: (*To AGAR.*) You looked at him and nodded as if to say 'start your talking now'.

AGAR: I'm just another committee member Mrs Harrison.

WARCLIFFE: (*To AGAR.*) Shall I carry on.

(*WILLIAM and MAUDIE laugh.*)

Yeah?

AGAR: Oh God. Get on with it!

WARCLIFFE: Right. As the local chairman of the – [war agricultural.]

MAUDIE: – If you evict us, where we gonna live?

ALBERT: If any soldiers step foot on my land, I'll shoot them!

WILLIAM: When does the eviction order tek effect?

WARCLIFFE: Now.

AGAR: Oh God. Look. We haven't informed the army yet. The pragmatics of the situation are such that effectively you've still got two or three days. So, if I might make a suggestion, plough the bloody field.

ALBERT: What is it with you and that field? This is Harrison land. Where's it say I've gorr an obligation to feed the whole of bloody England?

WARCLIFFE: The Ministry of –

ALBERT: Fuck the Ministry. They only want us now cos there's a war on, any other time they're happy to see us go to hell, cos they know they can get their cheap imports.

AGAR: Very true.

WARCLIFFE: (*Reading.*) 'I issued a ploughing directive to Albert Orlando Harrison of Kilham Wold Farm with regard to seven and a half acres known as Spittle Garth – '

ALBERT: – them fields is me hay for the winter. That's how I'm gonna feed the herd through till next back end.

WARCLIFFE: – 'This directive was served on the twenty-third of March nineteen forty-four'. Last Tuesday. 'Subsequently – '

ALBERT: – worr I wanna know is, how does anyone get the right to tell a man what he can and can't do on his own land.

WARCLIFFE: 'Kilham Wold Farm was graded C by the committee, which is less than sixty percent efficient'.

AGAR: Someone has decided that the country needs corn. Not meat. Not milk.

MAUDIE: Why dint they get some stocks in then afore the war? They knew it was coming.

ALBERT: You've gorra barn full of corn. Piled high waiting for the right price.

WARCLIFFE: Lord Agar's estate's been inspected by the committee just the same as everyone else.

MAUDIE: Aye, and what grade did the estate get?

WARCLIFFE: Grade A.

(*To AGAR.*) Should I finish? It'll be all legal then. Yeah?
(*Reading.*) 'On 22nd March 1944, the farm was visited by the Chairman, Arnold Warcliffe, and a committee

member, Lord Primrose Agar. The acres in question
remained unploughed so an eviction – '

(*There is a knock at the door.*)

WARCLIFFE: Oh bloody hell!

LAURA: I'll go.

(*LAURA opens the door to a Women's Auxiliary Corps officer. She
is in full uniform and has a rifle slung over her shoulder.*)

ATS: Hello. Looking for a Mr Albert Harrison, or William
Harrison?

WILLIAM: Who are you?

ATS: Miss Collins, Auxiliary Territorial Service. I'll be quick.
This is serious. We've got instructions –

ALBERT: – Yer got no rights on this land!

ATS: Eh?

WILLIAM: I don't think this is owt to do with –

ALBERT: – That's enough! I'll hear no more!

(*ALBERT manhandles the ATS, which surprises her completely
and he takes the rifle off her.*)

WILLIAM: Albert!

ALBERT: (*Wielding the gun at the ATS.*) Gerr ovver there!

MAUDIE: Put that bloody thing down!

ALBERT: How many's out there?

ATS: What the hell's – [going on.]

WILLIAM: – Albert! This has nothing –

ALBERT: I've towld you!

(*To the ATS.*) How many?!

ATS: One. Mrs Dunn. On the motorbike. She's armed. We're
here –

ALBERT: – We know why you're here!

(*ALBERT smashes a pane of glass in the window.*)

WILLIAM: Get down everyone!

(*Everyone lies on the floor. ALBERT fires once.*)

Albert! Put that thing away will yer. Yer mekking things
worse.

ALBERT: Fuck off.

(*ALBERT fires again.*)

WILLIAM: What have you come here for Miss Collins?!

ATS: (*Frightened to death.*) Report of an escaped Prisoner of War! Armed. He's been shooting off a rifle at the Americans up on the tops.

WILLIAM: He's shooting rabbits.

ATS: The Americans rang through –

(*ALBERT shoots a third time. Then there is a crack of a rifle and the shattering of glass. ALBERT, shot through the head, slumps to the floor, dead.*)

WILLIAM: Tell your Mrs Dunn to stop firing will yer please love.

ATS: (*Crawling towards the door.*) Edna! Stop firing! Stop firing! Hold fire!

WILLIAM: Tell her to shout to say she's heard yer.

ATS: Edna! Did you hear me!

MRS DUNN: (*Off.*) Aye! I heard yer! I've stopped firing!

(*They all stand.*)

(*Silence.*)

MAUDIE: He's dead.

WILLIAM: Aye. He is that.

MAUDIE: What we gonna do now?

WILLIAM: Pigs.

(*To black.*)

(*Interval.*)

1958 MUCK DAY

(*1958. February. The farmhouse kitchen. The floor is now black and white vinyl tiles. There are signs of affluence, a fridge, a telephone. A family photo in a frame of four daughters in ascending heights. The table is still set as ever it was. WILLIAM is sat in his wheelchair writing on cards which he takes from an intricate looking colour coded card index system. Enter MAUDIE. In work clothes, no coat.*)

MAUDIE: Cawld!

WILLIAM: Wireless ses there's penguins at Scarborough.

MAUDIE: (*Knuckling him on the head.*) Yer pulling me leg again! I tell yer what though, that shed's warm. Finishing house.

WILLIAM: Aye, course it is.

(*MAUDIE hands over six or seven coloured cards which WILLIAM takes and inspects.*)

MAUDIE: Gorr a couple coughing mind. I've isolated 'em.

(*Enter LAURA from outside, nine months pregnant, and walking crab like.*)

LAURA: Chloe's ready.

WILLIAM: 'Chloe?'

LAURA: Orange six. And Blue ten, she in't in pig. Again.

MAUDIE: She's gerrin' on a bit now that one.

WILLIAM: That's it with her then! She's going out in a pastry coffin.

MAUDIE: Are you alright?

LAURA: I've had a little show.

MAUDIE: Oh love, yer wanna get yerself in yer room, have yer gorr a fire in there?

LAURA: Aye, I'll go and lie down in a bit.

MAUDIE: You and yer bloody cards.

WILLIAM: Gimme them others.

(*LAURA hands over six coloured cards.*)

LAURA: Red 4. Green 2. Indigo 15 and Indigo bloody 16.

WILLIAM: Have yer written the dead uns in? I ask, cos yer never do.

LAURA: Each of them litters there has got one dead.

(*WILLIAM writes in the data on the cards.*)

MAUDIE: A man sitting in a warm kitchen all day, while the womenfolk gerr on wi' all the graftin'.

WILLIAM: Shurrup yer barrel of spite! Yer used to be good fun, you did. When yer husband was still alive.

(*MAUDIE knuckles him on the head.*)

Ow! That's fucking twice yer've done that now!

MAUDIE: Don't curse in my kitchen!

WILLIAM: If yer let me swear I'll marry yer.

MAUDIE: I don't want yer to marry me! I've had a change of heart.

(*LAURA laughs.*)

WILLIAM: (*To MAUDIE. Offering a card.*) Go and get Chloe started. I'll send Stef in to help yer if he gets back in time.

(*To LAURA.*) You, go and have yer bath.

LAURA: I really want to do Chloe.

WILLIAM: Look at yer, yer can hardly stand.

MAUDIE: D'yer wann us to call Doctor Wilson?

LAURA: Aye, well mebbe I'm exaggerating.

(*MAUDIE leaves.*)

WILLIAM: We're all excited about 'Chloe'.

(*LAURA goes off and turns the taps on in the bathroom.*)

LAURA: (*Off.*) I bet she has eleven!

WILLIAM: Thirteen.

LAURA: (*Off.*) Imagine that. Thirteen.

(*The sound of a car pulling up. The horn is sounded triumphantly in a rhythm of honks.*)

(*Off.*) That'll be Steffie! Has he got the car Will?!

WILLIAM: No! He's bought the horn separate. He's gonna collect the rest of the car tomorrow.

(*Enter LAURA in dressing gown, she stands in the open door looking out.*)

LAURA: I'll feel like the bloody Queen sittin' up in the front of that.

WILLIAM: Don't slip on them flags! I don't want that little lass in there starting her life with a bang on the head.

LAURA: I wish you'd stop it with that little lass talk!

WILLIAM: I'm willing that bain to be a boy by a convoluted method of madness which I wouldn't expect yer to understand since it involves talking a lot of bollocks.

(*Enter STEFAN. He kisses LAURA. STEFAN is wearing a quality tweed suit and a bow tie. He still has some German in his tongue, though he has mixed this with Yorkshire. He carries car keys.*)

STEFAN: Are you alright?

LAURA: Come on! Let's go for a ride!

WILLIAM: Don't go gerrin her excited!

STEFAN: (*To WILL.*) Have you seen it?!

WILLIAM: Shoulda put the money in new sheds.

STEFAN: Sheds, sheds, sheds. I thought my father was a bore because all he talked about was Johan Sebastian Bach. I've swapped early baroque for pig housing.

WILLIAM: She's had a little show.

STEFAN: Bugger me! Really?

LAURA: It was nowt much. Let's go to Brid!

STEFAN: Maybe just up Fimber and back. The girls'll be home in an hour.

LAURA: (*To WILLIAM.*) D'yer wanna come for a spin?

WILLIAM: No. It's Thursday.

(*To STEFAN.*) Any road, you, you're busy according to this maintenance card here.

STEFAN: Yes, I know. Sorry.

(*STEFAN takes the card and reads it.*)

WILLIAM: If yer look under the fans yer'll see the asbestos has come away –

STEFAN: – I've done this already. Shed two?

WILLIAM: If yer've done it yer an't filled yer card in.

(*STEFAN starts to wheel WILLIAM out the house.*)

STEFAN: Come on. You'll have to show us.

LAURA: I'm in the bath.

WILLIAM: Oi, you, fill your cards in.

(*LAURA picks at food from the fridge. She then sits at the pig info system and completes her cards and files them. The sound of a tractor turning up and turning off it's engine. LAURA looks through the window. LAURA retreats to the bathroom. Pause.*)

Enter AGAR. He is now a man of forty-five, and still gloomy. His coat and the exotic trappings of youth have gone.)

AGAR: Mr Harrison! Mr Harrison!!

(He waits. Surreptitiously he looks at the pig information system. He goes over and looks. He touches. He looks closer. Enter LAURA from stage left.)

LAURA: It's normally kept under lock and key that.

AGAR: Thursday. Again.

LAURA: Aye.

AGAR: Comes around doesn't it. It's snowing on the tops. It's actually drifting across Nafferton way.

LAURA: You might have to stay the night then.

AGAR: Oh no, I don't think so.

LAURA: I'm having a bath. Have you gorr owt for me?

AGAR: No. Not yet. I've decided to change the ending. After what you said.

LAURA: That were six month back.

AGAR: Oh dear! Really? Time's winged chariot. Ha! I read it again and I agree with you. The denouement doesn't satisfy. It is merely morbid. I see you've got the telephone in. Maybe I could ring you.

LAURA: No, yer can't.

(LAURA leaves for the bathroom. AGAR goes back to fiddling with the pig system, but this time he seems to understand it. Enter WILLIAM.)

WILLIAM: Pigs! It in't nowt but mathematics. All yer need's a system.

AGAR: Does it work?

WILLIAM: Din't yer see that brand new Austin A90 out there?

AGAR: I did. I've heard you're buying in straw. I could trade you straw for the muck.

WILLIAM: Hard cash. That's the deal we have. No man on this earth can talk with any authority about happiness until he's sold shit to the aristocracy.

(WILLIAM pours a little whiskey for AGAR and one for himself.)

AGAR: I imagine you're buying in straw because you've no-one to work the arable.

WILLIAM: I'm not selling. A farmer who sells land is like a wrestler who chops his arms off.

AGAR: I've never heard that expression.

WILLIAM: I just med it up. How long have we bin doing this?

AGAR: Twenty years.

WILLIAM: Any road, Maudie'd kill me. She likes to walk the circuit, meks her feel like a Queen. I don't wanna be the Harrison who sold his inheritance and left the Harrisons with nowt to work. If I do that they'll tek me portrait off the landing and stick it in the scullery.

AGAR: Do you have a portrait?

WILLIAM: I thought you of all people'd spot a metaphor.

AGAR: I've bought a small feed company. Fimber Feed.

WILLIAM: Oh aye?

AGAR: Yes. They've always bought my corn, and now I've bought them.

WILLIAM: Can't see how yer can mek money out of animal feed.

AGAR: There's a lot of farmers watching what you do.

WILLIAM: Yer can't keep a secret farming. To find out what someone's up to all yer gorra do is look over the hedge.

AGAR: If they look over your hedge they'll see a brand new car. A telephone.

WILLIAM: If they tek up pig farming they'll need a system.
(*AGAR fiddles with the pig info system.*)

AGAR: It's a little like playing God I imagine. What would He have written on your card?

WILLIAM: That I'm the happiest man alive. What's He gorr on yourn?

AGAR: That I complicate life.

WILLIAM: Life's easy enough. Weddings on a Satdi, Births on a Mondi, funerals on a Fridi.
(*WILLIAM pours more whiskey.*)
I've heard that driving down here for your muck every Thursday, to stand in this kitchen, is all the farming yer do.

AGAR: She is the most compelling individual female I have ever met.
(*Enter STEFAN.*)

STEFAN: Hello sir!

AGAR: Guten tag.

STEFAN: (*To STEFAN.*) It's muck day is it?

(*To WILLIAM.*) Guess Will! Go on guess!

WILLIAM: Thirteen?

STEFAN: Fifteen!

WILLIAM: (*In awe.*) Bloody hell.

STEFAN: One of our sows has just had a litter of fifteen.

(*Enter MAUDIE in a state of joy. STEFAN exits to the bathroom.*)

MAUDIE: Fifteen! Will! Fifteen!

(*MAUDIE goes to wash her hands at the kitchen sink.*)

WILLIAM: Aye, I've heard. Yer'd better write to Harold MacMillan.

MAUDIE: Oh! Hello sir! Dint see yer hiding there sir, sorry.

AGAR: Good afternoon. Fifteen. What breed of boar?

WILLIAM: Secret project.

LAURA: (*Off.*) Fifteen!

(*There is a cry from the bathroom.*)

MAUDIE: God, that's all we need! That's our Laura, she had a show today. It must be all the excitement.

WILLIAM: Pig farms are well known for their dangerous levels of excitement. We should have warning notices up.

MAUDIE: Yer daft in the head you. Excuse me sir.

(*MAUDIE exits to the bathroom. WILLIAM goes to the pig information system and writes up Chloe's card. AGAR watches.*)

AGAR: This is a factory.

WILLIAM: Part factory, part genetic laboratory, part gold mine.

AGAR: When do you stop? You don't have the labour to run two thousand pigs.

WILLIAM: I'll hire a pigman. Pay wages.

AGAR: Mixed farming, for these little family units was a good system, you know. Feed the cereals to the livestock, use the manure to feed the fields, to grow more cereals, to feed to the animals. A cycle. There was poetry in it. The rhythm of life in accord with the seasons.

WILLIAM: It's nineteen fifty-eight. The poor want meat.

AGAR: Do they? Oh dear. They don't want meat every day do they?

WILLIAM: Why should they eat any less well than you?

AGAR: Let's not get political again William. I've got a sore throat.

(*Enter MAUDIE in a rush.*)

MAUDIE: She's bloody started! Phone the doctor, yer know I don't like using that thing. Sorry sir.

(*WILLIAM goes over to the phone and starts looking for numbers.*)

WILLIAM: Calm down, she's onny giving birth. Yer only at top pitch cos yer never had none yersen.

MAUDIE: You'll bloody pay for that William Harrison!
Sorry sir.

WILLIAM: Stop fucking 'sorry siring'!

(*Exit MAUDIE to bathroom.*)

(*On the phone.*) Hello love...aye, Doctor Wilson at Driffield –

(*Enter MAUDIE.*)

MAUDIE: Sorry sir, we need to lift her...

AGAR: I see.

(*AGAR exits to bathroom. MAUDIE stands by the phone stressing WILLIAM.*)

WILLIAM: (*On the phone.*) It's William Harrison here, Kilham Wold...aye, oh not so bad ta ...how are you love?...

MAUDIE: – gerr on with it!

WILLIAM: – it's our Laura she's started...aye...

(*Commotion as LAURA is carried in by AGAR and STEFAN.*)

LAURA: Put me down. I'm alright, I'll walk!

WILLIAM: (*On phone.*) – that's all them going mad...right you are. Tarra.

(*To MAUDIE.*) He's coming to the phone.

(*They set LAURA down, she walks crab like, with one hand on each knee, into the room. AGAR and STEFAN follow, the door closes.*)

(*Intense.*) Gerr him out that room.

(*MAUDIE goes off. During the next AGAR enters.*)

(*On the phone.*)...Hello Doctor Wilson...It's not me, no. Last time I had trouble wi' me legs Jesus was looking for work as a carpenter...It's our Laura...I wun't know if her waters had broken.

AGAR: Yes. They have.

WILLIAM: (*On the phone.*) Aye, they have...yer know the Agar estate, aye, well yer pass them gates and then yer go about three mile and our post is there on yer left burr it's gorra sack over it for the ket man. So you're looking for a post with a bag over it, alright?...righteo. Over and out.
(*Phone down.*)

WILLIAM: Half hour. And he'll get lost as usual an'all.

AGAR: What do you have for the ket man?

WILLIAM: Dead sow.

AGAR: I'll take it for the hounds.

WILLIAM: I get money off the ket man.

AGAR: I'll pay. I'll take it with the muck.

WILLIAM: Two shilling.
(*AGAR pays up. LAURA cries out off.*)
(*The squire doesn't move. Enter STEFAN.*)

STEFAN: (*To Agar.*) Thanks for your help, sir.
(*To WILL.*) What's happening?!

WILLIAM: He's on his way.

STEFAN: (*Panicking.*) Maudie's panicking Uncle Will!

WILLIAM: Oh aye? And you're not?
(*Cries from LAURA. Enter MAUDIE.*)

STEFAN: Sheisse!

MAUDIE: Steff! Come in here and hold her hand at least.
(*Exit STEFAN.*)

AGAR: Should I do some hot water Mrs Harrison? And towels?

MAUDIE: Yer can if yer like but what the bloody hell I'm supposed to do with hot water and towels I do not know!
(*AGAR goes to the sink and starts filling a kettle. WILLIAM pours MAUDIE a drink.*)
Oh Will! I've not got a good feeling about this one! What we need is someone who knows what they're bloody doing.

WILLIAM: He's set off. Yer've midwifed fifteen already today, so –

MAUDIE: – he's the wrong way round or summat! I'm at top pitch!

(*MAUDIE snaffles the drink. He pours her another. She snaffles that and leaves to go back in the bedroom. During the next there are further cries.*)

WILLIAM: (*To AGAR.*) Go. The sow is on the rully.

(*Big cry from LAURA.*)

AGAR: I love her.

WILLIAM: Yer don't know what love is. The real thing's a lot more fun but a lot more complicated than that med up stuff of yourn.

(*Cries off. Louder, desperate.*)

AGAR: William! I think I can help in there! I may not know anything about love but I do know about child birth!

WILLIAM: Yer 'separated' siamese twins on an ice flo with a cake knife and a bottle of rum.

AGAR: I researched that chapter thoroughly! I went to Barts in London! My friend was a doctor!

WILLIAM: Both them siamese twins died.

AGAR: In the book! I can help in there, I know I can!

(*Cries off. Desperate. STEFAN comes out.*)

STEFAN: Oh God, what are we gonna do Will?! The baby's stuck. I think he's the wrong way round.

WILLIAM: We can all help her, by keeping calm.

STEFAN: Does the doctor know where he's coming?

AGAR: (*To STEFAN.*) I have no medical training as such Mr Harrison, but I had to research child birth very thoroughly for my book. My very best friend was a doctor. Have you read the book?

STEFAN: 'Cannibal!?' Yes. I've read it. What – [is the relevance…]

AGAR: – The birth of the siamese twins?

WILLIAM: They both died!

STEFAN: What's this – [about?]

AGAR: – In the book, yes!

STEFAN: Can someone – [explain to me what you're talking about.]

WILLIAM: – I've tawld the squire to go!

AGAR: I can save Laura! Don't you see I can save her.

(*AGAR starts to move towards the room.*)

WILLIAM: Stop him!

STEFAN: (*Grabbing him.*) Sir! Please!

WILLIAM: I'm norr 'aving you seeing that girl!

(*The cry of a new born child silences them. STEFAN goes in.*)
She int the only woman in the world yer know. Yer family's gorr a big house in London, so tek yersen down there. What yer need is a concentration of women of yer own sort. Yer not gonna get that round here. I know all you big families talk to each other, but obviously they an't come up with owt suitable for you. It's London yer wanna be. (*Beat.*) So we're done. There'll be a new load of muck next Thursday. And yer'll find out then if this un's a boy or girl.

(*Exit AGAR. More baby crying. Enter STEFAN with a big grin on his face.*)

WILLIAM: What we got this time?

(*To black.*)

1979 A ROMAN ROAD

(*1979. Summer. Morning, about ten o'clock. The pig information system is still there. There is an array of white goods, and other signs of modernisation. Fluorescent lighting replaces bulbs. Four framed photos of four girls on separate graduation days hang on the walls. The sound of 'Another Girl Another Planet' by the Only Ones is heard from upstairs. ALAN enters from the toilet dressed in underpants and a Ramones T shirt. He pours himself a bowl of cornflakes with milk and lots of sugar. He starts eating them, as he goes back to his bedroom. Once in the bedroom he turns the music up, and closes the door. Enter TITCH. He is about thirty. A huge man. He wears denims and has a jeans jacket tied by the arms around his waist. His chest is covered by a red singlet with the logo of STATUS QUO. His hair is farmer's boy long in the cut of the day. He carries a small buff card.*)

TITCH: 'ello!

> (*He looks at the buff card in his hand.*)
>
> Mr Hohen…Hohenstauf…fuck! HELLO!
>
> (*He sits at the table which is set as it normally is ie: running lengthways from stage left to stage right. He lights a cigarette. He seems confused and annoyed by the positioning of the table. After some thought he picks up the table and, in one movement, turns it through ninety degrees so it is running upstage to downstage. ALAN enters from upstairs.*)
>
> How do!?

ALAN: You've moved the table.

TITCH: Aye! Felt all wrong! You a student? Student music. What yer studying?

ALAN: Psychology.

TITCH: Yer gonna be a psychiatrist then?

ALAN: Psychology is the study of normal behaviour.

TITCH: What's that then?

ALAN: What do you want?

TITCH: Come for the job. Where's yer dad?

ALAN: I'll get him.

> (*ALAN exits to the fold yard. TITCH sits and smokes. Enter LAURA from the bathroom. She jumps, seeing TITCH.*)

LAURA: Agh! Yer give me the fright of me life!

TITCH: Come for the interview.

LAURA: Who moved the table?

TITCH: Me. I tawld the punk.

LAURA: You moved the table?

TITCH: Aye, it dun't mek any sense running East to West.

LAURA: We don't have any jobs, I think –

TITCH: – What's this then?!

(*LAURA takes the card from TITCH but doesn't read it. Enter STEFAN, ALAN and Uncle WILL.*)

Eh up! Here we go!

LAURA: We an't gorr any jobs have we?

STEFAN: I put a card in the job centre for a pigman.

LAURA: We don't need a pigman.

(*TITCH stands, as if to go.*)

TITCH: Are yer watching?! That's me! I'm off! I've come all the way from Beeford. It's a fair distance you know. Yer wun't wanna be dragged by yer balls from here to Beeford!

STEFAN: Please, sit down. There is a job. I'm Stefan.

TITCH: Steve Bolsover. Titch.

STEFAN: This is Will.

TITCH: Alright Will! Got no legs eh?

WILLIAM: I'm an amputee.

TITCH: Above the knee or below the knee? Don't tell me I don't wanna know. Gives me the willies.

LAURA: Can someone tell me why I've not been told that we're advertising for staff?

STEFAN: Darling, I'm sorry but –

LAURA: (*To WILL.*) – Do you know about this?

WILLIAM: Aye.

STEFAN: Laura!

LAURA: I don't know why I bother.

STEFAN: – Laura! Please!

(*LAURA exits in a huff.*)

TITCH: Glad she's gone. All men together now. Swear, talk bollocks. Do what the fuck we like, eh!?

WILLIAM: Who moved the table?

TITCH: Look! I'm gerrin fucking sick of this table business! I did. If I don't get the job yer can move it back to where it were afore.

(*ALAN exits upstairs.*)

He's had enough. Is this an interview then?

STEFAN: It's not unfair for us to want a know a little more about you is it?

TITCH: I'm me. Titch. That's it. You had anyone else for this job?

STEFAN: Not yet.

TITCH: That's it then innit.

WILLIAM: Where do you live?

TITCH: I'm not tellin' yer.

WILLIAM: Where did you sleep last night?

TITCH: In me car.

STEFAN: OK So you've got a full driving licence?

TITCH: Course I fucking have.

WILLIAM: What was your last job?

TITCH: Bensons.

STEFAN: I half know Daniel. He's a wonderful character isn't he, and –

TITCH: – He's a bastard. If I ever see the fucker again I'll kill him.

WILLIAM: Why did you leave?

TITCH: Sacked us.

STEFAN: And why exactly did he dismiss you?

TITCH: He caught me nicking stuff.

WILLIAM: What were yer stealing?

TITCH: Red diesel.

WILLIAM: Do you have any of the relevant City and Guilds stockman qualifications?

TITCH: Fuck off! I like pigs.

STEFAN: What exactly is it that you like about working with pigs?

TITCH: They're intelligent animals. They're clever but not that clever. Just enough to mek it interesting but not enough to get yer worried.

STEFAN: Are you married?

TITCH: No woman's ever gonna get the better of me.

STEFAN: You're not married then?

TITCH: Look, if I need a fuck I know where to go, alright?!

WILLIAM: How many sows has Benson got now?

TITCH: He's running about three hundred Large Whites.
He's got three big fuck off Warcup sheds, concrete floors,
automatic feeding, ventilation, and a lot of people pressing
buttons. It's like the last scene in a James Bond film but
with no bikinis. Onny problem with Benson's place is him.
He's a total and complete fucking cunt.

STEFAN: He's in a scheme with Tescos, yeah?

TITCH: Aye, they've gorr him by the balls.

WILLIAM: How long does he take to gerr 'em to bacon weight?

TITCH: Six month by rights. What about you?

STEFAN: We're working towards that.

TITCH: I bet. One look at them sheds of yourn and I could tell
yer was amateurs. I bet yer've got one clapped out awld
boar who can't gerr it up unless you whack him on the arse
with a shovel.

STEFAN: Actually, we have seven Norwegian Landrace
boars. We collect ourselves and distribute using deep
catheterisation.

TITCH: (*Stands and shakes hands with them both.*) Worr I'm doing
now, is apologising. I was obviously fucking way off.
Alright. I've sat down again now. I'm impressed.

WILLIAM: Stefan went on a course at Bishop Burton college.

TITCH: I'm banned from there.

STEFAN: What for?

TITCH: Dunno. Apparently, I've repressed it. How d'yer catch
the sperm? Yer got a saddle?

STEFAN: Yes. We've had a few disasters but I've got them
trained now.

TITCH: Have you ever had a go on it yersen? The saddle?
Go on! You have an't yer! Course you have! Had a little go
on there when no-ones looking. Ha, ha! I have. Live fast
die young me! I'm worried about them sheds though. They
look fucked to me.

(*Enter* LAURA. *She messes about in the sink area aggressively, and then leaves.*)

Yer not gonna get rocked to sleep tonight pal!

STEFAN: My wife and I, and Uncle Will of course, we make all the decisions as a family, but this is a little delicate, er…I'm not well and er…actually it's quite a serious condition and –

TITCH: – don't tell me! Yer not well and you an't tawld her!? What yer got?

STEFAN: It's not unrelated to emphysema and –

TITCH: – Pal of mine had that, wheezing and coughing he wor, and he went to the doctor and doctor said it wor emphysema and BANG – three month later he were dead!

WILLIAM: I bought the sheds off the MOD They were good sheds, but needed lining.

TITCH: A cawld pig is a thin pig.

WILLIAM: I chose asbestos. Stef lined each one of them three sheds hissen.

TITCH: On yer tod?

STEFAN: Yes.

WILLIAM: Cutting, sawing, shaving.

TITCH: (*To* STEFAN.) Do you blame him then? Has that come between yer? I mean, it in't murder, obviously, he din't mean it did he. Now he's blaming hissen. How do you feel about that? Him blaming hissen?

STEFAN: No-one knew about asbestos then. Going back to Benson's, what's his feed situation? He's got no land that I know of.

TITCH: They're not his pigs you know. Fimber Feed own the pigs, Benson's just finishing 'em for him. They're the best Fimber Feed. They turn up once a month blow it into the bins and fuck off. What do you do for feed here?

STEFAN: We grow some of our own, mix it ourselves. For historical reasons, didn't want to get involved with Fimber Feed. Can you plough?

TITCH: (*Standing.*) I'm a specialist pig man. I'm not ploughing fields, and bloody harvesting, and pratting about mixing up feed. Yer'll have me fucking Morris Dancing next!

(*TITCH makes to go.*)

Are yer watching this!? I'm off!

STEFAN: Mr Bolsover!

WILLIAM: Titch! Please 'ang on.

STEFAN: We're gonna rationalise down to four acres!

WILLIAM: We've decided to sell the arable!

TITCH: What's stopping yer then?

STEFAN: It's a family farm.

TITCH: It's her in't it?

STEFAN: Laura hasn't yet understood the implications of my
    illness.

(*TITCH sits down.*)

TITCH: Did you see that? I was up and off, but now I'm sat
    down again. Burr I'm not ploughing! It bores the tits off
    me. Look – it's obvious what yer have to do here. Get shot
    of the arable, buy some Warcup sheds, and get yersen a
    contract with Fimber Feed. Do that, and I'm yours.

STEFAN: It's not that easy to sell one's inheritance.

TITCH: I'll tell yer summat for nowt, that punk son of yours in't
    gonna be farming this land after you've jumped the stick.

STEFAN: I'm very proud of my son. He's doing a PHD in
    Educational Psychology.

TITCH: Like I said, neither use nor ornament. Meks yer sick I
    bet, eh? Yer build summat up like this, pay for him through
    school, they fill his head with shit, and then you end up
    with no-one to pass yer business on to. Is he yer onny son?

STEFAN: Yes. I have four daughters.

TITCH: Oh aye?

STEFAN: They're all married.

TITCH: You're not facing up to realities here are yer. You're
    dying, you got no legs AND you're not a spring chicken,
    and milado up there's off with the fucking fairies. All yer
    gorr is me. In a few years time it'll be just me and her.
    (*Pause. Silence. STEFAN puts his head in his hands. He takes
    some time to recover.*)
    Have I upset yer? Sorry. But that's me, that's Titch
    Bolsover, I'm straight, I'm a fucking Roman Road.
    (*Pause. STEFAN recovers.*)

STEFAN: OK.

TITCH: I wanna live in, but listen, I'm not working Sundays.

STEFAN: Ah! You're a Christian?

TITCH: No. I've gorr a drink problem. I get very badly pissed most Satdi nights. I want me own room, double bed, teasmaid. I'm not sleeping on a couple bags of chaff in the barn like a fucking Paddy. I'm not interested in the money. It's living in I want. A fried breakfast, cooked dinner, and a decent tea. I'm not eating margarine. I work hard I want butter.

STEFAN: I'll need to discuss this with my wife.

TITCH: Aye you do that. I'll go have a look round and come back in ten minutes.

STEFAN: She might say no. We run the farm, er…collectively. Discuss everything.

TITCH: 'Cept you an't told her yer dying.

(*TITCH leaves. STEFAN puts his head back in his hands.*)

WILLIAM: Y'alright son?

STEFAN: Yes, thank you. What do you think of him?

WILLIAM: He's bloody perfect.

STEFAN: Yes. It's a kind of miracle.

(*Enter LAURA with two or three pig catheters. She starts to wash them at the sink and then pegs them up to dry.*)

LAURA: – Yer interviewing men to work on my farm and I don't know owt about it!

(*Enter ALAN from upstairs with a coffee mug.*)

STEFAN: We need to talk.

LAURA: Bloody right we need to talk!

(*ALAN puts the coffee mug in the sink and goes to get a clean mug from the cupboard.*)

Use the same mug! What do you think this is an hotel?

ALAN: Don't take it out on me!

LAURA: Don't put owt in there when these is dripping.

ALAN: Oh fuck!

LAURA: Don't swear in this house! You can leave your Surrey talk in Surrey.

ALAN: You're drying Artificial Insemination equipment over the kitchen sink.

LAURA: They're clean!

ALAN: This is disgusting.

LAURA: Aye, owt to do wi' work's disgusting to you.

ALAN: Do you want a coffee Uncle Will? Dad.

WILLIAM: No ta. Yer dad dun't want owt.

(*ALAN looks at his dad, head in hands. He searches in cupboards for biscuits.*)

ALAN: We got any biscuits?

LAURA: Second cupboard.

WILLIAM: We need new buildings Laura. We need to sell the arable.

LAURA: That's an old idea, and a bad'n an'all. Four acres in't a farm.

STEFAN: That's all we need.

LAURA: Thirty year back, I came to this farm of me own free will. I wun't have come here if it were a four acre pig unit. I don't ever wanna be in a situation where if I tek a walk round Spittle Garth meadow I'm trespassing. Yer brother died for that field. Maudie – last thing she done before she took to her bed was walk the circuit down there.

WILLIAM: Some of the best moments of my life have happened in that field.

LAURA: (*Laughing.*) Don't embarrass me.

ALAN: I think it's a good idea.

LAURA: Shurrup you. If you had any interest in this place then yer can have a say, but you ain't, you never had, so put a biscuit in it.

(*To WILLIAM.*) Sell the land and we're dependent on the feed companies.

WILLIAM: We're gerrin twenty quid a pig Laura, the margins are alright.

LAURA: I know. I like me holidays, I like me new cars, I like the fact that every single one of my daughters has upped and offed to university and become so bloody full of themselves that I never see them.

WILLIAM: We an't got the labour to run eighty acres.

LAURA: Stef manages. Don't yer? What's up? The doctor said it were nowt. Yer've bin mekking the most of that cough for the best part of ten years. Anyone would think you were on yer last legs.

ALAN: These biscuits have gone soft. Where are the chocolate digestives?

LAURA: I've buried 'em. Up on the tops. It's a three mile walk uphill and then you've gorra dig 'em out the hole. With a bit of luck it'll be raining. There's spades out the back. Why don't yer tek the Ramones up there with yer, they look like they could do with the exercise.

ALAN: Tut! I'm outa here.

(*ALAN goes off up the stairs.*)

STEFAN: I need to talk to you.

WILLIAM: I'll be in me barn then. If yer need me.

(*WILLIAM exits.*)

LAURA: All I'm saying is every morning I'm up at six, I cook you breakfast, and then I'm straight in the farrowing house. The least I expect from you two is an equal say –

STEFAN: – Laura!

LAURA: Having a cough is no excuse for becoming ignorant! There's no way we're selling the arable. Over my dead body.

(*STEFAN stands and goes to the foot of the stairs.*)

STEFAN: Alan!

LAURA: What's gooin on?

STEFAN: ALAN!!

(*ALAN opens his bedroom door. The sound of Joy Division's 'New Dawn Fades' is heard.*)

ALAN: What?

STEFAN: Come down here, I want to talk to you.

ALAN: What is it now?!

STEFAN: Just come down here!

ALAN: (*Quietly.*) Oh fucking hell.

LAURA: What is it Stef? Tell me! What's gooin on?

(*ALAN comes down the stairs and stands stock still.* STEF *can't find the words and his bottom lip starts puckering.* LAURA *softens and takes him in her arms. They hold each other to the sound of 'New Dawn Fades'.* ALAN *just stands there looking at the floor. Enter* TITCH. *He stands and watches, and actually manages to be unobtrusive.*)
(*To black.*)

1995 SUFFRAGETTE

(*1995. Autumn. Early afternoon. A CD player. A computer on a workstation stand with printer. A modern telephone and fax. The pig information system has gone. WILLIAM is not using the computer but is in a modern motorised wheelchair. A streamer on the wall declares – '100 NOT OUT!!'. WILLIAM is blowing up balloons. LAURA enters in coat, with shopping.*)

LAURA: Foggy.

WILLIAM: Eh?

LAURA: (*Louder.*) Foggy!

WILLIAM: We better call it off then. Did yer gerr a balloon pump?

LAURA: Bugger. I knew I'd forgotten something. I hope I've gorr enough food here. How many have you invited?

WILLIAM: There's a small village outside Mexico City called Quarrapas, population of about three hundred. They're all coming.

LAURA: Yer get worse you. Have yer heard?

WILLIAM: Aye. Went peacefully, unfortunately.

LAURA: Now, now, come on. His son's come up from London. Tekken ovver.

WILLIAM: What's he called?

LAURA: The same I think.

WILLIAM: Poor bugger. Finding out that yer dad's called Primrose must be bad enough but not as bad as discovering that you are an'all.

(*Enter a young woman VET, about twenty-six, a Kiwi. She knocks on the door even though it's open.*)

LAURA: Yer done love?

VET: I need to fill out the scheme form, yeah.

LAURA: Here, sit at the table.

VET: Thanks.

(*VET sits at the table. And starts completing some paperwork. LAURA pours her a tea.*)

Is he alright yeah. Your pigman?

LAURA: Titch? What did he do?

VET: He just seemed to get rarked up real easy, yeah?

WILLIAM: He doesn't like women.

LAURA: Three reasons he wouldn't warm to you. One – yer a young lass and he thinks yer don't know what yer talking about. Two – yer a foreigner. And three – yer educated.

WILLIAM: And on top of all that – he's dead ignorant.

VET: You're quite incredible for a hundred Mr Harrison.

WILLIAM: Ta. Are yer courtin' love?

VET: (*Laughs.*) No.

WILLIAM: D'yer like ten pin bowling?

LAURA: Shurrup will yer! She might not like older men.

WILLIAM: I'm not auld. I just bin here longer.

VET: What do you feel about a young Kiwi 'lass' telling you what you can and can't do, yeah?

LAURA: We'd do owt that supermarket asked us to do to get that sustification stamp. Me, I'd cut me right hand off. What would you do Uncle Will?

WILLIAM: I'd streak naked through Woolworths. Again. If yer don't stamp us she'll have to go work in the Little Chef. (*Silence. The VET gets back to filling in her form, rather self-consciously since LAURA and WILLIAM do nothing but watch her.*)

VET: I didn't get a sense, yeah, that Titch knew what the broken needles protocol was, is, yeah? (*LAURA stands and goes looking for a file on the shelf.*) Did you get a telegram from the Queen, yeah?

WILLIAM: About broken needles? No. She's not that keen on pigs. She's more horses.

LAURA: Behave! (*Passing a file over.*) That's the needles book. It in't a telegram no more. It's a letter. (*LAURA shows her the letter. She looks at it, the envelope etc.*)

VET: Wow. Thank you. Fantastic. Do you have any tips on longevity?

WILLIAM: Get yer legs chopped off when you're twennie one. Are them sheds alright? (*She hands it back to LAURA. She goes back to the form.*)

VET: They're excellent buildings.

WILLIAM: Ta.

VET: Can I see your feed delivery records, yeah?

(*LAURA goes to get another file.*)

How much credit do you have with Fimber Feed?

LAURA: What right has that supermarket got to ask about my finances?

VET: It's a question on the form, I'm sorry, yeah.

WILLIAM: We got three months credit with 'em.

VET: (*Writing.*) And your feed bill is thirty-three thousand pounds a month. So you owe them ninety-nine thousand pounds, yeah?

WILLIAM: It's ovver an 'undred as it happens. It got to an hundred afore I did.

VET: Aren't they worried about that?

WILLIAM: It's exactly what they want.

LAURA: They've gorr us right where they want us. The squire in't gonna be worried about a hundred thousand pounds when Brussels chucks two million quid a year his way – money he don't even need.

VET: I beg your pardon, who's the squire?

LAURA: Fimber Feed.

VET: Right. Yeah, you'd be in a better position if you could grow your own feed.

LAURA: (*Looks at WILLIAM.*) D'yer hear that?

VET: (*Incredulous.*) Why do you do this? Pig farming?

WILLIAM: It's a good laugh. (*Laughs.*) When one of them gets out! Kaw!

LAURA: D'yer remember when that gilt escaped and ran down the main road?

WILLIAM: (*Laughing.*) Aye. 1976 that hot summer! Aye, that's me favourite!

LAURA: (*Laughing.*) Ran half way to Driffield!

VET: You're losing thirty pounds for every finished pig. That's three thousand pounds a week. I just don't see why you do it, yeah?

WILLIAM: We can't all be conceptual artists – there'd be nowt to eat.

LAURA: It's not what we do. It's what we are. We're farmers.

WILLIAM: That's not her talking there. That's summat someone said in the Guardian.

VET: I can't give you the accreditation stamp.

(*Pause.*)

You're using stalls for the dry sows. That's illegal – now, yeah.

LAURA: You tek the backs off them stalls and I'll guarantee yer, they don't go nowhere. We got 'em trained to it. All our pigs is happy pigs, in't they Uncle Will.

WILLIAM: Aye. Yer didn't mention this to Titch did yer?

VET: I'm not saying they're suffering. They look fine to me but what I'm saying is, you're still using stalls, yeah, and the date has gone, yeah. Stalls are illegal in the UK.

LAURA: We're in the European Community. Stalls aren't illegal in Europe.

WILLIAM: (*To LAURA.*) Leave her be Laura! It in't her doing. (*To the VET.*) Sorry love, she's got all political.

VET: This is British law. Your government – [they've chosen to...]

LAURA: – We went to Blackpool yesterday!

(*The VET is puzzled and looks to WILLIAM for clarification.*)

WILLIAM: Aye, we did.

VET: I'm sorry, I don't understand. We were talking about the Animal Welfare legislation, yeah, and then you tell me that you went to Blackpool yesterday.

LAURA: To see the minister.

WILLIAM: A lot of us in a bus.

LAURA: The government want us all to go out of business!

WILLIAM: She's been hell to live with ever since she went and got hersen politicised.

LAURA: You had your war, I've got mine!

WILLIAM: There's ovver much meat out there!

LAURA: We're gonna picket Hull docks tomorrow –

WILLIAM: – I'm not gooin! I'm having a lie in!

LAURA: – You're coming with us!

WILLIAM: – I'm an 'undred fucking years awld and I'll have a fucking lie in whenever I fucking want!

LAURA: (*To VET.*) There's forty thousand carcasses come in
  every week through them docks –

WILLIAM: – Leave her alone. Yer embarrassing!

VET: We inspect those carcasses. They're Dutch. It's all legal.

LAURA: – Dutch my arse. They're onny butchered in Holland.

WILLIAM: It's not her fault!

LAURA: Mark my words, all them Polish, or Yugoslavian pigs'll
  be tethered.

WILLIAM: She's come from the other side of the bloody world
  and she's going round Europe in a camper van tomorrow.
  So give her a break.

LAURA: Yer not gonna stamp us are yer?

VET: How can I stamp you, yeah?

WILLIAM: We're illegal! All of a sudden.

VET: If you remove the stalls, and convert to loose housing,
  I'm sure you'll be considered for the scheme in the future.
  The sheds are in good condition. You could run this place
  as a finishing unit for a feed company. I know Fimber Feed
  do –

LAURA: – I'm not working wage labour raising pigs for
  the bloody squire. Any pigs on this farm are gonna be
  Harrison pigs! I've never had a penny in grants from
  Europe and yet him up the road with forty thousand
  fucking acres gets two million quid a year he dunt need.
  (*Enter TITCH quickly. He is carrying a rope made into a noose.
  He climbs up on to the table and puts the rope round a hook and
  the noose round his neck. The VET stands and backs off.*)
  Titch? Titch!?

WILLIAM: What yer doing?

TITCH: Killin' mesen.

VET: Oh my God!

WILLIAM: Don't worry love, he's all mouth and no trousers.

TITCH: That lass there, she's insulted me.

LAURA: What's she said?

TITCH: She ses I'm mistreating my girls.

VET: I never said that.

TITCH: You tek the backs off them stalls, and none of 'em'll go nowhere. I've never used tethering. None of my fucking girls have ever been tethered.

(*To LAURA.*) Have yer got me dinner?

(*LAURA takes his dinner out the oven and passes it up to him. He eats as he talks.*)

VET: I've recorded that. The sows are no longer tethered.

TITCH: I've never had 'em tethered.

LAURA: Aye, that's true. We've never tethered 'em.

VET: Alright, I'll put something in the margin, yeah?

(*She writes.*)

TITCH: You've hurt me feelings. Look at me! Is this normal behaviour?

LAURA: Don't kill yersen Titch.

WILLIAM: It's yer pub quiz tomorrow.

TITCH: Don't try psychology on me. It's never worked, never will.

(*Re: the meal, to LAURA.*) This is good this Laura, ta.

LAURA: Thanks Titch.

WILLIAM: Who's yer pub quiz match agin?

TITCH: Old White Hart. Them fucking bastard cheating paraplegics.

LAURA: Come down Titch love.

TITCH: No. I'm a suffragette.

WILLIAM: Yer can't kill yersen until yer've fixed me up a string to the fuse box in the porch. (*Pause.*) Like yer promised.

(*TITCH looks over to the porch.*)

LAURA: Yer've forgotten about that an't yer?

TITCH: Sorry. I'll do it when… Look! She in't gonna stamp us is she?

LAURA: We'll borrow the money off the bank and convert to loose housing.

WILLIAM: Yer can play football with 'em then.

TITCH: Aye?

WILLIAM: Aye.

TITCH: No. I'm gonna kill mesen. (*Pointing at the VET.*) Cos of you!

LAURA: We love yer Titch.

TITCH: Who fucking does?

LAURA: Everyone. Yer brilliant. Yer light up our lives.

TITCH: I din't set out to try an' light up anyone's life. I'm just fucking me.

LAURA: That's what we like. You. Yer great.

WILLIAM: Yer lovable.

TITCH: I'm not fucking lovable, I'm fucking upset!

LAURA: We can see yer upset.

WILLIAM: She's onny doing her job.

TITCH: My girls are happy! If you tek the backs off them stalls –

VET: – I know. They won't go 'nowhere', yeah?

WILLIAM: She can't stamp us. We're illegal.

TITCH: What we gonna do then?

WILLIAM: Yer could retrain as a computer game designer.

LAURA: Shurrup! It's no laughing matter – he's gonna kill hissen.

WILLIAM: He 'eckers like gonna kill hissen!

TITCH: I will. I'm gonna jump now! Here tek me plate.

(*The VET runs out.*)

WILLIAM: Yer an't gorr an audience now.

LAURA: Come down Titch love. I'll put yer favourite record on. I'll dance with yer.

(*LAURA goes to the CD player and puts on Dr. Hook's 'When you're in love with a beautiful woman'. TITCH slips his head out the noose.*)

TITCH: Dint wanna upset her. People can tek things the wrong way, eh?

(*Dr. Hook's 'When You're In Love With a Beautiful Woman' plays. He dances close with LAURA.*)

This song's fucking brilliant Uncle Will. Listen to the lyrics.
(*Singing along.*) When you're in love with a beautiful woman,

You watch your friends.

(*Explanatory to WILL.*) You watch your friends.

(*Singing.*) When you're in love with a beautiful woman,
You know it's hard.

(*Explanatory to WILL.*) You know it's hard.

Are yer having a good birthday Will?!

WILLIAM: Aye. Ta.

LAURA: Happy?

WILLIAM: I'm happy that Maudie never saw this day.

TITCH: Count yer blessings!

WILLIAM: I got me health. You two have gorr each other.

(*TITCH and LAURA dance.*)

(*End of scene.*)

A SONG IN YOUR HEART

(2008. A January evening. It's dark. Some of the windows are broken; some are boarded up. Ivy and weeds are growing freely on the outside of the house and some ivy has crept in through a window. The table has gone. On the floor are lots of plastic ready meal containers; unopened post; and Tesco plastic carrier bags. The carrier bags are taped to the windows, on the floor. On the floor is a single mattress. The TV has a lottery ticket taped to the screen. The room is in darkness. The sound of breaking glass off stage left in the bathroom area. Enter DANNY, a young man of about twenty-five. He turns the light on.)

DANNY: *(Shouted.)* 's only me!! *(Laughs.)*

> *(DANNY goes over to the gun cabinet and tries the door. It's locked. Enter BLUE, a man at least one generation older than DANNY.)*

> Filth in here! Farmers eh? They're fucking animals. The gun cabinet's over there.

> *(BLUE tries the door of the gun cabinet. He then runs his hand along the top of the kitchen cabinets looking for a key. DANNY finds a bottle of whiskey and slugs from the bottle. BLUE pulls out a drawer from the kitchen cabinet puts it on the floor, in the light, and starts sifting through it. DANNY does the same with a second drawer. BLUE watches him.)*

BLUE: Look through them drawers. I'm driving back. You were doing eighty-five miles an hour in a thirty limit.

DANNY: I was thinking about sex. You know that massage parlour down Humber Street, top of the old fruit market?

BLUE: I've never been.

DANNY: They got this really old Chinese tart there, bowt twennie stone. Smells like an horse what has been eating Chinese food. Always got a dirty arse. I love it.

BLUE: I'm not working with you again. Fost time last time. I'm gonna have a word with Daz, he didn't tell me you were mentally ill.

> *(BLUE's mobile phone goes off.)*

> *(On phone.)* Alright Debs…I'm working…I'll be back about two in morning…I'm sorry Debs…I'll come straight back to the flat…is our Phil there?…alright…I'm sorry.

(*BLUE turns the phone off. Sits and stares into space.*)

Gissa shot of that whiskey.

(*He takes it and swigs.*)

That was our Debs.

DANNY: Didn't think you was married.

BLUE: Me sister. Me dad's died. Ten minutes ago. Just now. What's the matter with you Danny? I said, me dad's just died.

DANNY: Are you gonna get summat in the will? Who gets his flat?

BLUE: He told me yesterday that I'm out the will, unless I dig his grave. Said he wants to teach me the dignity of labour.

DANNY: That's weird man.

BLUE: He gorrit from an old book he picked up in a car boot sale. Novel about cannibalism

DANNY: Get him cremated, that'll learn the bastard. Spreading is easier work than digging.

BLUE: What do you know about work? You've never had a job.

DANNY: I have. I was a drug dealer for two years.

BLUE: Me dad always wanted me to be a trawler skipper. But that was all over by time I was old enough. I think fishing woulda suited me.

DANNY: What are we looking for?

BLUE: The key to the gun cabinet.

DANNY: No keys in there. Come on let's make the best of a bad job and get back to Hull. I don't like the country, it's dark.

(*DANNY puts the drawer back and inspects the kitchen. He finds a laundry bag in a draw and sets it in the middle of the room and fills it with anything he finds he likes, which is very little.*)

BLUE: This place was a pig farm. Do you know how much a bacon sarnie should cost?

DANNY: What do you mean should cost?

BLUE: Twenty-seven pound. Over time farmers have developed the perfect bacon pig. So you get cheap meat. But do you ever say 'Thank God for the genius of the British farmer, he's just saved me twenty-four quid'? No, you say, – two pound fifty for a poxy bacon sarnie, that's

a bit of an ask!' If I won the lottery I'd buy meself a little
farm, hobby farming they call, it. Some cattle, they look
beautiful cattle. Dogs. Aye. Key!

(*BLUE produces a small key. Walks over to the gun cabinet and
tries the lock. It doesn't fit.*)

I believe that is the key to an electric socket safe. Check
the sockets. Here.

(*BLUE hands DANNY an electric screwdriver. DANNY starts on
the sockets. BLUE lights a cigarette.*)

They don't have to do it, farmers. They could get out of
bed one morning and say 'fuck this for a game of soldiers, I
think I'll sign on and do a bit of nicking'. We don't respect
the farmer in this country. In France 'Peasant' is a term
of endearment. And the mad thing is compared to our
farmers the French are useless. A big French farm is three
cows, two chickens and a duck.

DANNY: I like to listen to you talking. You could stand for
Parliament. Go on, why don't yer?

BLUE: Cos I'm a burglar. You need to get out of the city more
Danny. Gerr a bit of air in yer lungs. Bit of green. Gerr a
garden.

DANNY: I'm never having another garden. Gardening! It's a
fucking minefield! Here we go!

(*DANNY has found a double socket behind which is a small safe.
BLUE gives the key to DANNY and DANNY opens the safe. He tips
the money on the floor.*)

Wedding ring. It's a couple of quid. It's a pint. Medals.

(*DANNY gives the ring to BLUE. DANNY picks up three first world
war medals.*)

BLUE: First world war.

DANNY: Kenny'll have them. What they worth?

BLUE: Nowt much. They all got these campaign medals. Put
'em back. Giss that one.

(*BLUE looks at the Military Medal. DANNY has found an envelope
and is opening it.*)

DANNY: Picture of the Queen, cheer up love it might never
happen. (*Reading.*) 'William Harrison. Her majesty is

much interested to hear that you are celebrating your one hundredth birthday bla, bla.'

BLUE: No key.

(*BLUE looks at the Queen's letter, checking the date.*)

DANNY: The old bird must be walking about with it.

BLUE: Put the safe back.

DANNY: In a minute. I need a shit.

BLUE: Go for a shit then.

DANNY: I'm gonna shit in here, screw it back in the wall. It's funny, what's the matter with yer?

BLUE: Don't. This is my job, I'm telling you 'no'.

(*BLUE walks down stage and makes a phone call. DANNY waits until he's on the phone then secretly he shits into the safe.*)

(*On the phone.*) Kenny?…Look on your phone it says who it is…yeah, I'm working hard…got a 1917 Military Medal, two bars…Really?…the good news for us is he's dead, he was hundred years old in nineteen ninety five…I might see you Monday…Tarra.(*To DANNY.*) Battlefield bravery award, that's what Kenny says.

DANNY: Worth a bit then?

BLUE: Fifty quid.

DANNY: We'll have some of that!

BLUE: No. Put it back in the safe.

DANNY: I'm not putting fifty quid back in the wall!

BLUE: We've come here for the guns. That's all. Gimme that.

(*DANNY hands over the safe. BLUE looks at the shit in it.*)

You're sick in the head.

DANNY: I get tense.

(*During the next DANNY laughs as he puts the safe back and screws it back into the wall.*)

BLUE: Shh!! Car!

DANNY: Fuck!

BLUE: Kill the light! Get rid of that whiskey! Get upstairs!

(*BLUE and DANNY go up the stairs. Enter LAURA, now eighty-five, with YOUNG AGAR. LAURA looks in a poor state, like a bag lady. She takes her coat off revealing a Little Chef waitress uniform.*)

LAURA: (*To AGAR.*) Yer don't want the house then?

AGAR: No.

LAURA: It's a good house. Been good to me. You get Uncle Will's barn chucked in. All me furniture, 'cept that good big table, they nicked that. Them hooks, is five quid each in Beverley antiques.

AGAR: What's the photograph?

LAURA: Titch. That's where he hung hissen. He threatened a few times, which was always funny, and then one time he did it. Daft bugger.

AGAR: I have no interest in the house. I expect your solicitor will advise you correctly to wait for someone from town with more money than sense.

LAURA: You just want the sheds then? They're good Warcup sheds.

AGAR: We have been over this so many times Mrs Harrison. Yes. I just want the sheds.

LAURA: I coulda been your mother.

(*Pause.*) I'm not signing. Not tonight.

AGAR: (*Big sigh of frustration.*) I'm going. In future, you can phone me, but I'm not coming out to negotiate. You're wasting my time Mrs Harrison, and I have to say there feels as if there's something deliberate about it. Why will you not sign tonight? What's tonight's reason?

LAURA: It's the lottery tonight. I might win. I been feeling lucky all day.

AGAR: Goodnight.

LAURA: Ta for the lift. I'll sign tomorrow if I don't win.

(*AGAR leaves. LAURA fiddles with the TV. She finds the Saturday night Lottery show. The boys creep down the stair. LAURA prepares for a bowl of cornflakes with sugar on top. She sits and eats them. The door opens slowly and BLUE peeks out. BLUE walks up to behind LAURA and then steps in front of her.*)

BLUE: Shhh!

(*LAURA stands, uttering nothing but a whine.*)

Sit down love. We're not gonna hurt you. If you do what we say, you won't get hurt. We both got mothers we love. We want the guns, and then we'll be off, alright?

DANNY: We can't find the key. Where's the fucking key!?

BLUE: Shut it you daft chav. Chill alright. Sorry Mum. Now
then, where's the key?

(*LAURA has the key round her neck on a chain. She lifts the chain
over her head.*)

Lovely. Sweet.

(*BLUE goes over to the cabinet and opens it. There are no guns
in it.*)

DANNY: Alright love? Finish your cornflakes.

BLUE: Where's the gun, Mum?

DANNY: Where's the fucking gun?!

(*LAURA whines a bit more and then DANNY grabs her by the
lapels and shouts at her.*)

You want some, eh!?

(*BLUE drags DANNY off her, genuinely angry. BLUE throws
DANNY across the room.*)

BLUE: What you fucking doing? Show some respect! Alright!?

(*To LAURA.*) I'm sorry love. He's well out of order.

(*To DANNY.*) Get over there.

DANNY: It was only a little smack Blue.

(*BLUE walks over to DANNY and takes him downstage.*)

BLUE: (*Whispering.*) What's my name?

DANNY: (*Whispering.*) Fuck. Did I? Sorry.

BLUE: Once we got the gun we're off. Where is it love? By
law you gotta keep it in the case. I'm not gonna hurt you
love, but just tell me where the gun is. I'm a decent bloke.
I respect you.

DANNY: Just give her a fucking slap, what's the matter
with you.

BLUE: (*To LAURA.*) Trust me. You're dealing with me Mom, not
him. Now, where's the gun?

LAURA: (*More of a whine than anything.*) No.

DANNY: Oh fucking hell!

(*DANNY picks a knife from the kitchen top and puts the knife to
LAURA's neck.*)

Where's the fucking gun! Tell us or I'll rip yer head off and
shit down yer neck!

BLUE: Get off her!

DANNY: Get back or I'll do her. Stay back there you. Right back! You've been on my fucking case all day. Now, I'm gonna have a bit of fun.

(*DANNY pushes LAURA on to the mattress, all the time holding the knife. He stands unzips his jeans.*)

Right. Lie back love. Come on, you done it before.

(*DANNY pushes LAURA onto the floor and straddles her. The lights and TV go to black suddenly.*)

What the fuck's going on?

BLUE: You on a meter?

LAURA: No.

DANNY: Where's the fuse box?

LAURA: In t'lobby.

BLUE: Shh! I can fucking hear someone. Shh!

(*DANNY goes over to the door in the back wall, and opens it, knife in hand. WILLIAM is in the doorway sitting in a motorised wheelchair, dressed in pyjamas, in the dark. He is now 109 years old with long white hair. He rests a shot gun in his lap. He has one hand on a length of string which goes to the fuse box above his head. He pulls the string and the lights flash on. There is a moment of tableau. Then WILLIAM shoots DANNY at very close range, and DANNY collapses dead.*)

No mate, please mate no. I an't hurt no-one. She's alright. Please mate. We're just doing a bit of nicking. She ant been touched, mate, honest, I an't touched her. Please mate, please.

WILLIAM: Don't call me 'mate'. It's annoying.

BLUE: I been decent with the woman, ask her please.

LAURA: I'm alright Dad.

WILLIAM: (*To LAURA.*) Who was that in the car?

LAURA: The young squire.

WILLIAM: What's he want?

LAURA: Dad. You know very well what we're doing.

WILLIAM: Who's gerrin the sheds?

LAURA: I told yer. The squire'll buy the sheds. Best to try and gerr a townie to buy the house.

BLUE: Don't shoot please.

WILLIAM: Worr about my barn?

LAURA: House and barn for the townies. Land and sheds for the squire.

WILLIAM: Did we win lottery?

LAURA: They an't had it yet. I've felt lucky all day.

WILLIAM: Empty your pockets. Mate.

(*BLUE complies, taking out the wedding ring, and the war medals.*)

BLUE: Military medal. That'll be yours yeah?

WILLIAM: Well it in't yours is it.

BLUE: I respect you. I honour you. You lost your legs in the war yeah? I respect that. How did you lose your legs?

WILLIAM: Tank ran over them.

BLUE: Filthy Germans eh.

WILLIAM: Germans din't have tanks.

BLUE: We don't do enough history nowadays do we? You didn't die though, eh.

WILLIAM: There's an angel for farmers. Obviously there in't one for burglars. Where's me letter from the Queen?

BLUE: I an't touched your letter Mister.

WILLIAM: It's still in the safe then?

BLUE: Yeah.

WILLIAM: Open the safe up love.

(*LAURA takes a screwdriver from the drawer and opens the safe.*)

BLUE: Oh no. You're not gonna like this. Before you get upset let me tell you that it was Danny, him, who did this, in the safe. It was him.

(*LAURA brings the safe over, looking at the contents as she does.*)

LAURA: That filthy beggar's done his toilet in the safe. I've read about that kind of thing with burglars.

BLUE: He was a nutter.

(*WILLIAM has a look in the safe.*)

WILLIAM: Where's me letter?

BLUE: It's underneath. It wan't really about you. He never liked the Queen. His sister's half Irish.

WILLIAM: Go pick that kitchen knife up off the top there.

(*BLUE picks up the knife.*)

BLUE: Please. Don't shoot. I'll do anything.

WILLIAM: Oh aye. Hold it t'other way round. Like yer stabbing.

BLUE: No, please. Don't shoot.

(*BLUE turns the knife around.*)

WILLIAM: Kneel down. Shuffle towards me. That's enough.

BLUE: Please don't shoot! My father died today.

WILLIAM: Don't you dare lie to me sunshine.

BLUE: I'm not lying. He'd been ill for months. Emphysema.

LAURA: I'm sorry to hear that love. He's alright, you killed the bad un.

WILLIAM: You comfortable?

BLUE: Yeah. Thank you.

WILLIAM: Good. Cos I'm gonna watch the lottery.

(*The lottery draw is done, in silence. They get one number somewhere in the middle of the draw. This is seen by a glance between LAURA and WILLIAM. LAURA doesn't need to check her numbers, she knows them off by heart, but she does hold her ticket. She turns the TV off.*)

You ever worked for a living?

BLUE: What?

WILLIAM: We got good sheds, but we an't got no labour.

LAURA: We need a pigman.

BLUE: What do you want me to do?

WILLIAM: Raise pigs.

BLUE: I like pigs.

WILLLIAM: Have you ever used a steam pressure washer?

BLUE: I could learn.

WILLIAM: It's all hard work, pigs, but it's fun.

LAURA: If one of them gets out. That's funny, in't it Dad.

WILLIAM: Always med me laugh.

BLUE: Me dad's sister had a dairy farm near Hornsea. I used to go up there on me holidays. Loved it.

WILLIAM: Pigs is different.

LAURA: Yer'll stink of pigs.

BLUE: I don't mind.

LAURA: Yer car stinks of pigs.

WILLIAM: Yer wife stinks of pigs.

BLUE: Yer can get used to owt if yer have to!

LAURA: Yer DVD player'll stink of pigs.

WILLIAM: Yer DVDs'll stink of pigs.

LAURA: Yer DVD disk cleaning kit'll stink of pigs.

(*WILLIAM and LAURA laugh. WILLIAM levels the gun as if to shoot.*)

WILLIAM: (*Serious again.*) Yer could live like that and still keep a song in yer heart could yer? Cos if yer couldn't do it with a song in yer heart I'll shoot yer dead now.

BLUE: I'd sing all day. I can, I can do it.

LAURA: Could you collect sperm from a boar?

BLUE: Yer catch it in a flask.

LAURA: And if you have to, yer give it an helping hand.

WILLIAM: Could yer check yer sows, see if they're 'ot.

LAURA: Press her back, see if she's ready.

BLUE: I could learn.

WILLIAM: Could yer open yer post in a morning?

LAURA: From the bank?

WILLIAM: From the feed company?

WILLIAM: From the ministry eh?

BLUE: Yes.

WILLIAM: Yer could open yer bills from the vet and still be fun to live with?

BLUE: Yeah.

LAURA: Yer could open yer post from Brussels, could yer?

WILLIAM: Aye, that's a good un. Open it, read it, read it again, read it a third time, and still not understand it.

LAURA: Tek it to your solicitor, pay him to read, and explain it yer.

WILLIAM: And still you don't understand it.

LAURA: And he don't understand it either!

WILLIAM: All you know for sure is that the whole world's gone mad.

LAURA: And next morning, could you get out of bed, put your gear on –

WILLIAM: – and with a song in your heart, go round your sheds and look at each and every pig, and really care –

LAURA: – not cos yer love the pig itself, but because if yer
    don't yer not doing yer job.

WILLIAM: – cos if yer don't look at every pig every day then
    one day one of them'll have P double R S or swine fever
    and yer wiped out over night –

LAURA: – And yer wife'll have to go and work in the Little
    Chef. Though that's not worr happened to us.

WILLIAM: Could you do that son?

LAURA: And keep singing?

BLUE: I imagine, it's a hard life, is it?

LAURA: It's enough to mek a monkey bite its young.

WILLIAM: And you wunt let all of that worry get to yer, and
    you could make love to your wife?

LAURA: Could yer make love to yer wife?

BLUE: Yes. I think I could.

WILLIAM: You could adore her; worship her; and make her
    feel beautiful and blessed and glad she married a pig
    farmer and not James Bond. Yer could do that could yer?
    (*BLUE breaks down and cries. He's beyond it.*)

BLUE: Yes! I'll do it. I'm serious. I wanna give it a go. Give me
    a chance. I won't let you down.
    (*WILLIAM puts his gun down.*)

WILLIAM: I think we just gorr ourselves a new pig man.
    (*To black.*)
    (*The End.*)

IN THE CLUB

Characters

PHILIP WARDROBE MEP
ALEXANDRIA TOGUSHEV (SASHA)
FRAU FLUGELHAMMERLEIN
MEHMET AZIZ
BEATRICE RENARD
EDDIE FREDERICKS
ANDRÉ PICQ
NICOLA DAWS

Also:
GENDARME, DOCTOR, ARCHBISHOP, PRIESTS

SET

The function suite of a superior Strasbourg hotel. In the back wall there are double doors which are the main entrance doors to the suite. When these double doors are open the doors to a lift can be seen. Downstage right is a door which leads to a double room with a picture window view of the Strasbourg Parliament building as a feature. This is Bed 1. This room also has an en-suite bathroom – Bath 1. Downstage left is a door which opens into a smaller bedroom with en-suite bathroom (Bed 2 and Bath 2). Upstage right is a door to a walk-in linen cupboard. Against the wall stage left are two side tables. On one of these is a laptop computer and various papers, a fax and phone etc. On one wall is a pull-down (i.e. rolled-up) film projector screen. A sofa, armchair and coffee table are set downstage centre.

In the Club was first performed at Hampstead Theatre on 25 July 2007, with the following cast:

PHILIP WARDROBE James Fleet
SASHA Siân Brooke
FRAU FLUGELHAMMERLEIN Carol Macready
MEHMET AZIZ Gary Oliver
BEATRICE RENARD Anna Francolini
EDDIE FREDERICKS Richard Moore
ANDRÉ PICQ Huw Higginson
NICOLA DAWS Carla Mendonça
GENDARME Dermot Canavan
ARCHBISHOP / DOCTOR Roderick Smith

Director David Grindley
Designer Jonathan Fensom
Lighting Designer Jason Taylor
Sound Designer Gregory Clarke

The play was subsequently revived for a UK tour, beginning at Richmond Theatre on 12 February 2008.

°

Act One

(*The present. Early morning. A mobile phone goes off in the central area. Enter PHILIP WARDROBE (MEP) from Bed 1, in dressing gown. He has a can of athlete's foot powder in one hand. He searches for the mobile.*)

PHILIP: (*On the phone.*) Nicola! Darling! I'm here now, in Strasbourg... For the last time I'm not having an affair!
(*Enter SASHA through the main doors, with newspapers, work stuff etc. She is looking sexy, efficient. They acknowledge each other as work colleagues do.*)
I am totally and incredibly not interested in other women.
(*He sneaks a lech at SASHA's bum.*)
...yes, every other 'male member' of the European Parliament does have a 'Strasbourg Wife' and some of them have a 'Brussels Wife' on top, or underneath, but I do not, I have you, a 'Kettering wife'... Nicola!? (*Off the phone.*)
(*PHILIP reaches for a packet of cigarettes. SASHA snatches them away from him. She gives him a coffee. He begins to powder his toes with athlete's foot powder.*)
How the hell did I find this place last night?

SASHA: Les Aviateurs nightclub closes at three in the morning so I sent a car with instructions to collect a man sitting on the kerb singing 'You'll never Walk Alone'.

PHILIP: Sasha, you're a credit to the whole concept of illegal immigration.
(*He starts having a look around.*)
This place must be costing me an arm and a leg.

SASHA: It's not costing you anything.
(*He opens the main double doors to reveal a group of PRIESTS / VICARS standing by the lift.*)

PHILIP: Bonjour!
(*Closes doors. Opens cupboard door and looks inside.*)

SASHA: It's the most expensive hotel in Strasbourg.

PHILIP: You know, I love being an MEP. It's a win-win situation. The people of Northamptonshire don't know who I am, and I don't know who they are.
(*Pulls down the screen.*)
Classy place this!

SASHA: There's a problem with the plumbing in my room. And the icer's not working. I've told the management.

(*PHILIP just glances into Bed 2 without going in.*)

And the Turkish Ambassador wants a meeting this morning.

PHILIP: No politics today! Nicola's flying in this afternoon for...you know.

SASHA: Today?

PHILIP: Yes! Monday the twelfth of March two thousand and eight will go down in history as the day that Philip Wardrobe MEP personally intervened to reverse the disaster of Europe's falling birth rate.

SASHA: He wants to know, quote, 'What the hell did you say to Prime Minister Erdogan?'.

PHILIP: I only asked him which one of his barking mad mullahs came up with the idea of three years in prison for slagging off Turkey.

SASHA: Article 301 was Erdogan's own idea.

PHILIP: Bugger! There's me, busting a gut, going round telling Europe that Turkey is an incredibly cuddly liberal democracy and what do they do, start banging up any Turk daft enough to say 'Actually, I think Turkey's a bit shit!'.

SASHA: See the Turkish ambassador, the man paying for this room, this morning and –

PHILIP: – Yes! But put a box round the afternoon and call it 'face to face' meeting, me and Nicola, one on one.

SASHA: You know, if Turkey joins the EU one in four Europeans will be Muslim.

PHILIP: One in four! Bloody hell! That's nearly a quarter.

SASHA: Why don't you embarrass the Democrats over their split on Turkey? If the Parliament, the MEPs, demand an opportunity to discuss Turkey's accession rather than just accepting what the Commissioners say –

PHILIP: – unelected Commissioners –

SASHA: – the debate would turn into an open season on the EPP. It would destroy them and then the socialists could step into the vacuum.

(*Knock at the door. SASHA opens the door. ANDRÉ stands there in a boiler suit. He has a moustache and the trappings of a plumber.*)

ANDRÉ: Bonjour Mademoiselle.

SASHA: Bonjour.

ANDRÉ: Il y a un petit problème de plomberie?

SASHA: Dans la deuxième chambre. Deux minutes s'il vous plaît.

(*SASHA goes off to change into the room stage right.*)

PHILIP: Elle a besoin de…

ANDRÉ: – D'accord! English?

PHILIP: Yup. Sit down. Philip Wardrobe.

(*They shake. ANDRÉ and PHILIP sit on the sofa. PHILIP administers powder to his foot.*)

ANDRÉ: André Picq. I'm Belgian.

PHILIP: Oh. Bad luck.

ANDRÉ: Athlete's foot?

PHILIP: Yes.

ANDRÉ: Me too. You have it on both feet?

PHILIP: Yup.

ANDRÉ: Me too. Athlete's feet.

PHILIP: In English we don't say 'athlete's feet'. Technically what I've got here is athlete's foot twice.

(*ANDRÉ takes two twiglets from the bowl, and gives them to PHILIP.*)

ANDRÉ: Put a twiglet between each toe. You need to get air to the skin.

PHILIP: That's actually an incredibly not bad idea.

(*PHILIP sticks twiglets between his toes. SASHA comes out of Bed 2 carrying her washbag.*)

SASHA: D'accord.

(*SASHA stares at PHILIP's twigletted feet.*)

PHILIP: I'm aerating my toes.

SASHA: I've had a brilliant idea.

PHILIP: No! You're my personal assistant. When you have a brilliant idea, it is actually my idea. So tell me, what is this incredibly brilliant idea of yours that I've just had?

(*During the next SASHA takes a jiffy bag from her desk.*)

PHILIP: It was raining, and I didn't have anything else to do. (*Beat.*) But I resisted.

SASHA: You resisted?!

PHILIP: Hard to believe isn't it. She's been chasing me ever since.

SASHA: (*Reading email.*) 'I would love coffee with you this morning.'

PHILIP: Get rid of her! Tell her I died.

(*The phone rings. SASHA answers.*)

SASHA: (*On phone.*) She's on her way up is she? Thank you. Who would you least want to see you like this?

PHILIP: The Socialist whip? Frau Flugelhammerlein. Aaaagghhh! (*Goes into Bed 1.*)

(*SASHA does a bit of tidying up, hiding foot powder and twiglets. Knock at the door. Enter FRAU FLUGELHAMMERLEIN. She oozes power.*)

FRAU F: Morgen Sasha. Where is he? I don't have long.

SASHA: Yes Frau Flugelhammerlein.

(*SASHA knocks on Bed 1 door.*)

Mr Wardrobe! Frau –

(*Enter PHILIP immaculately dressed and looking brilliant.*)

PHILIP: – Guten Morgen Freda. Wie geht's?!

(*FRAU F hands PHILIP a document. She notices ANDRÉ.*)

FRAU F: Es geht mir gut, danke! Philip, ve socialists have a big problem.

PHILIP: What? Socialism? I've been meaning to – [talk to you about that]

FRAU F: – Turkey! Ve embrace Islam. But, look at Holland. When that medieval madman killed Theo Van Gogh, that was Europe's 9/11, it's changed everything.

PHILIP: Yes, I remember the good old days when a Muslim didn't mind living next door to a live sex show. He either kept his head down, or joined in!

FRAU F: If it was the Methodists going around blowing themselves up, trying to kill us all, we'd have to think twice about letting the Welsh in wouldn't we?

PHILIP: Oh come on Freda, you can't compare Turkey with Wales. Turkey is a modern, civilised, secular democracy.

(*Beat.*) Look, I'm having some success with Erdogan. He's now scrapped adultery as a criminal offence.

FRAU F: Gut! But I am told that virginity testing is still practised, and honour killings are rife!

PHILIP: You can lead a horse to water, but you can't make it windsurf.

FRAU F: Ve Germans don't like metaphor. Ve don't see the point in beating around the bush.

ANDRÉ: (*To PHILIP.*) Tuesday! She rings me at work, I have to put my tools back in the bag, and go home and fornicate!

PHILIP: Excuse me André, but I'm in a meeting now. The plumber. He's trying for a baby with his girlfriend and so am I.

FRAU F: With his girlfriend?

PHILIP: No, with my partner, Nicola.

FRAU F: You and Nicola are not married?

PHILIP: No.

ANDRÉ: (*To FRAU.*) She's flying over today, to be serviced! We men are nothing to you women. We are the cheap form of IVF!

(*ANDRÉ goes into Bed 2.*)

PHILIP: Not even a good plumber, I've known serial killers use less duct tape.

FRAU F: I'd like you to write a report. It's called 'virk' Philip.

PHILIP: That word's always sounded a bit German to me.

(*Enter ANDRÉ.*)

ANDRÉ: – (*To PHILIP.*) We play fantasy games. Lorry driver / waitress. Pilot / air hostess. Magician / magician's assistant – that's my favourite. It is the only way I can get an erection.

PHILIP: Look André! You were very good on the athlete's foot but I do not have erection problems and if I did, I wouldn't call a plumber! And, I'm in a meeting right now!

(*ANDRÉ is pushed into Bed 1.*)

FRAU F: Belgian?

PHILIP: This is an idea of Sasha's which I thought of this morning. If we Socialists propose a vote of censure of the

Commission for being out of touch with the people of Europe in agreeing to Turkish accession –

FRAU F: – the Islamophobes in the Christian Democrats would support that.

PHILIP: – but the democrat Democrats, the free marketers, would oppose it.

FRAU F: And the Democrats' split would fatally widen. The EPP / ED alliance would be –

PHILIP: – Kaput!

FRAU F: Tot!

PHILIP: Gesundheit!

FRAU F: And we could finally deliver a truly socialist Europe.

PHILIP: But to do this we need a Democrat who is both a) Islamophobic, and b) mad enough to work with us to destroy his own party.

FRAU F: Beatrice Renard! The Chair of the Women's Committee.

PHILIP: I had an informal meeting with her last night.

FRAU F: You were dancing on the tables in Les Aviateurs. She in bra unt knickers; you were down to your unterpants.

PHILIP: Boxer shorts. There's a world of difference.

FRAU F: Set up a meeting with her today –

PHILIP: – not today! Today is about –

FRAU F: – Philip! Why did you come into politics?

PHILIP: Because I like telling people what to do.

FRAU F: I will be making my nomination for President of the Parliament this week.

PHILIP: Me? President of the European Parliament?

(*FRAU F makes to leave. At the door she turns.*)

FRAU F: For the Presidency you would need to be married.

(*FRAU F leaves. PHILIP spins into action.*)

PHILIP: Me! President! Ha, ha! Get Beatrice Renard on the phone! Tell her I would love to have coffee with her, here, now.

SASHA: No! Mehmet will be here any minute. How about Beatrice at ten o'clock? Can I remind you, the Parliament register will be open now?

PHILIP: I can't be arsed to sign today.

SASHA: Pederast! You earn a hundred and eighty euros just for signing your name! Some of my people in your country are picking tomatoes all week for less than what you get paid for two seconds' work!

PHILIP: Okay. I'll go and sign. Don't call me a pederast. I know it's a common Russian swear word but it's really not appropriate. Arsehole, twat, wanker – I wouldn't argue with any of those.

(*PHILIP leaves.*)

SASHA: (*On the phone.*) 'Allo.

(*ANDRÉ appears, checks out SASHA, and sits on the couch and lights a cigarette. SASHA watches him as he smokes and spreads out.*)

Je vous appelle de la part de Philip Wardrobe...oui, Sasha, c'est moi...cela lui ferait plaisir de prendre un café avec vous ce matin...dix heures?...parfait Ciao. (*To ANDRÉ.*) It's no smoking in here.

ANDRÉ: We need to talk.

(*ANDRÉ tears off his moustache.*)

SASHA: Is that a false moustache?

ANDRÉ: No. It is a real moustache which I tear off my face when I feel like a change. I am a master of disguise. They call me 'The Chameleon'. I created a plumbing problem in your room so that I could get access.

(*He shows her his ID.*)

You know what OLAF is I presume?

SASHA: It's the fraud investigation department of the Commission. Despite the fact that nine billion euros has gone missing, you have never successfully prosecuted anyone.

ANDRÉ: The longer an animal goes without killing and eating, the hungrier it gets.

SASHA: Why are you interested in me? I am a student.

ANDRÉ: Your student visa ran out on March the first this year.

SASHA: (*Genuinely distressed.*) Please don't deport me! My mother is a lorry driver, and my father assembles sunglasses on the kitchen table. I want to buy them both a home in the country so they can retire.

ANDRÉ: – my telescope is not focused on you. OLAF is not the immigration service, although I can always make a phone call. Are you going to help me today?

SASHA: Do I have a choice?

ANDRÉ: Mr Wardrobe employs this Nicola Daws, his partner, as his 'full time' Office Manager in the UK. Pays her eighty thousand euros a year. However, Nicola Daws is the 'full time' Secretary General of Human Rights Now! I have a good nose for a bad stink.

SASHA: I'm not involved!

ANDRÉ: I understand there is not much in the way of employment in your home town of Murmansk. Fish processing.

SASHA: Suka! Tva-ya mama sa-syot sobachie khuy-ee!

ANDRÉ: I was not aware that my mother has sex with animals.

SASHA: You speak Russian?!

ANDRÉ: Chameleon and polyglot.

SASHA: I've never met Nicola.

(*ANDRÉ places a transmitter under the coffee table.*)

ANDRÉ: This is an omni-directional condenser microphone.

SASHA: You can't do that, can you?

ANDRÉ: Do you wish to see the paperwork? This will be my office.

(*He goes into the linen cupboard and closes the door. Enter PHILIP, carrying a bouquet of roses.*)

PHILIP: I think I've shook the bastard off!

SASHA: Who?

PHILIP: Mr Squeaky Clean. Hans Peter Martin. He was hiding in a rubber plant filming all the MEPs signing in and leaving on a golf trip. Eight of us had to sneak out through the kitchens.

(*During the next PHILIP goes into Bed 1, and puts the flowers in a vase, and reappears having taken his jacket off.*)

Is Beatrice coming up then?

SASHA: Ten o'clock yes. Turkish ambassador at nine.

PHILIP: (*Off.*) Just time to do my expenses from yesterday.

SASHA: Now is not a good time to do expenses.

PHILIP: (*Returning.*) Anytime is a good time to do expenses!
Kerching! Most important job of the day! Come on!

SASHA: (*Loud.*) Okay! Yesterday. Travel! Brussels to Strasbourg.
You shared a car so I'll claim twenty euros petrol money.
(*SASHA nods violently.*)

PHILIP: Are you mentally ill?! Yes, I shared a car, but we claim
Air France club class return. Should be near enough fifteen
hundred euros.
(*SASHA is mouthing 'No!', and 'Shh!!'*)
What?! Hard earned money that. You want to try sitting in
the kid's seat of a Renault Espace for five hours while six
drunk Dutchmen run a sensationally well-organised farting
competition. Grandad Wardrobe was a miner, but he never
had to work in those conditions. My canary committed
suicide before we'd left Belgium.
(*PHILIP stands.*)
I'll get the receipts.
(*PHILIP exits to his bedroom closing door behind him. ANDRÉ
comes out of the cupboard wearing headphones, note book in
hand.*)

ANDRÉ: I have my fish on ze hook. I look forward to seeing
you in court. À la prochaine.
(*ANDRÉ leaves. Enter PHILIP from Bed 1 with receipts in
hand.*)

PHILIP: Tractor Bar, thirty seven fifty; Mickey Mouse bar –
eighty five ten; Kitty O'Shea's –

SASHA: – I'm going down to the lobby now to leave this bomb
with reception.

PHILIP: Goodo! (*On phone.*) Nicola, listen, I've got an idea…
how about a role-play game this afternoon?
(*PHILIP shoos SASHA out the room.*)
…lorry driver / waitress?…pilot / air hostess?…magician /
magician's assistant!?… Well what's your fantasy?… That's
not going to work is it!… Because I'm not in it!… President
and tart?… Yeah! You speak French, can you do Parisian
whore?… Great. Et, quand nous enconterons, tu dois
m'appeller 'Monsieur Le President'. See you later.

(*Off the phone. There is a knock at the door. PHILIP opens it to
EDDIE FREDERICKS, an MEP and Yorkshire pig farmer of about
fifty-five. There is a copy of the* Daily Mail *in his jacket pocket,
visible. He is carrying a briefcase and a sleeping bag.*)

EDDIE: How do?

PHILIP: You can't stay here Eddie!

EDDIE: – Yer not a man of yer word then?

PHILIP: Oh bugger. What did I say?

EDDIE: 'If yer bring me post up from Brussels yer can sleep on
the floor.'

(*EDDIE hands over a pile of post in which there is a large jiffy
bag.*)

Kaw! I'm worn out. Three weeks in Brussels, and then
every bloody fourth week pack up and off to Strasbourg.
Barmy! Twelve million euro down the pan every month for
nowt. If you paid an architect to design you an 'ouse and
he put the bedroom in Leeds and the bog in Scarborough
you'd think he were mad wun't yer?!

PHILIP: The Brussels / Strasbourg thing is a symbol of the
reconciliation between Germany and France.

EDDIE: If they want a symbol of reconciliation they can 'ave a
framed photograph of my arse.

(*Enter SASHA.*)

SASHA: Hello Eddie.

EDDIE: Hello Sash love. Looking gorgeous!

PHILIP: Why don't you just pay for your own hotel and claim
it back?

EDDIE: Cos as the UK Independence Party MEP for the East
Riding of God's Own Country I made a commitment that
if I won a seat on this disgusting gravy train I would travel
in the guards' van. (*He takes out a snap tin and a flask.*) What
do you think?

PHILIP: What do I think about what?

EDDIE: Winston Churchill – cigar; Margaret Thatcher –
'andbag; Eddie Fredericks – snap tin and flask. Iconic
symbols of thrift and incorruptibility.

PHILIP: Utter genius. You can't stay here! The Turkish
Ambassador is due any moment and will be incredibly not

impressed when he discovers that I spend my leisure time with a direct descendant of Cro-Magnon Man.

SASHA: Eddie, you get on well with the British Tories don't you?

EDDIE: I wunt trust 'em as far as I could chuck 'em.

SASHA: What I mean is, on policy, you're close?

EDDIE: Only cos they nicked our policies.

SASHA: (*To PHILIP.*) There's twenty-seven British Tories affiliated to the EPP, that's potentially twenty-seven anti-Turkish votes for the Censure, they won't talk to you, you're a Socialist but they'll talk to UKIP, here, at lunchtime, if there's a free buffet.

PHILIP: Eddie! Let me show you to your room!

EDDIE: It's a bog I need! I've had a couple of prisoners due for parole since Luxembourg.

(*Leads him to Bed 1. EDDIE goes off into Bath 1.*)

PHILIP: This is the third incredibly brilliant idea of yours I've had today already. Email all those Tories, and invite them here for lunch.

SASHA: But what about Nicola?

PHILIP: She doesn't get here until four.

(*PHILIP picks up the jiffy bag that EDDIE brought in.*)
What's this?

SASHA: That's not our bomb.

PHILIP: Okay.

SASHA: Suka! Look at this!

(*SASHA hands PHILIP a copy of the* Daily Mail.)

PHILIP: (*Reading.*) 'MEP IN TURKISH ORGASM STORM. Beatrice Renard' – oh no! – 'Chair of the Women's Committee, bla bla bla, said she won't vote to let Turkey into the EU until Turkish men improve as lovers, and learn to provide the thirty-six million women of that nation with the orgasms which are their right as citizens of a modern, liberal, democracy. Women's position in Islam, bla, bla, bla…' OH BUGGER! Trust her!

(*Toilet flush is heard. Enter EDDIE from Bed 1.*)

EDDIE: That's trap one out of action for ten minutes.

PHILIP: So half an hour tops with Mehmet and get him out
the building sharpish cos if he bumps into Renard there'll
be blood on the carpet, my blood! Easy! Mehmet at nine,
cigarette break, Beatrice at ten.

(*SASHA takes his packet of cigarettes from him.*)

– a quick siesta and then an afternoon of baby making.

(*EDDIE looks questioningly at SASHA.*)

SASHA: Nicola's flying over.

EDDIE: Are you on a promise?

PHILIP: Nicola and I are trying for a baby.

EDDIE: I know, you told me that last back end. She still not
pregnant? Who's the problem?

PHILIP: We're both fine, it's just one of those unutterably
tedious modern city living overworked stressy things.

EDDIE: Sperm count.

PHILIP: Eddie, I am ignoring you.

EDDIE: King Arthur, my Suffolk Old Spot boar, well, I was
gerrin a lot of sows not in pig after service, so I took to
packing his balls with ice.

PHILIP: We're a bit short of ice.

EDDIE: Sperm are like cod or haddock. They love the cawld.

PHILIP: This morning I have a negotiation with the Turkish
Ambassador, followed by a meeting with Madame Renard,
Chair of the European Parliament Women's Committee.
Instinct alone tells me that I would not perform at my best
in either of those delicate situations if I were to sit there
with my testicles packed in ice.

EDDIE: This in't important, yer know – Politics. Kids is the
only job in the world any of us have to get right.

SASHA: It can't do any harm can it? Give it a go.

(*SASHA begins to prepare a beermug-style glass with ice.*)

EDDIE: Gerra glass of water, put some ice in and then
whenever yer can, five minutes at a time, nip into the bog
and just give 'em a little dip.

SASHA: Still or sparkling?

EDDIE: Personally I'd go for sparkling. And bung a slice of
lemon in.

SASHA: What does the lemon do?

EDDIE: Nowt. Burr if yer drink it accidentally, it tastes better.

(*SASHA stands before PHILIP with the glass.*)

SASHA: Does it work?

EDDIE: Every squirt'll have ten thousand sperm and everyone of them'll be a swimmer.

SASHA: This is the last of the ice. That's your ration for the day.

PHILIP: (*To EDDIE.*) Little dip, whenever I can?

(*EDDIE nods. PHILIP takes the glass and goes into Bed 1 and closes door. There is a knock on the main door.*)

SASHA: Mehmet! Quick! Give me that paper!

(*EDDIE hands her the* Daily Mail *which was on the table.*)

EDDIE: This one or...

(*SASHA snatches it and turns away. EDDIE takes out his own copy and looks at it to see what might be interesting. SASHA puts the paper in her bin under the desk. She then lets in the Turkish Ambassador MEHMET AZIZ. He is a handsome man in a western suit, carrying a briefcase which is identical to EDDIE's. He also carries SASHA's jiffy bag 'bomb'.*)

MEHMET: Bonjour mademoiselle.

SASHA: Good morning, I'm Sasha, Mr Wardrobe's assistant. This is –

EDDIE: – Eddie Fredericks. Yorkshireman, Pig Farmer, and UKIP member – in that order.

MEHMET: You are Yorkshire not English?

EDDIE: Forget yer Islam, forget yer Christianity – there's onny three sorts of folk in the world; Yorkshiremen; them as wanna be Yorkshiremen; and them what lacks ambition.

MEHMET: – Is Mr Wardrobe here?

SASHA: He's just having a little dip.

MEHMET: There is a pool? Mmm. It is a magnificent hotel. Very old Europe.

SASHA: Please sit down.

(*MEHMET and EDDIE sit at the coffee table. MEHMET seems to be nursing the briefcase.*)

MEHMET: The receptionist asked me to give you this envelope.

SASHA: Oh! They should have brought it up themselves.

EDDIE: So Mohammed, what do –

MEHMET: – Mehmet.

EDDIE: What do you think of the European Union then?

MEHMET: We Turks are very positive about Europe.

EDDIE: Gerr out while yer can son.

MEHMET: We're not even in yet.

EDDIE: That's the best time to gerr out.

MEHMET: It has brought peace. Through trade we make friends – do you make war with your friends? No. You musn't forget that Turkey has been in NATO for over fifty years.

EDDIE: I an't forgorren Gallipoli.

MEHMET: We are a young nation, we look forwards.

EDDIE: So you're trying to get membership of an exclusive club when you hate the guts of one of the members.

MEHMET: Cyprus, my friend, does not exist.

EDDIE: How are yer gonna trade with a nation what dun't exist then?

MEHMET: People like you, you have these 'objections' to Turkish membership, ha! They are a smoke screen to hide your racism.

EDDIE: I'm not a racialist and I've got nowt against Muslins. If it weren't for them you cou'n't gerr a pint of milk on Christmas day.

(*PHILIP appears from door of Bed 1 with the glass of iced water in his hand which he puts on the coffee table.*)

PHILIP: Mr Aziz!

MEHMET: Good to see you.

PHILIP: Some coffee for Mr Aziz.

MEHMET: Water please.

PHILIP: A glass of water please Sasha!

(*SASHA prepares a glass of water for MEHMET and delivers to stage right on the coffee table.*)

– Eddie! Do you want to unpack? In 'your' room.

EDDIE: Unpack? What's that? Polite for bugger off?! Done.

(*EDDIE goes into Bed 1 and closes the door. PHILIP sits next to MEHMET, who shuffles along the sofa towards the medicinal water. PHILIP is now in front of MEHMET's water (no lemon) and MEHMET is in front of the medicinal water, with lemon. PHILIP*) *drinks from the clean glass, but realises his mistake. MEHMET sees him take the drink and takes a hold of the medicinal water but doesn't drink. PHILIP is like a rabbit in the headlights.*)

MEHMET: Prime Minister Erdogan is concerned about the growing volume of anti-Turkish rhetoric stirred up by this London-based organisation, Human Rights Now. We pay you to counter these racists.

(*MEHMET pauses and raises his glass. PHILIP holds his arm.*)

PHILIP: Hang on! Did you want lemon?

MEHMET: Yes, I like lemon, this is fine.

PHILIP: Sasha, Mr Aziz doesn't want lemon!

MEHMET: This is perfect, ice and lemon.

(*There is a tug of war with the glass.*)

SASHA: Oh my God! It's a hair!

(*SASHA whips it away. SASHA puts the glass in the fridge.*)

PHILIP: Carry on, sorry!

(*He passes over a photocopy of a letter.*)

MEHMET: It's a letter to Prime Minister Erdogan from Nicola Daws –

PHILIP: – Nicola!

MEHMET: Do you know her?

PHILIP: Nicola Daws? Rings a bell.

MEHMET: She's the Secretary General of Human Rights Now!

PHILIP: Ah, yes, her, yes, she's –

MEHMET: – a real bitch. She says that our harmonisation laws are a sop to the EU and that our police are still torturing people with impunity.

PHILIP: I'll sort her out this afternoon.

MEHMET: You will, good. Now. Money.

PHILIP: My second favourite word. Ha!

MEHMET: What's your favourite word?

PHILIP: Cash!

MEHMET: This is cash!

(*He clicks open the case which is full of notes in bundles.*)
A million euros.

PHILIP: Wow! It's a nice case too, isn't it.

(*PHILIP takes out a bundle and fondles the money, taking a rubber band off the wad.*)

MEHMET: (*With a nod in SASHA's direction.*) Can she be trusted?

PHILIP: One step out of line and she's on the next train back to Murmansk.

MEHMET: Don't bank it, just spend it.

PHILIP: You've chosen the right man, I know what to do, I've spent money before. Do you want the rubber bands back?

MEHMET: Get Turkey in the EU and each year we will receive *twenty-five billion euros* in subsidies. But each year that we sit in the waiting room –

PHILIP: – is twenty-five billion down the pan?!

MEHMET: Exactly! We will pay you a bonus of a million euros for each year we don't have to wait.

PHILIP: So if Turkey got the green light next year, nine years earlier than you expect, my bonus would be nine million euros.

MEHMET: Correct.

PHILIP: For nine million euros I'll get you in the club even if you're wearing trainers.
(*They shake hands.*)
Twenty-five billion should sort out the Turkish debt mountain, eh?

MEHMET: (*In a panic.*) Shhh!!! No-one is allowed to say *Turkish Debt Mountain!*

PHILIP: You just said *Turkish Debt Mountain.*

MEHMET: Those three words are now illegal under article 301 of the Turkish Penal Code.

PHILIP: I'm not Turkish.

MEHMET: You work for us! What the hell is this!

PHILIP: What?

MEHMET: 'MEP in Turkish orgasm storm'! What!?

PHILIP: You don't want to read that.

MEHMET: (*Reading.*) No! Beatrice Renard. That crazy whore!

PHILIP: I didn't think it was too much to get excited about, I mean she's –

MEHMET: – this is the kind of thing which makes us question your consultancy work for Turkey. I may have to take my case back.

PHILIP: (*Grabbing case.*) I've worked tirelessly for Turkey! Only people who are effecting change, make enemies.

(*SASHA gives him the jiffy bag.*)

Oh no! Not another one!

MEHMET: What is it?

PHILIP: A jiffy bag bomb.

(*They all stand. PHILIP leaves the letter bomb on the coffee table.*)

Don't panic Mehmet. I've had a few of these.

MEHMET: Really?

PHILIP: Oh yes, usually racists. Sasha, run a bath please. When I started putting the case for Turkey, kaw! that's when the hate mail started.

(*SASHA goes into Bath 1 and starts to run a bath.*)

You have to isolate the bomb, submerge in water.

(*SASHA comes out of Bed 1.*)

SASHA: It's running.

PHILIP: (*To MEHMET.*) Excuse me.

(*PHILIP exits into Bed 1 with the bomb. EDDIE comes out of Bed 1. SASHA dials a number.*)

EDDIE: I'm not staying in there.

SASHA: (*On the phone.*) Allo! La Police s'il vous plaît... Oui, c'est pour vous signaler que M Philippe Wardrobe a reçu un autre jiffy bag bomb...merci, il n'a pas eu mal.

(*PHILIP re-appears from Bed 1. There is a knock at the door. PHILIP opens the door. It is Madame BEATRICE. A fortyish, not unattractive French woman, well-dressed in a rather downbeat way. PHILIP takes a look at her, and then slams the door and locks it.*)

PHILIP: For our own safety can I suggest we all go into Sasha's bedroom out the way. That's the biggest jiffy bag bomb we've had so far.

(*PHILIP pushes MEHMET, EDDIE, and SASHA into Bed 2. He then opens the main doors again and BEATRICE enters.*)

Hello Beatrice. You're an hour early?!

BEATRICE: I slept with your tie last night. We are both exhausted.

PHILIP: If it was that good, keep the tie.

(*BEATRICE pushes past him and gives him a big, lumpy jiffy bag.*)

BEATRICE: Your post. The boy on reception asked me to bring it up.

PHILIP: Look, I've got a proposal to make to you. Get in there. Quick!

BEATRICE: In the bedroom? For an English quickie!?

PHILIP: No, I've got to talk to you about your party, the EPPPP. But not out here it's dangerous. This could be a jiffy bag bomb.

BEATRICE: OH!! I didn't realise you were important enough to get jiffy bag bombs. And look at you, you are so brave, so English.

PHILIP: Stay in there! Sasha!

(*PHILIP runs across the room, opening the door to Bed 2. He is confronted by SASHA. At that moment BEATRICE opens the door to Bed 1 and PHILIP slams the Bed 2 door shut.*)

BEATRICE: (*Holding flower and card.*) They are beautiful flowers Philip, thank you, and Chanel Number Five, and the card, well! What a message!

PHILIP: Shut that door!

(*She shuts the door. SASHA comes out.*)

Beatrice has turned up an hour early! We've got to get rid of Mehmet now, before they tear each other to bits. And! She thinks Nicola's flowers and that furry fox message are for her.

SASHA: Beatrice Renard! 'Renard' is the French word for 'fox'. I get it! She thinks, she's your furry fox.

PHILIP: Oh bugger! Right, I've got to find a way of committing suicide.

SASHA: All we have to do is get Mehmet out the building. I'll call the lift and hold it on this floor, doors open. Lock Renard in your room.

PHILIP: …lock Renard in there…

SASHA: – then knock twice on my bedroom door,

PHILIP: …my door, your door!

SASHA: – and then either me or Eddie, I'll tell Eddie the plan.

PHILIP: – Eddie!

SASHA: – one of us will run Mehmet straight out the doors into the lift, and out the building.

PHILIP: They musn't see each other Sash!

(*SASHA goes out through the main doors and is seen calling the lift. PHILIP goes to Bed 2 door.*)

Eddie! A word!

(*Enter EDDIE from Bed 2.*)

EDDIE: What's gooin off?

PHILIP: Renard is here!

EDDIE: Bugger me.

PHILIP: Tell Mehmet the police want the whole suite evacuated because of the bomb, but wait for me to knock twice on the door, cos I've got to get Renard locked in there first, somehow.

EDDIE: Jam a chair again the 'andle.

PHILIP: Good.

EDDIE: So yer gonna knock twice?

PHILIP: Yeah.

(*EDDIE goes back into Bed 2. Enter BEATRICE from Bed 1.*)

BEATRICE: Philip, chéri.

PHILIP: Madame Renard! Get back in there!

BEATRICE: I cannot stay in here when there is a bomb!

PHILIP: The bomb is in the bath. It won't go off!

BEATRICE: Philip, the whole world knows me as the Chair of the Women's Committee, as a tough nutter –

PHILIP: – tough nut, but go on –

BEATRICE: – a feminist, but that does not mean that I do not feel. I have a dark secret, Jean Claude is not a real man –

PHILIP: – he's still your husband!

BEATRICE: I never wanted a French husband, French men are dogs with no back legs. Always rubbing something against the floor. But I spent ten years in Basingstoke and I have had my eyes opened!

PHILIP: Was it just your eyes you had opened?

BEATRICE: English men 'ave a key for everything.

PHILIP: And what about Turkish men? You don't mind telling the world about them do you?

BEATRICE: Mehmet!? I was just another butterfly he pricked with his pin. I have had my revenge.

PHILIP: Tell me about it. Look! I prefer blondes, my girlfriend of *ten years*, Nicola, she's blonde –

BEATRICE: – I could be blonde for you!

PHILIP: No! I wanted to see you to talk about a vote of no confidence in the Commission on the Turkey accession. I need the votes of a hundred Christian Democrats.

BEATRICE: I can't tell them how to vote.

PHILIP: You could, the women. You're Chair of the Women's Committee.

BEATRICE: I will get as many votes as you like if you do what you said you would do last night. Make love to me.

PHILIP: Stay in there!

(*He pushes her into Bed 1 and shuts the door. He jams a chair up against the door, but it is too big/or small. Bed 1 door opens and BEATRICE comes out.*)

BEATRICE: You can't push me about. Have you got another woman in here?

PHILIP: NO!

BEATRICE: I think you do.

(*She knocks on Bed 2 door twice.*)

PHILIP: Shit.

BEATRICE: What?

PHILIP: Okay. Let's make love now, in that room. Eddie!

(*PHILIP scoops BEATRICE up in his arms. EDDIE comes out first, pulls down the film screen so that when MEHMET comes out he is looking at the screen and PHILIP's legs.*)

MEHMET: Goodbye Mr Wardrobe.

PHILIP: (*From behind the screen.*) Bye, bye Mehmet.

MEHMET: I really didn't realise that you had put yourself in personal danger in the service of the Turkish people.

PHILIP: (*From behind the screen.*) Oh you know, all in a day's work! See you!

MEHMET: I will tell Prime Minister Erdogan that in you he has chosen well. I would like to shake your hand to express my gratitude.

(*PHILIP comes out from behind the screen and shakes hands with MEHMET.*)

PHILIP: You must leave, the police are getting incredibly jumpy about the bombs.

MEHMET: Bombs? Plural?

PHILIP: Yes, I think we're up to three at the moment and counting.

(*MEHMET leaves. PHILIP closes the doors. EDDIE sends the screen back up revealing BEATRICE balancing on the picture frame.*)

EDDIE: (*To BEATRICE.*) Are you Chair o' Women's Committee?

BEATRICE: Oui.

(*EDDIE helps her down from the wall.*)

EDDIE: I'd like to gerr on the committee, I don't mind not being Chairman, burr I gorra few good ideas.

BEATRICE: Some other time, monsieur, at the moment I am busy. Philip!

(*BEATRICE goes into Bed 1 and closes the door.*)

EDDIE: Wahey! You're in there kid!

PHILIP: I'd rather jump out of a plane wearing a parachute folded by Peter Mandelson.

EDDIE: I can only deliver yer 27 Tories.

PHILIP: Today was supposed to be about me, Nicola, and trying to make a baby. Simple, good, honest life. All of a sudden it's turned into a race for the Presidency, and the chance of picking up nine million euros!

EDDIE: Do what you like when you're President.

PHILIP: Oh God! I hadn't put the two together. If I become President, I can greenlight Turkey, *and* pick up nine million.

(*Enter BEATRICE.*)

BEATRICE: Your furry fox is getting impatient. I will wait in your chicken coop and try not to break the eggs.

(*BEATRICE exits to Bed 1. A muffled mobile phone is heard.*)

PHILIP: Is that your mobile?

EDDIE: 'ant gorr a mobile.

(*PHILIP shuts the lid and picks up the jiffy bag brought in by EDDIE and listens with his ear close up.*)

PHILIP: It's this one!

(*PHILIP rushes into Bed 2 and through into Bath 2. There is an explosion off.*)

(*To black.*)

Act Two

(*Later that day at about 3.45pm. There are bottles of wine and the remnants of a buffet set out on one of the side tables. EDDIE is eating a ham sandwich from his snap tin, and having a cup of tea from the flask. PHILIP is sitting on the chair squinting. Both hands are amateurishly bandaged and occasionally he sticks a finger in his ear as if his hearing is affected. Enter SASHA through the main doors.*)

SASHA: The hotel doctor will see you in ten minutes. How do you feel now?

PHILIP: Someone somewhere wants me killed. I cannot tell you how sensationally happy this has made me! I feel important! Relevant! Effective! Why did you go into politics, Eddie?

EDDIE: I got to' top o' Young Farmers and there were nowhere else to go.

PHILIP: Westminster was so fantastically pointless. The only time I actually felt I'd achieved anything was 1997 when I managed to claim more expenses than Keith Vaz. This is my first taste of real politics and it is sensational! I love it! I want to be President of the European Parliament.

EDDIE: I know you, you want that nine million an' all for shoeing in Turkey sooner rather than later.

PHILIP: A modern, secular, democratic Muslim nation embraced by Europe would help to stifle terrorism.

EDDIE: Saving the world now are we?

PHILIP: Yes, actually. So Eddie, how many of those Tories we've just fed and Beaujolayed will be voting to censure the Commission?

EDDIE: Don't believe a worr anyone ses while yer feeding 'em!

PHILIP: Still, it's another twenty-seven votes.

SASHA: What about the third jiffy bag? It might be another bomb.

EDDIE: Where is it? Lightning don't strike twice.
(*EDDIE heads off for the bathroom of Bed 1.*)

SASHA: It's no smoking in here. Is your vision normal?

PHILIP: My vision is normal IF at this moment we are in a discotheque halfway through an indoor fireworks display.

SASHA: You should go to the hospital.

(*Enter EDDIE carrying wet jiffy bag. He's opened it already.*)

EDDIE: It's not a bomb. It's summat much worse than that.

(*He takes out a vibrator and handcuffs.*)

One set of handcuffs, and one prick. It's a start your own police force kit.

SASHA: Is there a letter?

EDDIE: (*Producing a wet letter.*) Aye.

(*He reads.*) 'Dear Mr Wardrobe MEP,

– I purchased this 'vibrator' for my wife to commemorate the sixtieth anniversary of VE day. As an electrical engineer I can say that the wattage ratio of the electric motor is inadequately torqued to drive the action of the head during normal use. Also, my wife, who is a Health and Safety officer, tells me that the fluffy bits of the handcuffs are not made from flame retardant material, which could be dangerous because we're on gas. Tommy Jeffers, the landlord of the Cricketers in Oundle, told me that you are my local member for the European Parliament –'

PHILIP: (*To SASHA.*) – take Jeffers off the Christmas card list.

EDDIE: '– I would like you to pursue this issue in the European Court of Human Rights. Yours sincerely Abbas Ali Belhadj.'

PHILIP: It's those pissheads in the Cricketers!

(*EDDIE offers the vibrator to SASHA.*)

SASHA: I'm not touching it!

EDDIE: Maybe it's the lads in the Cricketers who sent the letter bomb an' all.

PHILIP: Na! The bomb will have been IslamoPHOBES, IslamoPHILES, or IslamoISTS.

EDDIE: What yer saying is yer an't gorr a clue?

PHILIP: Who would you blame Eddie?

EDDIE: Gippos.

SASHA: Eddie!

EDDIE: I'm a farmer, I blame gippos for everything.

PHILIP: You're talking about a significant racial minority with an amazingly rich culture.

EDDIE: Since when has nicking fences and eating hedgehogs been culture?

PHILIP: And what exactly is UKIP policy on the Romany Peoples?

SASHA: Is it in a document called 'The Final Solution'?

PHILIP: That's shut you up Eddie.

EDDIE: I'm unshutupable. Time for another dip!

(*EDDIE gives PHILIP the medicinal glass. The main doors open, it's ANDRÉ in a suit.*)

PHILIP: (*Puzzled.*) Are you looking for your brother, the plumber, with the moustache?

ANDRÉ: I am my brother. You need to know, I work for OLAF, the fraud –

PHILIP: – I claim only my legal entitlement of expenses!

ANDRÉ: Relax! I 'ave instructions to use you, Mr Wardrobe, the little fish, to catch a bigger fish, a sprat –

PHILIP: – oh steady on –

ANDRÉ: – to catch the shark, Beatrice Renard. She is registered as married, and yet I have always suspected that her husband was a chimera and now I can prove it. She is romantically interested in you. I plan to record your pillow talk.

PHILIP: No way! It would be incredibly not in my interests for you to arrest Beatrice since she has a key role in my plans to be President.

ANDRÉ: Then I will have this *illegal alien* deported back to Murmansk where the only employment is working as a whore on the brothel ship which services the Russian fishing fleet.

PHILIP: (*To ANDRÉ.*) What do you want me to do again?

ANDRÉ: Invite Beatrice to rendez-vous here and make her talk about her husband.

PHILIP: Okay Beatrice talks about her husband, you get your information, BUT you don't arrest her until after the vote tomorrow.

ANDRÉ: You are a proper politician aren't you?

PHILIP: I must be. I've had three letter bombs already today and we haven't had the second post yet.

ANDRÉ: This is a deal.

(*They shake on it. ANDRÉ opens the linen cupboard, goes in and closes the door.*)

PHILIP: He's just gone in the linen cupboard.

SASHA: That's his office.

EDDIE: Why don't you take Beatrice up on her offer?

SASHA: And what exactly is her offer?

EDDIE: 'I will get you as many votes as you like if you make love to me.'

SASHA: (*Amazed.*) NO!

PHILIP: She's nuts about me, I mean that is understandable, but I'm not going to actually ever sleep with her. Ring her up! Go on! I want it over and done with before Nicola turns up.

EDDIE: Come on! One last time! Cawld bath for Cannon and Ball!

(*PHILIP goes into Bed 1 with medicinal glass. SASHA gets on the phone.*)

SASHA: (*On the phone.*) 'Allo?… Madame Renard?… C'est encore moi, Sasha. Monsieur Wardrobe se demande s'il-peut changer son rendez-vous avec vous. Vingt minutes. Très bien, à bientot.

EDDIE: How much was these bottles of wine?

SASHA: Seventy euros.

EDDIE: Fifty quid. Not bad for a case.

SASHA: Seventy euros each.

EDDIE: Fifty quid a bottle! Bloody hell. There's some left in the bottom of this one.

(*EDDIE pours himself a glass of wine.*)

SASHA: Excuse me, Mr Incorruptible.

EDDIE: (*He drinks.*) Aye. There's a difference in't there between yer fifty quidder and yer five quid Tesco's Frascati.

(*There is a knock on the door. EDDIE opens it. It is a bespectacled GENDARME, in uniform.*)

GENDARME: Bonjour Monsieur! Je m'appelle Popineau, Sécurité Nationale. Il pourait qu'il y a eu une petite bombe ce matin. Est-ce que vous étiez ici a l'exact moment a l'explosion? J'espère que vous allez vous montrer cooperatifs envers mon enquête aujourd'hui. Il est vrai que vous êtes des representants du Parlement european mais Strasbourg est sous jurisdiction française.

EDDIE: Look son, I'm a great believer in supporting minority and dying languages like French burr I don't speak it mesen.

GENDARME: You speak English?

EDDIE: No. Yorkshire. It's a lot like English, but there's norr as many words. Burr if we ever do say owt, we fucking mean it.

GENDARME: You 'ave a small bom'?

EDDIE: Thank you. I used to do a lot of cycling. Now, do you want a glass of wine?

GENDARME: Zank you.

(*EDDIE pours a glass of wine for the GENDARME and one for himself. The GENDARME drinks.*)

EDDIE: Chateauneuf de summat or other.

GENDARME: – Pape.

EDDIE: Oh, I thought it were quite good mesen.

GENDARME: I have a need to probe everyone who was in zis room. Names s'il vous plaît.

SASHA: Mehmet Aziz, Beatrice Renard, me, that's Alexandria Togushev, Sasha, Edward Fredericks –

EDDIE: Eddie.

SASHA: – Philip Wardrobe, and this man, I don't know his name.

(*SASHA opens the cupboard door.*)

GENDARME: Why are you hiding in ze cupboard?

ANDRÉ: I'm not hiding. They know I'm here.

(*Beat. ANDRÉ shows him his ID card.*)

GENDARME: OLAF!

ANDRÉ: D'accord!

GENDARME: Continuez.

(*Enter PHILIP, with glass in hand from Bed 1, not noticing the GENDARME.*)

PHILIP: I think it's actually incredibly working. But I want to squeeze one more dip in just before Nicola gets here okay, so I'm putting the glass back in the fridge okay to keep cool. Brilliant Eddie, my testicles feel amazing. Hello. Who are you?

GENDARME: Inspecteur Popineau. I am ze chef here now. No-one is leaving zis chamber unless zey are asking me for permissions first. I will probe you all. First, Monsieur Wardrobe.

PHILIP: That's me.

EDDIE: Can I nip down to the Parliament for five minutes please? I've gorr all of this week's voting slips to tear up.

GENDARME: Okay, but you are not going inside ze Parliament chambers.

EDDIE: No fear, I did it once, kaw! I'd rather have someone brek coal on me head.

GENDARME: (*To SASHA.*) Zis Beatrice Renard, when is she arriving?

SASHA: (*Checking her watch.*) In fifteen minutes.

GENDARME: Bien! And ze Turk, ring him up and get him to come back 'ere for 'is deep probing.

(*The GENDARME starts to leave.*)

PHILIP: Sasha, Nicola will want a bath. But for God's sake don't let her bump into – [bloody Renard, it –]

SASHA: – Nicola's not due for another hour.

GENDARME: Monsieur Wardrobe? Zis way please. MEPs… huh! You are coming 'ere inside my town, you are thinkings 'ow can I make ze laughter, ha! Maybe we drive ze wrong way round ze one-way system, oh yes, funny! Maybe we climb up to ze top of ze bridge and piss into ze river – very funny! Bien! I am ze one laughing now.

(*GENDARME leaves, closing door.*)

SASHA: Eddie, what does Nicola look like, I've never met her. And Renard, I've not met her either.

EDDIE: Didn't you see Renard this morning?

SASHA: No, I was in my room, and then –

EDDIE: Nicola's blonde and English, and Renard's brunette and French. Righteo. I'm offski.

(*EDDIE finishes off his glass of wine and leaves. SASHA goes into Bed 1. ANDRÉ comes out of the cupboard and surreptitiously*

pours himself a glass of wine before returning with a glass to the
cupboard and closing the door. There is a knock on the door.)

SASHA: (*Looking at her watch.*) Tvoiu mat!! This Beatrice Renard
is crazy about him. Fifteen minutes early!

(*SASHA opens the door. It's NICOLA. She has a small valise with*
her. Her new hairstyle is brunette.)

Vous êtes en avance!

NICOLA: Bonjour. Sasha?

SASHA: Oui. C'est moi.

(*SASHA pushes NICOLA towards Bed 2.*)

NICOLA: Où est Philip?

SASHA: Il parle de la lettre piégée aux gendarmes. Il a un
rendez-vous avec le –

NICOLA: – Est-ce que vous préférez parler en anglais?

SASHA: Sorry, yes I forgot, of course you speak perfect English
don't you! From all that time you spent in Basingstoke.

NICOLA: I've been to Basingstoke, yes, but I don't remember
learning anything. Phil told me about the letter bomb, is he
alright?

SASHA: It's nothing really. Actually the Gendarme wants to talk
to you.

NICOLA: And in what way am I involved?

SASHA: You were in this room when the bomb went off.

NICOLA: I'm sorry, I was not in this room when the bomb
went off. I was –

SASHA: – No! You weren't were you. You were – [in there]

(*NICOLA's mobile phone goes off. She answers it.*)

NICOLA: Excuse me. (*On the phone.*) Claude, how are you?…
Good, well done… Once I've got the Women's Committee
up to speed we can run it past the Turks…let's embargo it
until tomorrow… Ciao!

(*Turns off phone.*)

SASHA: I think your Women's Committee could do more for –

NICOLA: – It's not *my* Women's Committee AND I've just
given myself the afternoon off, thank you.

SASHA: Come on. You're in here.

(*She closes the door on NICOLA in Bed 2. There is a knock at*
the door.)

(*Looks at her watch.*) Who's this? Bliat!! It must be Nicola! If these two meet!

(*SASHA opens the main doors and we see BEATRICE standing with a new blonde hair-do. At that moment NICOLA opens the door to Bed 2 and comes out. SASHA closes the door in BEATRICE's face.*)

NICOLA: Sasha, there's another woman's clothes in here.

SASHA: Yes. It's my room.

NICOLA: But what's wrong with Phil's room?

SASHA: It's a crime scene. The police said.

NICOLA: Oh okay. The letter bomb?

SASHA: Yes.

NICOLA: And you don't mind me being in your room?

SASHA: No.

NICOLA: That's very kind of you.

(*NICOLA goes back into Bed 2.*)

SASHA: (*Under her breath.*) Tart.

(*SASHA jams a chair up against the handle of Bed 2 then unlocks the main doors and opens them and lets in BEATRICE who this time breezes past her.*)

Hi! Nice to meet you at last.

BEATRICE: Sasha isn't it? Can you send an email to my office to let them know where I am. I'm expecting a phone call from the London office of Human Rights Now! I had my mobile phone stolen last night.

SASHA: Yes. Whatever you want, just ask. You're in here, the master suite, Philip suggested I run you a bath.

(*SASHA goes into Bath 1 and starts running a bath.*)

BEATRICE: He wants me to have a bath? Well, well.

SASHA: He's always talking about you.

BEATRICE: Is he?

SASHA: Yes, he's crazy about you!

BEATRICE: Did he say that?

SASHA: What's that? Chanel number 5!

BEATRICE: Yes, it's Philip's favourite isn't it?

SASHA: Only because it's your favourite.

BEATRICE: Has Philip told you why I'm here?

SASHA: Oh yes, don't worry, I understand. My Aunt Irena wanted a son to take over the farm, but my Uncle Sergei is impotent so Uncle Alexander stepped in. They have five daughters and they're still trying. In Russia sex is like agriculture, a functional thing. Philip is with the Gendarme. We had a jiffy bag bomb –

BEATRICE: – I know. Is he alright?

SASHA: We've booked a doctor. He got you some flowers.

BEATRICE: I've seen them. Sasha, could you please send that email?

SASHA: Of course. Have a nice long soak.

(*SASHA shuts the door behind her, and takes the chair from Bed 2 door and jams it against the handle of Bed 1. She then goes to the linen cupboard and opens it.*)

(*Indicating Bed 2.*) What's she doing in there?

ANDRÉ: You know you've made a – [mistake –]

(*The door to Bed 2 opens and SASHA closes the linen cupboard door quickly. NICOLA is wearing a dressing gown. She goes straight to the fridge and pours herself a glass of white wine from an open bottle.*)

NICOLA: No ice. That's a serious problem.

SASHA: Why?

NICOLA: I'm a modern working woman. I can't relax unless my body mass is at least eighty-seven per cent white wine spritzer.

SASHA: We don't have any ice to spare and there's no soda water.

NICOLA: You and I seem to have got off on the wrong foot. I've had a very stressful morning, and I like a bath and a glass of fizzy, that's all!

SASHA: There's no point in you having a bath! He's not going to go through with it. I don't think it's decent, what you're doing!

NICOLA: So that's it! We have to be married do we? Look, I'm forty-two. I've got to make the most of my opportunities.

(*NICOLA makes her way to Bed 2.*)

I'll be in the bath.

(*NICOLA shuts the door of Bed 2. Enter PHILIP through main entrance doors.*)

PHILIP: You've got to go and see the Gendarme.

SASHA: (*Fierce whisper.*) Nicola's here! In there!

PHILIP: She's an hour early? She's never early.

SASHA: The bad news is – Beatrice is here too.

PHILIP: Oh no! Oh no, oh no, no, no, no. I'm going to lie on the floor, you get a sharp pencil and stick it in my eye and then bang it in with a heavy book. Bugger!! Where's Beatrice?

SASHA: In my room.

PHILIP: So Nicola's in here?

(*PHILIP knocks on Bed 1 and goes in.*)

Darling?!

(*He comes out again.*)

She's in the bath.

(*PHILIP opens the cupboard. SASHA leaves.*)

PHILIP: What's Beatrice doing in there?

ANDRÉ: They are both having baths. It is not an issue for me but –

PHILIP: – Why is Beatrice having a bath? That is incredibly not good news.

ANDRÉ: I have some vital information…

(*PHILIP closes the door on ANDRÉ. Enter EDDIE through main doors. PHILIP assesses the situation and looks at his watch.*)

PHILIP: Eddie! Got a little job for you.

EDDIE: An't you gorra go see the doctor?

PHILIP: Yes, exactly, but we've got a tricky situation here. Nicola…

(*NICOLA comes out of Bed 2 unseen. She's wearing a dressing gown. She's not yet got in the bath. PHILIP approaches Bed 1.*)

…is in here having a bath, and –

(*PHILIP notices NICOLA.*)

– Nicola! Bloody hell! Your hair! You look gorgeous!

NICOLA: I was worried, I know how much you need me to be blonde.

(*They kiss. It's a real hug and kiss.*)

What the hell is going on? The place is swarming with
people. I've flown over here today, so we can try and make
a baby, but it looks like you've been selling tickets to a live
sex show.

PHILIP: Listen, it's complicated –

NICOLA: – there's nothing at all complicated about it. The
thermometer's looking good.

PHILIP: Alright, I'm ready, nearly – you're not very 'French
tart'.

NICOLA: You're not very 'President'.

PHILIP: I'm a lot more 'President' than you would imagine
actually.

NICOLA: I've got fishnet stockings in my case.

PHILIP: Ah, bonjour Mademoiselle, c'est combien, complête?

NICOLA: Monsieur Le President, vous n'avez pas besoin de
payer.

(*They kiss. EDDIE coughs.*)

PHILIP: This is Eddie Fredericks.

NICOLA: UKIP Eddie Fredericks?

EDDIE: Aye, aye. Guilty as charged.

NICOLA: I wrote to you about the comments you made about
Travellers in the *Daily Mail.* Did you ever read it? I didn't
get a reply.

EDDIE: I got your letter and purr it in me caravan, which is the
farm's office, intending to read it next morning, but that
night a coupla gippos pulled up in a transit and nicked the
caravan.

NICOLA: I don't believe you.

EDDIE: You can ask our lass, they nicked her computer an' all.

NICOLA: Do you employ *your* wife to run your UK office?

EDDIE: Na! She's gorr enough on her plate running a pig farm.
Has he got you doing that then?

NICOLA: I don't do anything.

PHILIP: (*Conscious of ANDRÉ in the cupboard.*) Shh!

NICOLA: It's immoral, claiming eighty thousand euros for me
when I do bugger all.

ANDRÉ: (*From cupboard.*) Ha ha ha!

PHILIP: Ha, ha, ha. Oh God. Shutup!

NICOLA: – excuse me Eddie. I can't make love in that room. You promised me a view, and a jacuzzi. All I can see out the window is a skip, and the kitchen bins.
(*She heads to Bed 1. PHILIP stands in front of the door. NICOLA puts her ear against the wall.*)

PHILIP: This is our room but it's a crime scene. There's a policewoman from forensics in there.

NICOLA: Having a bath?

PHILIP: She's doing a reconstruction. I was just about to throw the bomb into a full bath of water when it went off.

NICOLA: (*Holding up the vibrator.*) I suppose you confiscated this off the maid.

PHILIP: One of my constituents –

NICOLA: – You're up to something Phil. Get rid of these people, go and see your doctor, then you can try and get me pregnant.
(*She goes back into Bed 2.*)

PHILIP: Agh! Sasha's put Beatrice in here with the bath, the card, the flowers.

EDDIE: Leave it with me son. Come on, let's get you to that doctor.
(*EDDIE opens the main doors, leaves them open, and calls the lift, then he comes back into the main room having left the main doors open.*)

PHILIP: You're the best mate I've got over here Eddie. You're sensationally misguided politically of course, but you're funny, sincere, honest. I'm sorry I said those things about you in the *Guardian.*

EDDIE: That dint even prick the skin kid. All my life I've had people coming up to me and saying 'You smell of pig muck'. That's what hurts. If yer wanna see me upset, Phil, if yer ever wanna get me really upset, four words – 'You smell of pigs'.
(*EDDIE closes the lift doors and then the suite doors. He pours himself another glass of wine and sups it. Then he knocks on the door of Bed 1 whilst still holding on to the handle. BEATRICE opens the door. She is half-undressed.*)

The Gendarme wants to interview you. Down the corridor, but there's a photographer from *Paris Match* in that bedroom waiting to take a snapshot of the Chair of the Women's Committee, half-naked in a Socialist MEP's bedroom.

BEATRICE: Merde!

EDDIE: (*Going into Bed 1.*) I've gorr a plan to get you out the room without yer being seen.

(*BEATRICE lets him in. NICOLA comes out. She walks around the room. She listens at the door to Bed 1. EDDIE comes out of Bed 1 and opens the main doors and goes out into the corridor and returns pushing a large chambermaid's linen trolley on wheels.*)

NICOLA: What are you doing?

EDDIE: Just helping out. Can't help gerrin' involved me. Nice bath?

(*EDDIE pushes the trolley into Bed 1.*)

NICOLA: Yes, thanks.

(*NICOLA goes back into Bed 2 not quite closing the door behind her. Noises from Bed 1 suggest someone climbing into the trolley. EDDIE comes out pushing the trolley. NICOLA is suspicious. He gets as far as the main double doors before NICOLA shouts –*)

Stop right there! Okay! Let's see what she looks like!

(*NICOLA goes over to the trolley, and with her back to the room, lifts the lid and looks in. BEATRICE sprints out of Bed 1 carrying her high heels, fully-clothed, and hides downstage of the sofa. NICOLA turns and then goes into Bed 1 to have a look, closing the door behind her. EDDIE pushes the trolley out of the way down the corridor. BEATRICE sprints out from downstage of the sofa and goes out through the main doors. NICOLA reappears, closing Bed 1 door behind her, just as EDDIE closes the double doors.*)

EDDIE: Glass of wine?

NICOLA: Why not.

EDDIE: Nicola, why don't you move in there? It's a much nicer room.

NICOLA: I think I will.

(*NICOLA goes into Bed 2 and picks up her things and moves into Bed 1 leaving the door open. EDDIE picks up a bottle and rather groggily moves to Bed 2.*)

EDDIE: I'm gonna gerr a bit of shut eye in here.

(*EDDIE goes into Bed 2 and closes the door. Enter SASHA. She sees NICOLA in Bed 1.*)

SASHA: What are you doing in there?! Get out!

(*NICOLA comes out of Bed 1.*)

NICOLA: Nice flowers.

SASHA: They're for his girlfriend.

NICOLA: Really.

SASHA: Yes, an English woman. He's known her for years.

NICOLA: (*Sits, genuinely shocked.*) English? I thought some attractive PA maybe, but... – is she young?

SASHA: No. She's your age.

NICOLA: Hell, it would be easier to understand if she was young.

SASHA: Age is not the issue. Love, commitment, and children, that's what it's all about.

NICOLA: Children?!

SASHA: Yes! They're going to get married and have children.

NICOLA: That's it. I'm going. I'll get changed in the corridor if I have to. You can tell him it's all off.

(*NICOLA takes her bags and goes out through the main doors.*)

SASHA: That will give me pleasure!

(*SASHA closes the doors. The main doors open and BEATRICE enters. She makes her way erratically towards Bed 1 as if hiding from the photographer still.*)

Are you alright?

BEATRICE: I am trying to avoid the photographer.

SASHA: There is no photographer.

BEATRICE: Eddie said – ah, when Phil suggested we get together this afternoon I thought we would be alone!

SASHA: You musn't be embarrassed! This is so important! It is the right time of the month for you, isn't it?!

BEATRICE: It's not the wrong time of the month.

SASHA: Then you simply must have sex!

BEATRICE: I like you, I like your attitude. I don't know how much Philip pays you but if ever you feel like a change, just give me a call.

SASHA: You know I'd really like to work for Human Rights Now! and –

BEATRICE: – I can't help with that, but I have business ventures of my own which always need entrepreneurs, risk takers. Tell the cockerel, I'm ready.

(*BEATRICE gets into bed. SASHA closes the door. Enter PHILIP wearing bandages on both hands and bandages around his eyes and ears. A doctor is with him.*)

DOCTOR: Bonjour. Are you Sasha?

SASHA: Yes, hi.

DOCTOR: I'm the doctor on call, it looks worse than it is, ha! The bandaging is preventative. The eyes are not damaged but they need a chance to rest, so he should keep the pads on overnight. Sit down here Monsieur Wardrobe. This is the sofa!

(*PHILIP feels the back of the sofa.*)

PHILIP: (*Too loud.*) IS THIS THE SOFA?

DOCTOR: He's a bit deaf because I've applied soothing ear drops to both ears.

PHILIP: WHERE'S NICOLA?

SASHA: SHE'S WAITING FOR YOU IN THE MASTER BEDROOM!

PHILIP: What?

SASHA: (*To DOCTOR.*) Is he allowed to get excited?

DOCTOR: The eyes and ears need resting. Otherwise he's perfectly healthy. Now, I charge the hotel who charge the room and they require a signature and Monsieur cannot sign because he cannot read it and –

SASHA: – You want me to come down and sign your contract?

DOCTOR: Not my contract, the hotel's.

(*Enter EDDIE.*)

EDDIE: Bugger me sideways! It's the invisible man. Alright?

SASHA: Renard's gone, so we can all relax. Nicola's in there, ready.

(*SASHA exits with the doctor.*)

PHILIP: IS NICOLA IN THE BEDROOM?

EDDIE: I'LL TEK YER THROUGH. COME ON.

(*EDDIE gets up and puts the vibrator in his pocket then pulls on PHILIP's arm.*)

PHILIP: SASHA GOT THEM MIXED UP EARLIER.

EDDIE: IT'S ALL SORTED.

PHILIP: WHAT DID YOU SAY!?

EDDIE: IT'S ALL SORTED!!

(*EDDIE leads him to Bed 1 and knocks on the door.*)

Hello love. You've gorr a visitor!!

BEATRICE: (*Off.*) Je suis toute nue!

(*Door is closed.*)

EDDIE: That's funny, she's speaking French. JE SUIS TOUTE NUE. WHAT DOES THAT MEAN?

PHILIP: Nicola said she'd role play a French tart.

EDDIE: Wahey!

(*BEATRICE opens the door, EDDIE deliberately turns away.*)

BEATRICE: Faites entrer le jeune coq tout seul. Je saurai m'en occuper.

EDDIE: Go on my son!

(*PHILIP is ushered in by BEATRICE. EDDIE shuts the door. He has a little listen with ear against the door. Then he finds a 'Do Not Disturb' sign and hangs it on the door handle. He pours a glass of wine and opens the cupboard door. EDDIE gives ANDRÉ the glass of wine and takes the headphones from him and puts them on. He does this standing outside the cupboard. The story on his face tells the story of Bed 1. Enter NICOLA on the phone. EDDIE turns and sees her, keeping the headphones on, big double-take. During the next NICOLA looks around the room searching for her Blackberry.*)

NICOLA: (*On the phone.*) Torture and ill-treatment in detention; impunity; criminalisation of dissent; and that old Turkish staple – violence against women. Hang on Claude.

EDDIE: Hello love.

NICOLA: I left my Blackberry. Have you seen it?

EDDIE: Yer bramble?

NICOLA: It's a handheld computer.

EDDIE: Nothing handheld round here.

NICOLA: Sorry Claude… I've got some free time this afternoon now and I thought I might try and get to see the Chair of the Women's Committee. I'll speak later. Bye!

(*NICOLA finds the handcuffs. And picks them up with a heavy question mark.*)

EDDIE: Is that it love?

(*NICOLA is alerted by noises within Bed 1 and goes over and sees the 'Do Not Disturb' sign. She then tries the door but it is locked. She goes over to EDDIE.*)

This is OLAF, he's a kind of spook, anti-fraud squad.

NICOLA: Nice to meet you Olaf, could you turn the volume up please?

(*EDDIE says nothing but the sounds of love-making come through the open speakers of the headphones. NICOLA opens the headphones up so they act like speakers. Enter SASHA.*)

SASHA: (*To EDDIE.*) What's she doing here?

EDDIE: You know this is Nicola don't yer?!

(*SASHA looks slowly towards Bed 1. The door of Bed 1 opens slowly. PHILIP stands there still bandaged fully, then he starts to unravel the bandages as he talks.*)

PHILIP: We've got champagne somewhere. Or do you want one of your spritzers? You know, I think that doctor's overreacted. I caught a bit of flash alright but I'm not wearing these bloody bandages. They itch!

(*He takes the pads of his eyes and looks across at EDDIE, SASHA and NICOLA.*)

Oh no.

NICOLA: Oh yes.

PHILIP: (*Looks to SASHA.*) Oh no.

SASHA: Oh yes.

PHILIP: (*Looks to EDDIE.*) Oh no.

EDDIE: Oh yes.

PHILIP: Oh fff – !

(*To black.*)

Act Three

(*One hour later. They're all smoking. PHILIP is pacing with twiglets between his toes. He is half-dressed, i.e. bare feet, vest and suit trousers held up by braces. EDDIE's half-drunk and opening another bottle. SASHA is ironing shirts. The iced water glass is set in the fridge.*)

PHILIP: I've lost Nicola! I'm forty-six and there's been a lot of women, and I'm not ashamed of that. I'm incredibly proud of it, actually, in a kind of immature adolescent sort of way, but she's the only one I've ever really loved. I wish I understood women. I went to boarding school where *Club International Magazine* was our only source of information. I've still not recovered from the disappointment of realising that women don't wear shoes in bed.

SASHA: (*Holding Blackberry.*) I've found her Blackberry. She'll come back for this. She's got a mobile, I'll ring her.

PHILIP: No! Text her.

(*SASHA texts.*)

EDDIE: And when she comes back – propose. Marriage. Get down on one knee and do the right thing.

SASHA: Did you get down on one knee to propose Eddie?

EDDIE: I'd already been on me knees for twennie minutes. Worst case of carpet burns I'd ever had. Stop sulking! At the end of the day, when all's said and done, what's happened? Yer've accidentally fucked the wrong woman. It's easily done. At least you haven't married the wrong woman like most of the rest of humanity.

SASHA: Did you marry the wrong woman Eddie?

EDDIE: I married the right woman. Me and our lass started when we was sixteen. Mind you she's always been a frisky one. You only had to sneeze twice and she had twins.

PHILIP: – Too much information Eddie!

EDDIE: Hysterectomy's med her worse. She blames the operation. She ses all it did was convert the workshop into a playroom.

PHILIP: (*Covering his ears.*) – I'm not listening!

EDDIE: Even with the change –

PHILIP: Shutup!

EDDIE: Mind you it's tekken me forty years to find out what our lass really wants in bed.

PHILIP: And what does she want in bed?

EDDIE: George Clooney. My generation in't the problem, it's you youngsters. All this women's rights malarkey –

SASHA: Oh!

EDDIE: Don't get me wrong. I'm a bit of a 'new man' mesen, it's quite right that our women have careers, work, but that means they have kids much later, or not at all, whereas yer Muslims are knocking 'em out –

PHILIP: Eddie!

EDDIE: – mark my words, hundred years' time Europe'll be Eurabia, unrecognisable, and then what!? Well, yer gays and yer Jews –

(*Enter ANDRÉ from the cupboard interrupting.*)

ANDRÉ: – Messieursdames.

PHILIP: Did you get what you needed? What did Beatrice say?

ANDRÉ: (*Reading, from note book.*) 'Encore, encore, non, à gauche, voila! Oh, oh, mon dieu, mon dieu, oui, oui, oui, ooooohhh!'

PHILIP: That's not gonna stand up in a court is it?

ANDRÉ: 'owever, when she was alone in the room she rang the family physician. Her father is, it seems, on his deathbed as we speak. Her father is Mister Monsieur Bricolage.

PHILIP: Mister Monsieur Bricolage?!

ANDRÉ: Yes! That's 300 DIY stores throughout France.

PHILIP: That is a lot of nails.

ANDRÉ: Madame Renard should inherit the fortune but the father has stipulated that she will get nothing unless she marries before he dies!

PHILIP: But she's already married!

ANDRÉ: Exactement! I am right! How you say, once in a row! Jean-Claude Renard, her supposed husband, the chimera, lives in the Dordogne.

PHILIP: Why? Is he English?

ANDRÉ: There are still some French people left in the Dordogne.

SASHA: But Beatrice is the MEP for Strasbourg.

ANDRÉ: Her husband is a tobacco farmer with eighty-three hectares of land. Each year he receives two hundred thousand euros from the Common Agricultural Policy.

EDDIE: Last year I fraudulently claimed sixty thousand quid's worth of setaside.

PHILIP: What – for land you were still farming?

EDDIE: For the A64 to Scarborough. I give the money back. Onny did it to prove me point.

ANDRÉ: And what exactly is your point?

EDDIE: That you're all fucking idiots.

ANDRÉ: To prove that Madame Renard is not married to this Jean-Claude we will have to squeeze more information out of her.

PHILIP: I've done enough squeezing for one day.

EDDIE: You're obsessed with Madame Renard aren't yer?

ANDRÉ: Batman had the Joker; James Bond had Goldfinger; the Man from UNCLE had THRUSH. I want you to ask her to marry you.

PHILIP: What?!

EDDIE: Yeah, don't yer see, if she agrees to marry yer, that proves that she's single.

ANDRÉ: And confirms that the tobacco farm is a sophisticated criminal fraud.

PHILIP: Fantastic for you, you've only got to catch her, I've got to marry her and run an imaginary tobacco farm!

SASHA: Which doesn't exist.

ANDRÉ: Just propose to her. If she says *yes* that will be the end of it, I will have my catch.

PHILIP: I'm sorry this is a sensationally bad idea and I'm not having anything to do with it.

ANDRÉ: You forget, I now have solid evidence of your misuse of the expenses budget, particularly in relation to the employment of Miss Nicola Daws who, in her own words, earns eighty thousand euros a year for doing 'bugger all'. And I can 'ave Sasha put on the next train back to Murmansk.

EDDIE: What you're really saying is you've got him over a barrel?

ANDRÉ: I do not understand.

EDDIE: You've got him over a fifty litre non-elliptical container generally used for the transportation or storage of wet goods.

ANDRÉ: Exactement!

PHILIP: Alright, I'll do it. But remember the deal is you don't arrest her before tomorrow and the vote in the Parliament.

ANDRÉ: D'accord!

(*ANDRÉ goes back into the cupboard door slams. Main doors open and NICOLA comes in. She's obviously been shopping and is carrying a plastic carrier bag with 'Doctor Love' on it.*)

NICOLA: Did you have sex with that woman in there?

PHILIP: Define sex.

NICOLA: Did you have full penetrative sex?

(*Beat.*)

PHILIP: Define full penetrative sex.

NICOLA: Did you put your erect penis inside her vagina?

PHILIP: – Oh, I see what you mean! Yes.

NICOLA: This is for you.

(*She produces a box, not gift-wrapped, and puts it on the coffee table.*)

The shop assistant said it was the perfect gift for a 'wanker'.

PHILIP: Really, you shouldn't have. A card would have been enough.

(*NICOLA exits to Bed 2.*)

That went quite well.

EDDIE: At least you're talking.

SASHA: You see, she loves you! Why else would she come back?

PHILIP: I know her, she'll be planning a revenge event spectacular.

EDDIE: 'Doctor Love'. That's that sex shop on the island. I'm banned from there.

SASHA: What for?

EDDIE: Fighting.

(*PHILIP has opened the box and taken out a silicone female hand with painted nails and a rubber sucker on the base. He reads from the box.*)

PHILIP: 'The Helping Hand'.

EDDIE: (*Reading from the box.*) 'This textured silicone hand has
been moulded from a beautiful model to give you the
not-so-solo-sex-sensation of a lifetime. Warning – highly
inflammable. Batteries included. See diagram for standing
use. The Helping Hand has a variable stroke facility. For
slow sensual arousal set to Slow –'
(*PHILIP sets the hand on the table to Slow. They watch.*)
'– switch to Fast for rapid satisfaction.'
(*PHILIP switches it to Fast and they watch it as it moves faster and
works its way to the edge of the table and eventually falls off.
Enter NICOLA with Blackberry in hand.*)

NICOLA: Sasha, since I now have some free time, I would like
to meet with the Turkish Ambassador.

PHILIP: Why do you want to see Mehmet?

NICOLA: I'd like to discuss Article 301 of the Turkish Penal
Code.

PHILIP: Nicola, please keep your work separate from my work.
Do you really think now is the time –

NICOLA: – now is the time for making babies but when I
turned up for that meeting you'd started without me!
(*NICOLA goes back into Bed 2.*)

PHILIP: Bugger! It's revenge. She's trying to screw up my deal
with the Turks.
(*EDDIE attaches the Helping Hand to a door upstage at about
groin height. Then he takes the vibrator and puts it in the Helping
Hand, standing next to it as if it were his own penis.*)

EDDIE: Oh I gerr it!
(*Enter the GENDARME. He sees EDDIE. He watches EDDIE.*)
Don't bother knocking then!

GENDARME: I am nearly concluding ze deep probing wiz
Madame Renard. Ensuite, I have a need of Monsieur
Mehmet Aziz.

SASHA: I've called him half an hour ago and he's on his way.

GENDARME: Zank you. May I remind you zat no-one is to
leave zis chamber wizout my permissions. (*To EDDIE.*) You
must be careful wiz zese rubber 'ands monsieur, zey are
highly inflameable…apparently. Please, continue.

(*Exit GENDARME. EDDIE sits leaving the vibrator in the Helping Hand stuck on the door.*)

PHILIP: Nicola thinks I'm a complete wanker. She hates me.

EDDIE: This is nowt! Yer know they really hate yer when yer gerr a paper shredder for Christmas.

SASHA: She loves you! You love her! Ask her to marry you and if she loves you then she may forgive you. It was an honest mistake.

PHILIP: Alright! I'll ask her.

SASHA: Yes!

(*SASHA kisses PHILIP.*)

PHILIP: Nip out and buy a simple gold ring. Save the receipt – I'll put it on expenses.

(*SASHA heads for the exit doors.*)

EDDIE: (*To SASHA.*) More booze an' all. Sash!

PHILIP: Champagne. Yes! And ciggies.

EDDIE: Don't get any cheap muck.

SASHA: (*In the doorway.*) I'll do all of those things for you, if, one of you boys will get rid of a certain glass of water in the fridge. There's no further use for it, and I'm not touching it. Okay?!

PHIL: (*Stands.*) Stop! Beatrice, she might be pregnant!

EDDIE: Aye, mebbe a swimmer got through.

PHILIP: Sasha, we're going to need a morning after pill.

SASHA: You can't just *buy* morning after pills. There's a form to fill in and everything.

PHILIP: Fill the form in then!

SASHA: I'm not doing that, it's –

PHILIP: – Murmansk!

(*SASHA leaves with an angry slam of the door.*)

I just wanted a nice quiet day with Nicola.

EDDIE: Everything's going well. Yer've got Beatrice to recruit an 'undred Democrats to vote for the Censure –

PHILIP: – Ninety-seven.

EDDIE: – you've pretty much secured the Presidency, and that means nine million euros off the Turks and yer've had a shag, and that alone meks it a good day in my book. All we need now is for you to ask the lass yer love to marry yer.

(*Knock at the door. PHILIP leaps up and grabs his clothes off the ironing board and elsewhere.*)

PHILIP: Bugger! That'll be Frau Flugelhammerlein!

(*ANDRÉ opens the cupboard door.*)

ANDRÉ: You will be safe in ze cupboard with me!

PHILIP: Great! (*To EDDIE.*) Can you amuse her for a minute? Don't upset her Eddie, please.

(*PHILIP goes into the cupboard closing the door behind him. The Helping Hand is still stuck on the outside of the cupboard door. EDDIE opens the main doors once PHILIP is in the cupboard.*)

FRAU F: (*Striding in.*) Guten Tag!

EDDIE: Norr exactly a beautiful language is it, German? Ever been to Lille International railway station?

FRAU F: Ja! Selbsverstandlich!

EDDIE: Yer waiting fer the Eurostar and yer always get the fost announcement in English. 'Attention please, the next train for Brussels will be arriving at platform three in two minutes'. Then next, yer French – 'Attention s'il vous plaît, le prochain train pour Bruxelles...' whatever. And then yer get yer German – 'ACHTUNG! ACHTUNG! DER NECHSTE ZUG...!!!!' I nearly shit mesen.

(*PHILIP slowly opens the cupboard door and puts a hand round the door feeling for the Helping Hand. He gets the vibrator which he puts in his jacket pocket. Then he picks the Helping Hand off the door.*)

FRAU F: Who are you?

EDDIE: Eddie Fredericks, UK Independence Party.

FRAU F: Wo ist Philip?!

EDDIE: He's putting a tie on. Do you want a drink?

FRAU F: Water please. Train stations remind me of my grandfather. He was murdered in the camp at Dachau.

EDDIE: Jewish eh?

FRAU F: Communist.

EDDIE: Just a different kind of fascism.

FRAU F: He worked against the Nazis. He had a vision for Europe, the kind of vision you backward-thinking independence parties hate. He dreamt of a continent of peoples living peacefully together, trading, enjoying each other's cultures and all working together –

EDDIE: – to rip off the English.

FRAU F: He understood that the kind of blind, stupid nationalism which you Europhobes so love, has created the wars that have blighted this continent. You, your party of little Englanders – you're ridiculous, you have no policies, you have no leader, you have no principles.

(*During the next EDDIE starts preparing a clean glass of water with ice.*)

EDDIE: I'm democratically elected love, unlike the Commissioners. I feel sorry for them Eastern Europeans. Soon they'll realise that they've swapped dictatorship from Moscow for dictatorship from Brussels, Joe Stalin for Peter Mandelson. Stalin was a fascist and a mass murderer, but at least he din't bat for the other team.

FRAU F: Homophobic too! Like everyone in your ridiculous party you're a myopic, small-minded, racist moron –

(*EDDIE has prepared the drink and is about to offer the glass of clean water to FRAU F.*)

EDDIE: – you can't upset me love.

FRAU F: – and you smell of pigs.

(*EDDIE freezes.*)

EDDIE: D'yer wanna reconsider that last remark?

FRAU F: Wiz you comes a distinct smell of pigs.

(*EDDIE goes over to the fridge and picks out the 'medicinal water' and offers it to FRAU F. She takes it. PHILIP has surreptitiously opened the cupboard door and unseen is watching the scene.*)

EDDIE: Cheers!

(*EDDIE clinks glasses, though FRAU F doesn't want to. EDDIE drinks. FRAU F raises the glass and drinks. EDDIE picks up the 'medicinal twiglets' and offers the bowl to FRAU F.*)

Twiglet?

(*FRAU F eats a twiglet. PHILIP comes out of the cupboard, fully-dressed but looking dishevelled.*)

FRAU F: Why have you come just out of the cupboard?

PHILIP: I…er…go in there to…do my Tai Chi.

FRAU F: In a cupboard?

PHILIP: 'Cupboard Tai Chi'. It's like 'Travel Scrabble'. It's the perfect activity for people who like Tai Chi but don't like being watched. Is that water alright?

FRAU F: Fine. Cold, and just a hint of salt.

(*FRAU F drinks again.*)

PHILIP: And the twiglets?

FRAU F: Excellent, I didn't know they did cheese-flavoured.

PHILIP: Are they cheesey?

FRAU F: Try one. Go on.

(*FRAU F takes the bowl of twiglets from EDDIE and pushes it towards PHILIP. PHILIP baulks at the offer.*)

Come on! I value your opinion. When you're President, which looks very likely, you'll need to form opinions on everything on the spur of the moment!

(*PHILIP eventually takes one and eats it.*)

PHILIP: (*With a full mouth of twiglet.*) There's a hint of brie.

FRAU F: Correct! Now, everything's going fantastically well Philip.

PHILIP: Is it?

FRAU F: Jawohl! The Democrats are split in two! Their left wing is blaming their loony right wing for the jiffy bag bomb. Now, all you need is a wife.

PHILIP: I'm going to propose to the woman I love as soon as she's calmed down.

FRAU F: Gut! I do not wish to mutter you Philip – but I never had any children of my own. I married ze party and virk has been my man. But your choice of bride is very important. Imagine dinner with Bush, Putin, Bono. It's vital to have someone who's not going to show you up.

(*Enter NICOLA from Bed 2.*)

NICOLA: I'm going to fuck the next man who walks through this door.

PHILIP: Nicola! Darling! This is Frau Flugelhammerlein, my boss, the socialist whip.

(*She closes the door.*)

FRAU F: You're marrying a tart?

PHILIP: Her!? No, No!!

FRAU F: You called her 'Nicola darling'.

PHILIP: That's her name – 'Nicola Darling'. She's Alistair
Darling's mother.

FRAU F: Mother?

EDDIE: Niece.

PHILIP: Niece!

FRAU F: The President of the European Parliament needs a
mature woman; sophisticated; charming; elegant and if
she's a linguist, I can't tell you what a bonus that is.
(*Enter BEATRICE, through the main doors, looking elegant,
wearing the blonde wig.*)

BEATRICE: Guten Tag Frau Flugelhammerlein. Wie geht's?

FRAU F: Es geht mir gut, danke. Und Sie?

BEATRICE: Prima! Vielen dank! Das Wetter hier in Strasbourg
ist so warm.

FRAU F: Enchantée. (*To PHILIP.*) Your partner reminds me just
a little of that Beatrice Renard who runs the Women's
Committee.

PHILIP: My what?

FRAU F: (*To BEATRICE.*) You're like an attractive, not mad
version. (*Laughs.*)

BEATRICE: (*Laughs.*) L'habit ne fait pas le moine! À la
prochaine.
(*BEATRICE goes into Bed 1.*)

FRAU F: (*To PHILIP.*) She speaks French too. Fantastisch! Now
she is the perfect wife for a President!

PHILIP: Isn't she!

FRAU F: You two getting married is the best news I've had all
day! (*To PHILIP.*) Brilliant work Philip!
(*FRAU F makes to go. Enter SASHA quickly with a plastic shopping
bag with wine bottles rattling. She doesn't notice FRAU F.*)

PHILIP: Apart from letting Turkey in, as President, what are my
other policies, what do I stand for?

FRAU F: Anti-corruption, anti-excess, family values.
(*SASHA empties the bags.*)

SASHA: Booze, fags, morning after pills.

FRAU F: Auf Wiedersehen.

EDDIE: Tarra!

(*FRAU F exits. PHILIP slams the doors closed and leans back against them for support. PHILIP goes to the cupboard opens it. ANDRÉ is revealed with headphones on.*)

PHILIP: (*To ANDRÉ.*) Are you ready to record this because I'm only going to propose once okay!

ANDRÉ: On y va!

(*PHILIP closes the cupboard door. He goes over to SASHA's desk.*)

PHILIP: Eddie, get me a drink of water. Clean, fresh water please. (*To SASHA.*) And give me one of those morning after pills.

(*SASHA gives him a morning after pill and EDDIE begins preparing the glass. PHILIP knocks on Bed 1 door. BEATRICE opens it.*)

Will you marry me? Come on make your bloody mind up!

BEATRICE: Do you love me?

PHILIP: Of course, I bloody love you. My heart aches when you're around.

BEATRICE: Not around, surely.

PHILIP: Eh?

BEATRICE: Say something romantic Philip!

PHILIP: Right! Compared to your beauty, roses are a bit shit. Well!? What is it?! Oui ou Non!?

BEATRICE: Oh yes! Let's get married!

ANDRÉ: (*Off.*) Ha ha ha!

BEATRICE: I think there is someone in the cupboard.

(*BEATRICE starts to move towards the cupboard. PHILIP grabs her.*)

PHILIP: We'll have plenty of time for looking in cupboards after we're married. Now, let me kiss you.

(*PHILIP is seen to put the morning after pill on the tip of his tongue. They begin a long, deep tongue kiss. NICOLA opens the door to Bed 2 and watches, unseen. She then returns to Bed 2 closing the door quietly. PHILIP slaps the back of his head and spits the morning after pill into BEATRICE's mouth. BEATRICE begins to choke. EDDIE is there with the drink.*)

Here, take a drink, swallow.

(*BEATRICE drinks and swallows and heads for the door.*)

SASHA: Madame! You can't leave, the Gendarme needs everyone to stay in this room.

BEATRICE: Gendarme?! Phuh! I have to see someone much more important. Philip, chéri, you have made me so happy.

(*She kisses PHILIP and leaves. PHILIP opens the cupboard door.*)

PHILIP: Did you get that?!

ANDRÉ: Oui! My fish is now off ze 'ook, and in ze keep net, all I have to do now is knock her on ze head with ze wooden priest.

(*NICOLA comes out of Bed 2. PHILIP slams the door of the cupboard.*)

NICOLA: Who is that woman? The one you were kissing?

PHILIP: That was incredibly not a kiss actually. That was a kissectomy. An emergency medical procedure.

NICOLA: I've seen hardcore pornography that was easier to watch!

PHILIP: It wasn't even a tonguey!

NICOLA: You were licking her kidneys! Sasha, I'm looking for scissors.

PHILIP: (*Backing off.*) Nicola, will you marry me? What happened earlier, in there, was an accident.

NICOLA: Did you enjoy yourself during the accident?

PHILIP: Yes, but only because I thought it was you!

NICOLA: Tut!

(*NICOLA searches SASHA's desk for a pair of scissors.*)

PHILIP: You're the only woman I've ever really loved. And I mean LOVE. I'm not just talking about good sex.

NICOLA: Asking me to marry you is a desperate attempt to win me back and you don't really mean it.

PHILIP: I do do mean it.

(*NICOLA cuts his tie in half, then his braces which results in his trousers falling down.*)

Nicola!

(*Enter MEHMET through the main doors.*)

Mehmet?!

NICOLA: Mehmet Aziz?

MEHMET: Yes?

NICOLA: I'm Nicola Daws.

    (*NICOLA offers her hand. MEHMET refuses it.*)

MEHMET: And the very worst enemy of the Turkish nation.

    (*To PHILIP.*) You are lovers? With this woman?

PHILIP: (*Shaking his head as if to say No.*) Yes.

NICOLA: Please, sit down Mr Aziz.

    (*During the next SASHA switches EDDIE's case for PHILIP's.*)
    In order to make Turkey pass for a civilised society you've
    rushed through these harmonisation laws, but they are
    a veil, if I might use that word, and human rights abuses
    against women...

PHILIP: – Mehmet, can I get you a drink?

MEHMET: (*To PHILIP.*) No! Turkey is a modern secular
    democracy with exemplary standards.

NICOLA: Try telling that to Mr Hrant Dink.

MEHMET: We did not kill Mr Dink, it was some boy, some
    idiot.

NICOLA: You charged him under article 301 of the Penal Code
    with insulting Turkey. Why didn't you just stick a target on
    his chest!

PHILIP: Nibbles? We've got some clean twiglets.

MEHMET: No thank you!

NICOLA: You made him wide open to any Islamist nutter with
    a gun.

MEHMET: What do you expect if you go around saying that
    Turkey killed a million Armenian Christians!

NICOLA: So you admit that it is not possible to speak the truth
    in Turkey?

MEHMET: It is not the truth!

NICOLA: Your Nobel Prize Winning author, Orhan Pamuk, has
    had to flee to Paris in fear of his life.

MEHMET: Reading his books anyone would think that Turkey
    is swarming with Taliban-style executioners shooting
    anyone without a beard, and that everywhere it is snowing
    all the time!

NICOLA: You and I know Turkey only want to join the EU for the grants. Money you desperately need to pay off the Turkish Debt Mountain.

(*MEHMET stands. Everyone stands and looks around for armed mullahs.*)

PHILIP: Shhh! You're not allowed to say *Turkish Debt Mountain!*

NICOLA: Article 301 does not apply to me, I'm not Turkish.

MEHMET: (*To PHILIP, standing.*) No! As an employee of Turkey *you're* not allowed to say *Turkish Debt Mountain.*

EDDIE: (*To MEHMET.*) That's twice today you've said *Turkish Debt Mountain.*

MEHMET: I would never say 'Turkish Debt Mountain' because that would be an insult to Turkishness which is a very serious crime for a Turk, and I might get my thumbs crushed.

NICOLA: So you admit that torture is prevalent in Turkey?

MEHMET: No! Turkey is perfect! Wherever Turks live together there is paradise! Have you never been to Stoke Newington?

(*MEHMET picks up EDDIE's case.*)

Our deal is off Mr Wardrobe!

PHILIP: What?!

MEHMET: I will take my briefcase back now!

PHILIP: Oh no please! I've bought shoes to match!

(*Enter GENDARME.*)

GENDARME: Ah voilà! Monsieur Aziz. Please arrive quickly zis way for ze deep probe in ze rear corridor.

MEHMET: Goodbye!

(*GENDARME and MEHMET leave, closing the doors behind them.*)

NICOLA: What was in that case?

(*SASHA has opened the remaining case. NICOLA can't see the contents.*)

SASHA: Ham sandwiches.

PHILIP: Yes!!!

EDDIE: Eh?

NICOLA: I don't understand.

PHILIP: Mr Erdogan was impressed with my consultancy work
for Turkey on the accession talks last December –

NICOLA: So he gave you some ham sandwiches?

PHILIP: Yes. Enough for a picnic.

NICOLA: Do I have a big neon sign on my head that says
Gullible Fuckwit? What's in that case there?
(*SASHA stashes the money case in the cupboard.*)

PHILIP: (*Ashamed.*) One million euros.

NICOLA: Ah! Money. I can never compete with that can I? The
next person I want to see –

PHILIP: – will you marry me? I love you. (*To SASHA.*) Ring!
(*Showing the band.*) Look! It's ninety-one carat gold.
(*NICOLA takes the band and turns it upside down.*)

NICOLA: Sixteen.

PHILIP: To get something as classy as that in England –

NICOLA: – you'd have to go to Argos. Some people can't be
bought Phil.
(*She gives the ring back. NICOLA goes into Bed 2 and closes the
door behind her.*)

PHILIP: (*To SASHA.*) How come we've still got the money?

SASHA: I switched briefcases.

PHILIP: You are the most incredibly gorgeous illegal Russian
genius babe. I fucking love you.
(*SASHA presents her cheek for a peck, but PHILIP grabs her in a
big squeeze. His trousers come down again. NICOLA opens the
door to Bed 2 and watches. NICOLA waits.*)

NICOLA: (*To SASHA.*) Sasha, when you have a minute, please.
(*PHILIP breaks off the snog and pulls his trousers up.*)
I'm having difficulty getting in touch with the Chair of the
Women's Committee.

SASHA: She's had her mobile phone stolen.

PHILIP: You don't want to see Beatrice – she's nuts.

NICOLA: And since when have you been an expert on mental
illness? (*To SASHA.*) If you could fix up a meeting that would
be brilliant. My flight's at nine so I'll have to leave here by
seven. (*To the room.*) If anyone has forgotten, I'm going to
fuck – [the next man who comes through that door]

PHILIP: – Yes, yes, we know.

(*NICOLA goes back into Bed 2. Enter BEATRICE through main doors. She is carrying some papers. EDDIE puts a chair up against NICOLA's door, i.e. Bed 2.*)

BEATRICE: Philip, my friend Roman is coming! He said he could do it!

PHILIP: Do what?

BEATRICE: Marry us. My father saved his life in the war. He was a Polish bomber pilot with the RAF.

PHILIP: Since when did Second World War Polish bomber pilots have the right to marry people?

BEATRICE: He's an Archbishop now. He's in the hotel for the conference! He'll be here in a minute. Mr Fredericks could you be a witness please?

EDDIE: Aye. And I'll be best man if yer want. I gorr a few jokes. This zebra walks into the farmyard –

SASHA: – wait! You can't get married just like that in France. The Lord Mayor has to perform a civil ceremony first. (*BEATRICE produces a wad of papers. PHILIP snatches at them.*)

BEATRICE: The Mayor of Strasbourg owes me seventy-three thousand euros and six favours. Today I cashed in the favours. You will see everything is in order.

PHILIP: (*Looking at the papers.*) You've forged my signature!

BEATRICE: This way we can be married today!

(*Enter ANDRÉ from cupboard.*)

ANDRÉ: – Enough!

BEATRICE: (*To PHILIP.*) I told you there was someone in the cupboard.

ANDRÉ: You are under arrest with OLAF.

(*Enter the GENDARME carrying handcuffs. He doesn't fully enter the room at first and BEATRICE is obscured from his view by the open door of the room.*)

GENDARME: I have a need of arresting Madame Beatrice Renard.

(*BEATRICE opens the cupboard door and goes in.*)

Ze cell phone on the insides of the jiffy bag bom' was registered in her name. Now, say to me where she is?

PHILIP: The last time I saw her she was in here.

(*PHILIP ushers the* GENDARME *into Bed 1, and shuts the door behind him.*)

If she gets arrested before the vote tomorrow, I'll never be President!

(*ANDRÉ opens the cupboard door.*)

ANDRÉ: This woman is going to be my scalp, not his!

(*ANDRÉ goes into the cupboard with* BEATRICE. *Enter* GENDARME *from Bed 1.*)

GENDARME: She is not in the insides zere. Why are you having a chair up 'ard against ze 'andle of zat chamber here?

(*PHILIP goes over to the door and blocks the* GENDARME's *path to the door.*)

PHILIP: Listen! You are in extreme danger of being shagged to death if you go in there.

GENDARME: Are you saying, zere is a woman inside zere who will force me to make love to her against my will?

PHILIP: That is incredibly bang on exactly what I'm saying officer. And you don't want that to happen do you, I can tell, you're a happily married man.

GENDARME: Step aside please.

(*PHILIP stands aside. The* GENDARME *moves the chair and opens the door, and looks in, he looks back, and is then yanked in by* NICOLA. *The door is slammed. There is screaming from the cupboard and* BEATRICE *falls out holding the Helping Hand.*)

BEATRICE: Ah!!! There are body parts in ze cupboard.

(*PHILIP takes the hand off her.*)

PHILIP: Calm down! It's nothing unusual. It's a perfectly normal masturbating hand!

(*Knock at the door.* SASHA *opens it. Enter the* ARCHBISHOP. *During the next* PHILIP *is conscious of holding the masturbating hand and he passes it on to* EDDIE *who passes it back to* PHILIP. *It's a hot potato and ends up back with* PHILIP *who slips on his jacket and secretes it up the sleeve of his jacket like a prosthetic limb.*)

BEATRICE: Roman! This is very kind of you.

ARCHBISHOP: (*Polish accent.*) I don't have long my Beatrice, I have to be in the plenary session in ten minutes.

(*BEATRICE kisses the* ARCHBISHOP.)

Dziendobry. I am Archbishop Roman Borowczyk.

EDDIE: Dziendobry.

ARCHBISHOP: Czy rozmawjasz po Polski?

EDDIE: Moy ojciec uciekl do Angli podczas wojny.
Scarborough.

ARCHBISHOP: I am sorry we are being rude, speaking Polish.

PHILIP: Eddie. You speak Polish?

EDDIE: I'm half Polish. Me dad were a Jewish refugee.

BEATRICE: So you're a Jewish pig farmer?

EDDIE: No love. With yer Jews it's the mother's line in't it?

PHILIP: But you're not a proper 100% Yorkshireman?

EDDIE: If it walks like a duck, and talks like a duck, it's a
fucking duck.

ARCHBISHOP: Are you Mr Wardrobe?

PHILIP: Yes sir, hello.

(*ARCHBISHOP offers his hand to shake. PHILIP thinks for a
moment and then shakes it with the Helping Hand because he
is holding his trousers up with his left hand.*)

ARCHBISHOP: A prosthetic hand? My son, I sympathise. I
have a false leg. I lost it in the war. How did you lose your
hand?

PHILIP: Er… Overuse. Too much of something.

(*Accidentally sets it to the Fast setting.*)

But this new hand is brilliant. I can do absolutely
everything I used to do before – only quicker.

ARCHBISHOP: Congratulations on your marriage! Can I see
the civil licence please?

(*BEATRICE shoves the paperwork into his hands.*)

All in order! Now I'm a little expensive, four hundred
euros an hour.

(*BEATRICE pays him a wad of cash which she produces from
her suit.*)

NICOLA: (*Off.*) Ohagh!! Oh yes, yes, oh yes, don't stop, yes,
Oh! Oh!

(*PHILIP listens at the door to Bed 2.*)

PHILIP: She's doing it. I didn't believe her. She's bloody well,
incredibly doing it. (*Sadly to the ARCHBISHOP.*) She's having
it off with the Gendarme!

(*PHILIP tries to open the door.*)
She's locked me out!
(*He bangs on Bed 2.*)
Stop, Nicola! Please! I love you!
BEATRICE: Who 'ave you got in there?
PHILIP: One of the bridesmaids.
ARCHBISHOP: You love one of the bridesmaids?
PHILIP: No! It's my mother.
EDDIE: Sister.
PHILIP: Yes, sister.
(*Enter GENDARME from Bed 2.*)
BEATRICE: Agh!
(*SASHA lifts the ARCHBISHOP's robes and BEATRICE hides in them.*)
GENDARME: I have 'ad a good look. And I am now satisfied that Madame Renard is not within the insides.
EDDIE: Here you go son.
(*EDDIE gives the GENDARME a cigarette and lights it for him.*)
PHILIP: Did you make love to Nicola, the woman, my sister, within the inside? Did you!?
GENDARME: I am asking ze probing questions today Monsieur.
(*He takes a drag of the cigarette, and:*)
Now! Attempted murder wiz a jiffy bag bom' is a serious crime within the inside of France. I will find Madame Renard, arrest her, secure zis chamber, and then phone for back up.
SASHA: (*To GENDARME.*) Have you looked in the cupboard!?
(*The GENDARME gives PHILIP his cigarette, which PHILIP takes with the Helping Hand. SASHA opens the cupboard door and takes out the money case. The GENDARME goes into the cupboard. SASHA shuts the door on him. EDDIE holds the handle up so the GENDARME can't get out the cupboard. Enter MEHMET through the main doors with briefcase.*)
MEHMET: Where is my money?!
EDDIE: Where are my bloody sandwiches?
(*SASHA opens the door to Bed 1.*)
SASHA: I think your money is in here Mr Aziz!
MEHMET: Thank you Miss.

(*MEHMET goes into Bed 1 and SASHA jams a chair up against the handle. The cigarette has set light to the Helping Hand but PHILIP hasn't noticed. BEATRICE comes out from under the ARCHBISHOP's robes. There is banging on the cupboard door.*)

GENDARME: (*Off.*) Let me out!

BEATRICE: Chéri! This is our happy day!

PHILIP: Get off me! I'm going in there.

BEATRICE: Non! It is me you love! Come on!

(*She tries to grab him and pull him over to the ARCHBISHOP but she comes away with the hand which has caught fire in the meantime.*)

Agh! Your wanking hand is on fire!

PHILIP: Eddie, Eddie!

EDDIE: Sasha! Fire!

(*The GENDARME comes out. SASHA throws the contents of the ice bucket at EDDIE holding the hand. The contents miss the hand and hit the GENDARME who loses his glasses on the floor. SASHA picks them up and pockets them.*)

GENDARME: Merde! Mes lunettes!

SASHA: Madame Renard is getting away!

(*SASHA opens one of the main doors and slams it.*)

She's escaping down the stairs!

(*The GENDARME finds his own way uncertainly to the main doors and goes through. SASHA slams the doors on him. ANDRÉ goes back into the cupboard again. She then packs one of the cases with A4 paper and dresses it on the top with notes. The rest is then packed in her own case and left on the desk.*)

BEATRICE: (*To ARCHBISHOP.*) Get on with it then!

ARCHBISHOP: Do we have two witnesses?

ANDRÉ: Oui! C'est moi!

ARCHBISHOP: (*To EDDIE.*) And you sir?

EDDIE: (*Drunk.*) Am I on? Alright! So this Zebra walks into this farmyard, and ses to the chicken, 'What do you do here? And the chicken ses 'I shit everywhere, quack, and lay the odd egg'. And the zebra ses to the pig 'What do you do here?' And the pig ses 'I shit everywhere, oink a lot, and then when I'm fat enough they turn me into bacon.' And

the zebra ses to the horse, 'And what do you do here?' And the horse ses, 'Tek yer pyjamas off and I'll show yer'.
(*EDDIE collapses totally drunk.*)

ARCHBISHOP: – Thank you! So, you are gathered here today to witness the joining in matrimony of –

PHILIP: (*To ARCHBISHOP.*) No, no, no, and incredibly not yet wait! Sasha!

SASHA: (*Tapping her nose knowingly.*) I've switched the cases.

PHILIP: There's only one woman I love, and there are no circumstances in which I would marry this woman today. No-one living on this earth could persuade me that it is a good idea.
(*Enter FRAU F.*)

FRAU F: Congratulations Philip! Wunderbar!

PHILIP: What's wonderbar?

FRAU F: You've got it! The Presidency! (*To BEATRICE.*) Congratulations my dear.

PHILIP: I've got the nomination? All I've got to do is marry… this woman? And then I'm the most powerful man in Europe.

FRAU F: Jawohl! Carry on Archbishop, sorry to interrupt.

ARCHBISHOP: (*To PHILIP.*) Do you have a ring?
(*PHILIP goes into his pocket searching for the ring and comes out with the vibrator which he hands to the ARCHBISHOP and continues searching for the ring. He comes up with the ring.*)

PHILIP: Will this do?

ARCHBISHOP: Holy matrimony. Which is an honourable state of life instituted from the beginning by God himself, signifying to us the spiritual union –

SASHA: – No! I will not allow this to happen.
(*There is banging on the door of Bed 1.*)
(*To BEATRICE.*) Mehmet Aziz is in here, and I'm going to open the door.

BEATRICE: No! I will kill him!

SASHA: Or he'll kill you.
(*BEATRICE dives under the ARCHBISHOP's robes again. MEHMET comes out of Bed 1.*)

Beatrice Renard is hiding between the legs of this
Archbishop.

(*MEHMET lifts the robes of the ARCHBISHOP to reveal
BEATRICE.*)

MEHMET: You have insulted all of Turkish manhood!

ARCHBISHOP: Beatrice. NO!!!

BEATRICE: Ahhhh!!!!

(*During the next BEATRICE leaps up from between the
ARCHBISHOP's legs holding his prosthetic leg which is now a
weapon. She attacks MEHMET and lays him out.*)

MEHMET: Agh!

ARCHBISHOP: Give me back my leg. I'm useless without it.

BEATRICE: You're useless with it!

SASHA: (*Indicating the cupboard.*) And OLAF is in there!

BEATRICE: Mon dieu!

(*BEATRICE leaves, running with the ARCHBISHOP's leg.*)

ARCHBISHOP: Come back!

(*BISHOP leaves, hopping. MEHMET gets up on his knees. SASHA
gives him the briefcase dressed with money on the top.*)

SASHA: I think you'll find all your money is in here Mr Aziz.

(*MEHMET leaves. Enter NICOLA from Bed 1. NICOLA and PHILIP
face each other. There is a hiatus of silence.*)

PHILIP: (*To FRAU FLUGELHAMMERLEIN.*) I resign, as President.

FRAU F: You can't do that, what about –

PHILIP: – What's the point of anything, without kids. I want to
be a dad. I don't want to be President.

FRAU F: You have let down Europe, me, the party, socialism.

PHILIP: For the record. French – Je suis desolé. German – Ich
entschuldige mich. English – I couldn't give a fuck. Now
go, please! I have something very important to say to this
woman here. Thank you!

(*FRAU F leaves.*)

(*To NICOLA.*) I heard you in there. I forgive you. Even
though what I did was an accident and what you did
was deliberate. I've only ever been any good at two
things. Screwing up, and apologising. Me and you eh?
You're like a part of me. Ten years, off and on. Always,
no matter where I am or what I'm doing, and I've even

known it when having dinner with another woman or even that time, you know, d'you remember her – bonfire night? Yeah, even then, whenever I think of you my heart leaps – you know like when you drive over a hump-backed bridge, your heart, no not just your heart your guts leap upwards – well, that's always happened. Just the thought of you. I think that's how I know it's real. The only reason I love me, is because you love me, or at least, I thought you did. Get Freud to chew on that one. Huh!

(*He looks sideways and sees* SASHA *standing there with the money case.*)

Money eh? It doesn't interest me much. I've never had to work for it. Can you honestly remember a time when I was ever short of money, me, a socialist. Huh!

(*He takes the case. He gives the money case back to* SASHA.)

Take it Sash, it's yours. Spend it, don't bank it. And thank you.

SASHA: Thank you Phil. My mother, and my father…thank you, thank you.

(*SASHA leaves.*)

NICOLA: I didn't do anything in there. With the Gendarme.

PHILIP: You didn't?

NICOLA: No. I faked it.

PHILIP: Will you marry me? Please!

NICOLA: Why? Why would I want to marry a sex-obsessed, self-obsessed –

PHILIP: I'm incredibly not self-obsessed. I sponsor a goat in Somalia.

NICOLA: You called the goat 'Philip Wardrobe'.

PHILIP: Okay! Okay! I want to marry you. I want to grow up.

NICOLA: It wouldn't work.

PHILIP: I'd make it work. I'd change.

NICOLA: People don't change. They stay the same and then they start to hate their partners who want them to change. Every day with you will be like this – alcohol, sex with strangers, and athlete's foot. Marry you? I won't even vote for you again.

PHILIP: I want to go to the Cricketers on a Sunday afternoon, walk there, hand in hand, over the fields, and have lunch, and you can leave me there, and pick me up later, like you usually do, and we can go to bed in the afternoon and have a Chinese takeaway later on, and do those crispy duck pancake thingies and watch some Jane Austen adaptation on telly which, at a subliminal level, reinforces our joint love of England. Oh for fuck's sake Nicola!

(*PHILIP turns away.*)

NICOLA: Alright then.

PHILIP: What did you say?

NICOLA: Yes.

(*They kiss – long and complicated.*)

But I don't want to be Mrs Wardrobe.

(*They kiss.*)

PHILIP: We could go the doubled-barrelled route.

NICOLA: Wardrobe-Daws?

PHILIP: What's wrong with that?

NICOLA: It would be unfair on the kids. What are we going to do now?

(*Another kiss.*)

PHILIP: I'm going to make love to you so slowly and for so long, that in years to come it's gonna look like a gap in your CV.

(*They edge towards Bed 1 and go in without closing the door. A moment later PHILIP comes out with EDDIE's sleeping bag and covers him with it. PHILIP goes to the cupboard and opens it. We see ANDRÉ there with his headphones on, crying. ANDRÉ picks up his things and goes to the door. They shake hands and ANDRÉ leaves. Then PHILIP, with a lift in his step, heads for Bed 1, and before closing the door, has a brief, satisfied scan of the room, and closes the door.*

To black.)

(*The End.*)

THE ENGLISH GAME

Characters

WILL 59	ALAN 45
LEN 89	REG 59
THIZ 55	THEO 55
PAUL 28	OLLY 28
NICK 25	THIEF 15
SEAN 40	RUBEN 13
CLIVE 35	BERNARD 55

SET DESIGN

A London park cricket pitch. The action takes place in and around a section of the boundary where The Nightwatchmen cricket team congregate. The wicket is not visible. There is no boundary line. Upstage is a wire or metal fence, with holes in it, and beyond that a small copse. The grass of the pitch is not well cut and lines of cut grass remain on the pitch. A fresh pile of dog dirt is set centre stage. Down stage right is the remains of a burnt out cricket pavilion. All that can be seen is the concrete foundations, and some charred wooden floorboards. The actors always take the field down the pavilion steps, it is a club tradition, and so a batsman going out to bat exits stage right and is heard to click with his boot studs on the concrete steps.

SOUND DESIGN

The audience in the stalls should feel that they are on the pitch, and that the game is going on around them. A character fielding at Deep Long On who shouts or says anything should sound as if he is diametrically opposite a character fielding at Deep Third Man. I guess the term is surround sound.

TIME

The Present. The first two acts take place in real time. Leaps of time in the third act can be indicated by an accelerated scoreboard. All three acts take place on the same very hot August Sunday.

The English Game was first performed at Guildford's Yvonne Arnaud Theatre in a Headlong Theatre production on 7 May 2008, with the following cast:

SEAN   Tony Bell
BERNARD   Peter Bourke
NICK   Rudi Dharmalingam
WILL   Robert East
ALAN   Andrew Frame
CLIVE   John Lightbody
LEN   Trevor Martin
PAUL   Ifan Meredith
THIZ   Sean Murray
OLLY   Marcus Onilude
REG   Fred Ridgeway
RUBEN   Jamie Samuel
THEO   Howard Ward

Director Sean Holmes
Designer Anthony Lamble
Lighting Designer Charles Balfour
Sound Designer Gregory Clarke
Assistant Director Jamie Harper

Act One

(*The sound of traffic mixed with bird song, then a cuckoo. A VW camper van pulls up off. The van's stereo plays 'And the Healing has Begun' by Van Morrison. This is turned off after a few bars, and* WILL *is heard humming/singing to himself the same song. He enters. He is a fifty-nine year old grey haired man. He is wearing shorts, leather sandals and has elasticated bandages on both knees. He wears a beaten up straw hat on his head, no sunglasses. He is carrying his own kit bag and a deck chair.* WILL'*s cricket bag, a Slazenger, contrasts with his persona in the sense that it is newish, sleek, in a loud red. He puts the kitbag down upstage centre at the point where the slope begins. He looks out to the pitch and up at the clear sky. He breathes. He then walks down stage left and in setting up the deckchair shows an awareness of the position of the sun. He turns to go back to the camper van and sees the dog dirt which he marks with a seagull feather. He exits back to the camper van. He re-enters this time carrying his father,* LEN. LEN *is eighty-nine and very frail. He is dressed in a white linen suit with a white bowling cap.* WILL *puts him in the deckchair and makes sure that the sun is not in his eyes.*)

WILL: I brought both sunglasses. Which ones do you want?

LEN: The Roy Orbisons.

(WILL *reaches into his pocket and puts a pair of black Ray-bans on* LEN'*s nose.*)

WILL: Have you got your water?

(WILL *finds the water bottle in his dad's jacket pocket.*)

LEN: (*Barely audible.*) Cup.

(WILL *exits to the camper van, walking deftly round the dog dirt.* WILL *returns with all the tea things. Folding table, ice box, and in his mouth is a polythene tube bag of paper cups. He puts the tea things down near his kitbag, extracts a cup and comes over to* LEN *with it.*

WILL *pours some water into the cup and puts it into* LEN'*s hand.*)

LEN: (*Hardly audible.*) Rain's forecast.

WILL: It's not raining now. It's very very hot. Put this sun block on.

(WILL *starts to apply sun block to* LEN'*s hands and ears, nose.* LEN *weakly pushes him away.* WILL *manages to dab some block*

161

on his nose. WILL turns and walks back to the camper van. Mid walk he breaks into a warm up jog, which doesn't go too well, so he goes back to walking. LEN, with a supreme effort, wipes the sun block off with his sleeve. WILL returns this time carrying the scoreboard which is a plain piece of black wood. It's a bit tatty, worn and past its best. The number plates are in their own home made box. WILL positions the scoreboard stage right. He turns to walk back to the camper van and stands in the dog dirt.)

Bugger!

(He slips his shoe off and walks up to the hedge and wipes it in the grass at the top of the bank. He exits to the van. LEN begins to unwrap a mint. WILL returns from the van carrying three bags of sandwiches all contained in the original bread bags, and his own chair which is a fishing style chair. There are also boxes of cakes from Tescos, enough for twenty-two but no more. The food he puts on the table. He then erects his own fishing chair. It looks as if he's going to sit in it and take a breather, but he changes his mind and exits back to the van.)

LEN: *(Looking at the sky.)* There in't no rain in that sky.

(Enter THIZ. His hair is thinning dyed blond. He wears sunglasses and hippy style cotton trousers and leather sandals. He is carrying his cricket gear in a quality leather holdall, not a cricket bag, and he has his bat which is brand new still in its polythene cover. He sits in the fisherman's chair. And lets out a sigh.)

THIZ: Alright Len?!

LEN: I said it'll never rain today.

THIZ: Don't want it to rain do we.

(THIZ rolls his trousers up and takes his shirt off. He has a new tattoo of a bass guitar on his left shoulder. He looks at it. He stretches out and points his body to the sun.)

Kaw! Lovely.

(WILL re-enters carrying the kit bag. It is a typical team cricket bag and should be carried by two men at least. He shuffles along with it.)

Bloke goes to the doctor, he says doctor I think I'm a moth. The doctor says, I can't help, you need to see a psychiatrist. The bloke says I know, I was on my way to see him when I saw your light on.

(*WILL laughs. THIZ waits a beat and then laughs louder.*)
Am I sitting in your chair?

WILL: I haven't finished.

THIZ: Do you want a hand?

WILL: Nearly done.

THIZ: I don't wanna help. I'm just saying. Good chair this. I'm gonna get one of these.

(*WILL exits to the camper van. He re-enters carrying the boundary markers, and other equipment.*)

WILL: You can put the stumps out if you want.

THIZ: Na, I'd get it wrong.

WILL: How could you get it wrong?

THIZ: I'd put four stumps at one end and two at the other. Lovely day.

WILL: Rain's forecast.

(*During the next WILL goes to the tea table and empties food from a plastic carrier bag. He takes the carrier in his hand and collects the dog dirt, and puts it in the dog dirt bin.*)

THIZ: This is why I'm in England you know. Cricket. Nothing else.

(*WILL picks up THIZ's new bat.*)

WILL: New bat?

THIZ: Two hundred and forty quid. Is that a lot?

(*WILL tries the bat, testing the pick up, two or three times, and once with just the left hand.*)

WILL: Nice pick up.

THIZ: Yeah?

(*WILL suddenly rocks back and like Brian Lara hooks an imaginary ball with extraordinary violence.*)

WILL: Have you knocked it in?

THIZ: Have I what?

(*WILL goes to the kitbag and returns with the knockerinner. He picks up the bat and knocks it five or six times. Then hands the bat and knockerinner to THIZ.*)

WILL: Twenty-five hours they say.

(*THIZ knocks the bat half heartedly several times, then stops.*)

THIZ: I'll pay our drummer. He likes that kind of thing.

(*WILL goes to the kitbag and takes out the stumps and the stump gauge and walks off stage right and down the pavilion steps. Enter ALAN. ALAN carries an ordinary sports kit bag in one hand and a large white wooden box in the other. This box is a new scoreboard which he has built. He is a man of about forty-five, fit, and wiry. He wears supermarket jeans and has a tattoo on one forearm of a lion.*)

ALAN: Hi.

THIZ: What's that Alan?

ALAN: I've built a new scoreboard.

THIZ: That's a shame. I was gonna build one. But you've done it now.

(*During the next ALAN opens out the scoreboard and sets it up. It's an ingeniously designed contraption with the box opening out to make a board and the inside of the box having the hooks for the numbers. The numbers are stored on the hooks.*)

Have you got enough sevens?

ALAN: Yeah.

THIZ: Seven hundred and seventy-seven for seven off twennie seven overs, last man made seventy-seven. That's...seven sevens. If we didn't have enough sevens, it'd be a disaster. We'd all have to go home.

(*ALAN goes up stage and sets up the new scoreboard next to the old one. THIZ continues sunbathing with his eyes shut. Enter WILL from the pitch carrying mallet and stump gauge.*)

WILL: (*Doubtful.*) Terrific Alan. Don't think I've ever seen a white one.

ALAN: It's marine ply. If it rains.

WILL: Rain's forecast.

THIZ: It's got enough sevens.

(*ALAN sits on the grass and starts to undress, and change into his cricket gear. THIZ watches him. Enter PAUL. He is a man of about thirty dressed in drainpipe black jeans and loafer style shoes. He is a bit Elvis, but not overly. He has newly dyed black hair. He carries a cricket 'coffin', a big black box, also new. He doesn't acknowledge anyone, or say hello. WILL, not expecting a hello, watches.*)

WILL: (*Mock surprised.*) Hello Paul!

PAUL: What?

WILL: Are you playing today?

PAUL: Yeah.

WILL: Nice to know.

(*WILL exits to the van.*)

PAUL: What's the matter with him?

THIZ: Time of the month. What's that?

PAUL: The vernacular term is cricket coffin. It's new.
Lillywhites.

THIZ: I'm gonna get one of them. I'm gonna get one twice as
big as that. Bloke goes to the doctor, he says doctor I think
I'm a moth. The doctor says, I can't help, you need to see
a psychiatrist. The bloke says I know, I was on my way to
see him when I saw your light on.

(*PAUL and THIZ laugh.*)

PAUL: Tell the bees joke.

THIZ: Na. Lovely day.

PAUL: Actually, I'm not suited to this heat. Genetically I'm
a Viking and living several hundred miles closer to the
Equator than my biological optimum.

THIZ: Monotonous drizzle. That would suit you.

(*During the next ALAN and PAUL open their kitbags and begin
to change into their whites. This is done on the grass edge with
some concessions to modesty, but not a lot.*)

PAUL: Is that a new tattoo?

THIZ: Fender Precision bass.

PAUL: Looks like a guitar from Woollies.

THIZ: I've never liked you.

PAUL: Who are we playing?

ALAN: Farringden.

PAUL: Teachers. Took me two hours to get here. Wandsworth
was gridlocked.

THIZ: Three minutes. I live just over there. How does that
make you feel?

PAUL: There's pitches in Crouch End. We could play a few
games in North London. Most of us live in North London.

WILL: Good idea Paul. You organise it.

THIZ: That's the end of that.

WILL: Where's Olly?

PAUL: He stayed at Barbara's last night.

THIZ: Barbara. Mmm. Nice.

(*Enter THIEF from stage right. He is a young man of about fifteen dressed in an ill fitting cricket sweater, white trainers and white tracksuit bottoms with a stripe down the side. He is holding a mobile phone in his hand though he's not talking on it. He walks across the pitch five yards in front of the team, and off stage left.*)

I bet he's a cunt.

(*Enter REG from stage left. REG is a fifty-nine year old man. He is wearing terylene trousers with a crease and a military white shirt with epaulets. He has tattoos on both arms, and an ostentatious ersatz Rolex. He has an intense, driven demeanor. He has his kit in a tennis bag.*)

REG: Reg Bowden!

WILL: We're the Nightwatchmen. Are you playing for Farringden?

REG: I'm Gary's next door neighbour. Gary Whattle? He can't play today.

WILL: So you're playing for us then?

REG: Gary said it'd be alright.

WILL: That's great Reg. Will, I'm the club skipper.

(*REG shakes hands. It is a crushing squeeze. He makes a point of shaking with everyone.*)

REG: Bit late. Sorry. Very bad RTA on the Chertsey Road.

THIZ: A what?

REG: Road Traffic Accident. Nobody gets in my way when I'm driving. Kaw!

WILL: They burnt the pavilion down. We change here now.

(*REG begins to change. He immediately starts stripping off standing up. It is a more ostentatious strip than the others. His kit consists of golf shoes with spikes, whites that are too big for him around the waist. He keeps on his military style white shirt.*)

REG: Glad to be out the house. The enemy's organised a poetry reading. Her own poems. Kaw! Any port in a storm!

THIZ: I like poetry.

PAUL: Do you bat or bowl?

REG: Bidda both. Used to play for British Telecom seconds. Won the Greater London Switch knockout cup three times on the dog – back in the old TXE4A days when telephones were red and smelt of piss.

WILL: Is Gary alright?

REG: His mother's pace maker's gone tits up. Sod's law eh?! That kind of thing never happens on a rainy Tuesday!?

(*Enter SEAN. SEAN is a man of about forty. Athletic but carrying a bit of weight. He carries a beat up old cricket coffin decorated with airline stickers.*)

SEAN: Who ordered sunshine!

THIZ: } Seanie!

WILL: } Good afternoon Sean.

ALAN: Alright mate.

SEAN: I see the lazy bastard's cut the grass. Have we got eleven?

WILL: Ruben's playing. And Paul is twelfth man.

PAUL: Twelfth man?!

WILL: You didn't ring.

PAUL: Took me two hours to get here.

SEAN: You can umpire. You're doing an umpiring course.

WILL: Gary can't play. Sean this is Reg.

REG: Hi matey!

(*REG shakes hands. It is another big squeeze. SEAN glances at THIZ questioningly.*)

PAUL: Two hours. I mean Wandsworth was absolutely chocca.

SEAN: Alright Len!

LEN: Keeps low this wicket. Always has.

SEAN: You got that big hundred against the Combined Forces here didn't you Len?

LEN: Hundred and forty-three.

SEAN: Not out.

LEN: And no chances.

SEAN: Still lost though didn't you! Ha!

(*SEAN rejoins the huddle.*)

REG: (*To THIZ.*) I know you don't I. Don't tell me! Rock Logic!

THIZ: Yeah.

REG: Hammersmith Palais nineteen…bloody hell, nineteen –

PAUL: – nineteen fourteen.

REG: Seventy-one? Seventy-two?

THIZ: Don't ask me. I can't remember a thing.

REG: Bugger me! One of Rock Logic! I've got the album with the seal on the front.

THIZ: Walrus.

REG: Is that a walrus?

THIZ: The album's called 'Plain Walrus'. It's not called 'Plain Seal' is it. That'd be crap.

PAUL: Why's it called 'Plain Walrus'?

THIZ: Drugs.

REG: They'll be playing 'Sunny Sunday' today!

THIZ: They'd better be. That song's my pension plan.

PAUL: Actually, I've always thought your 'Sunny Sunday' was a bit similar to 'Monday, Monday' by…er…–

WILL: – the Mamas and the Papas.

PAUL: (*Singing.*) Monday, Monday – da da, da da da. And Sunny Sunday, oh, ho, oh ho ho!

THIZ: One's about a Sunday and one's about a fucking Monday! Two completely different days of the week.

REG: Stone me! Rock Logic. What's the singer doing now?
(*Silence.*)

THIZ: (*Standing.*) Have I got time for a poo?
(*THIZ exits stage left.*)

WILL: We don't mention the singer.

REG: Goddit! Sorry.

(*SEAN goes for a piss. This involves him pissing through a gap in the fence into the copse. Enter NICK and OLLY from stage right. NICK is an energetic twenty-five year old British born Indian. He carries a Gunn and Moore cricket bag with a bat in the sleeve. He is wearing fatigue type shorts and hippy type sandals, and various rave style accessories. OLLY is about thirty, black British, and wearing summer casuals. OLLY is hung-over and crashes out next to his kit.*)

WILL: Niranjan! Welcome back!

SEAN: (*From the copse, mid piss.*) Hello Nick!

NICK: Hi team!

ALAN: Alright mate.

PAUL: You've been badly missed. We've lost the last three games.

WILL: Yes, we've struggled without the Hindu God of flawlessness.

NICK: Don't worry. Fifty today. My first ever fifty. I've had coaching. Lords.

WILL: Coaching?!

NICK: New scoreboard Alan. Fantastic! Look at it. It's a work of beauty. Art.

(*To WILL.*) He's not talking yet.

WILL: You're not talking Olly?

OLLY: No.

WILL: Heavy night?

OLLY: Don't shout man.

WILL: You're not opening the bowling then?

OLLY: No. Leave me alone.

PAUL: (*To OLLY.*) You left the iron on in your room. It's been on two days. I could've died.

OLLY: Did you turn it off?

PAUL: I'm going to have to get a new lodger, because you're getting married.

OLLY: Yeah, you are yeah.

(*REG heads to the lip of the stage and stares out at the pitch. He essays a huge forward defensive shot bringing the bat down like the white cliffs of Dover.*)

REG: Field of bloody dreams eh?

(*WILL shows REG the pavilion.*)

WILL: Reg. We have two club rules. Rule one is that we always take the field, and leave the field, by the pavilion steps. Tradition. Burning down public facilities for a laugh whilst out of your head on skunk is integral to yoof culture, and of course, I respect that, but if we allow them to change the way we live, then we have handed them victory.

REG: If I had my way, I'd lock 'em up, and throw away the door. What's rule two?

WILL: No woman is allowed to make the tea. We're a team of militant feminists. Niranjan, this is Reg, Gary's next door neighbour.

(*REG gives NICK his huge handshake, possibly firmer because he's Indian.*)

REG: Niramjam?

NICK: Nick.

REG: Alright mate? Are you an Hindu?

NICK: My parents are Hindu.

REG: I was in Bangalore only last year, yeah. Kaw! They're all mad aren't they!

(*NICK and SEAN hug. REG watches puzzled.*)

NICK: Hiya big fellah!

SEAN: Hi Nick. Hi Olly?! Is he alright?

NICK: Tequila –

SEAN: – Great.

NICK: Don't interrupt. And cocaine.

SEAN: Fuck.

(*Enter CLIVE. CLIVE is a well dressed man of about thirty-five. He carries a Newbury cricket bag with bat in the sleeve, a copy of the Sunday Independent and a hard back book. PAUL is reading a paperback.*)

CLIVE: Hello boys. No need to stand.

(*SEAN and CLIVE hug. REG watches even more puzzled.*)

SEAN: Good to see you.
ALAN: } Alright mate.
WILL: Clive!
NICK: Alright man!

CLIVE: Iceland?

NICK: Spectacular man! Got back Monday. In the nets at Lords Tuesday morning.

CLIVE: Coaching?

NICK: Yup. Fifty today, man.

PAUL: (*To CLIVE.*) Did you come through Wandsworth?

CLIVE: Yes, Paul, I did.

PAUL: I was stuck there for nearly an hour.

CLIVE: I find it somewhat churlish to complain about the traffic when one is a constituent part of same. But yes, concur, Wandsworth was a bitch!

PAUL: Rain's forecast.

CLIVE: We'd better all go home then. I didn't know you could read Paul.

PAUL: Steve Waugh's autobiography. Have you read it?

CLIVE: I wouldn't pay to watch James Joyce bat so I don't see why I should concern myself with Steve Waugh's prose.

PAUL: A psychologist helps him prepare mentally before he goes out to bat.

CLIVE: He should try having a shit and washing his hands, works for me!

PAUL: It's important to feel OK about yourself.

CLIVE: Feeling 'OK' about myself is not a state to which I aspire. Feeling fucking brilliant about myself might be worth the effort, but since that's how I feel anyway, I don't see the point.

PAUL: What are you reading?

CLIVE: I'm re-reading *The Odyssey*. Homer.

PAUL: Is that work?

CLIVE: Pleasure.

PAUL: Are you reading it in the original Latin?

CLIVE: So far he's sticking to the Greek.

WILL: Working Clive?

CLIVE: 'Yes', I'm working, 'No', I'm not being paid.

NICK: I saw it Thursday. It's really good man.

CLIVE: I didn't know you were in.

NICK: Cameron was tired. We decided to get an early night. (*REG visibly flinches.*)

CLIVE: I'm not overly offended.

OLLY: What is it?

CLIVE: It's a staggeringly bad translation of an incredibly poor French play. I play 'Man' and 'Dog'. An impossibly gorgeous and astonishingly intelligent actress called Katrina plays 'Woman' and 'Sparrow'.

SEAN: Does the dog shag the sparrow?

CLIVE: Not yet.

(*SEAN drops his pants and bends over his cricket coffin. CLIVE is left staring at his bare arse.*)

That's what I like about you. Your arse!

SEAN: Public school!

(*Enter RUBEN on his bike. He is a thirteen-year-old boy, already dressed in his cricket gear.*)

CLIVE: ⎫ Ruben!
ALAN: ⎬ Hello mate.
SEAN: ⎭ Hiya kid!

RUBEN: Hi. (*RUBEN goes over to WILL.*) Dad. Where's my bat?

WILL: In the van. Say hello to your grandad.

(*RUBEN walks off to find his kit. Having found his kit he plays with the new scoreboard.*)

SEAN: Here they are! Late.

(*Everyone looks towards stage right to see Farringden arriving.*)

WILL: (*Holding up a carrier bag.*) Valuables bag. I'll lock it in the van.

(*No-one takes any notice. He puts his own watch and wallet in it.*)

Are you getting changed Paul?

PAUL: You said I was twelfth man.

WILL: I was punishing you. It's a club rule and it's good manners. You ring by Thursday to confirm that you're playing. Get changed.

SEAN: (*To WILL.*) We don't want to field first in this heat.

WILL: What's his name, their captain? History teacher. Very pedantic. Good at spelling.

CLIVE: Bernard.

WILL: Always forgets to bring a new ball. Possibly because they cost fifteen pounds each.

(*They all now get changed if not already changed. SEAN's kit is none too clean. ALAN and REG are practising upstage, ALAN bowling to REG's batting. CLIVE approaches LEN. PAUL watches this with interest, with a glance towards OLLY.*)

CLIVE: What a beautiful day Len?

(*CLIVE shakes his hand.*)

LEN: Clive. Alright son.

CLIVE: Lovely. England.

LEN: Aye.

(*PAUL approaches.*)

PAUL: (*Ignoring LEN.*) I need someone to look at my best man speech for Olly's wedding.

CLIVE: Paul. Have you said hello to Len yet, today?

PAUL: Alright Len. Cos your like, a trained actor –

CLIVE: – I'm not like a trained actor, I am a trained actor.

PAUL: Alright, whatever, I thought it'd be a good idea if you had a look at it and er…made any suggestions, yeah?

CLIVE: And you want me to do this today?

PAUL: Yeah. Ta. Don't show Olly yeah.

(*He hands over three pieces of A4 stapled together, and walks back to the group. CLIVE opens the pages and has a quick look before putting the speech in his pocket.*)

SEAN: Who are we missing?

WILL: We have a quorum. Theo's here. Late, but here. Church warden you see.

SEAN: Is he?

WILL: I think he and Deborah are doing some kind of job share. Oh hell! I don't know. What's next?! Bernard.

(*WILL walks off stage right to meet the opposition. Enter THEO. He is a fifty-five year-old rotund man. He carries his kit in a Kookaburra cricket bag with a bat in the sleeve.*)

THEO: Hello boys, I'm late, sorry, *mea culpa*. After church went to Asda, big mistake, lost the will to live. Hello Sean. What a simply splendid day!

SEAN: Alright Theo.

(*Enter THIZ.*)

THIZ: Bloke goes to the doctor, he says doctor I think I'm a moth. The doctor says, I can't help, you need to see a psychiatrist. The bloke says I know, I was on my way to see him when I saw your light on.

THEO: Excellent! Are we going to get the bees joke today?

OLLY: Go on Thiz. Tell the bees joke.

THIZ: Na, not today.

PAUL: Actually, the British bee population is down seventy percent.

NICK: Why's that man?

THIZ: Tight underpants.

THEO: Thiz my dear, I never know why you spend your summers here when you could be in that lovely house of yours in the south of France.

THIZ: She got the Lot mate.

OLLY: You own a house in France don't Theo?

THEO: Indeed we do. In the Perigord.

OLLY: That's the Dordogne isn't it?

THEO: Yes, that's right Olly, inland from Bordeaux. It's beautiful.

THIZ: Too many bloody English for my liking.

OLLY: Do you rent it out, you know, like a holiday gite?

THEO: Normally, yes, we do, but next year, we're having the roof done. In the long term we plan to live there. Just a matter of when. Thiz, a new tattoo! What is it?

THIZ: Oh piss off.

(*THEO seeks out WILL.*)

THEO: Good luck today Will. I prayed for you.

WILL: Prayers? For…?

THEO: Your ten thousand runs for the club. How many more required?

WILL: Three.

THEO: Gosh, I remember your first century – I was umpiring. Your long black hair in that red headband, like whatshisname, that runner, David Bedford.

WILL: You prayed to God for me to get three more runs?

THEO: Oh I believe that He is absolutely fine about managing the tsunami of human trivia that must come his way.

WILL: Maybe it was the trivia which made him forget about the tsunami.

(*WILL realises he's hurt his friend, and touches his arm.*)

Thank you Theo. I appreciate that. I'll try not to let you down.

SEAN: What are they like, Farringden? I forget.

PAUL: They've got that fat bloke with his own tits opens the batting.

NICK: They never give him out. Never give LBWs.

SEAN: Oh yeah, I remember this lot.

OLLY: Last year he was wearing a tag. They're scared of him.

SEAN: I thought they were teachers.

THIZ: I might get a tag. Be useful, you'd always know where you were.

SEAN: Is Will going to skipper?

CLIVE: You know perfectly well that he'll ask you to skipper.

SEAN: Don't mind. We'll try and win for a change, eh?

CLIVE: Certainly. Shall we inspect the wicket?

(*CLIVE and SEAN put some distance between themselves and the others.*)

SEAN: Don't want to field first in this bloody sun.

CLIVE: *Mon brave.* What is it? You can tell me.

SEAN: No change. I don't want to become the bloke that I hate. The man who leaves his wife and kids. I can't stand it. I just can't stand it anymore.

CLIVE: If you left, no-one would blame you.

SEAN: How do you leave?

CLIVE: Plenty of people do.

SEAN: They've been playing football on here haven't they? Bastards.

WILL: (*To SEAN and CLIVE.*) Senior Professional, Senior Amateur! Boundary markers please.

(*CLIVE and SEAN take boundary markers off WILL, share them out, and CLIVE places sticks one in the grass in front of LEN.*)

CLIVE: See you in the middle.

SEAN: Yup.

(*CLIVE places a second boundary marker in front of the pavilion and exits stage right. SEAN exits stage left placing a marker just before the wings stage left. RUBEN approaches LEN.*)

RUBEN: Hi Grandad.

LEN: Are they gonna give yer a game Ruben?

RUBEN: Yeah.

LEN: Wear a cap, in this sun. The worst thing on an 'ot day like this is to drop a catch cos the sun's in your eyes. What do yer catch with?

RUBEN: Your eyes.

LEN: What do you bat with?

RUBEN: Your eyes.

LEN: (*Chuckling to himself.*) What do you bowl with?

RUBEN: Your arse.

LEN: Good lad! Ha, ha! Freddie Trueman, big arse; Darren Gough, big arse; I do not know how that Steve Harmison even gets the ball down yon end.

RUBEN: Drink some water Grandad.

(*RUBEN returns to the huddle.*)

REG: Is that the opposition?! Looks like the bloody United Nations.

NICK: Come on guys. Catching!

(*THIZ goes on to the pitch with his new bat. The others bar OLLY – who remains crashed out – form a horseshoe around him. They throw the ball to him and he bats it back to them as catching practice. RUBEN joins in. If there is a spectacular catch. Then there are cries of Test Class / Good catch etc.*)

THIZ: Where've you been anyhow?

NICK: Iceland.

THIZ: Fish innit?

NICK: They do have fish, yeah.

THIZ: Fish and blondes.

NICK: Yeah, they've got a lot of gorgeous boys.

THIZ: When Heaven 17 supported us in Reykjavik. They didn't want to go home.

NICK: Thiz, give Reg a go.

THIZ: But this is my new bat.

(*REG takes it and tests the pick up. And then essays an enormous forward defensive shot.*)

REG: Beaudiful. Look at that, English willow. This is the mark of craftsman! Not been knocked out by a bloody Chinaman has it!

(*THIZ starts to bat catches back to them.*)

PAUL: How much was it?

THIZ: Two hundred and forty quid.

NICK: Two hundred and forty quid!?

THIZ: Yeah, I got the last two they had.

(*They laugh. Enter WILL, SEAN and CLIVE from stage right.*)

WILL: (*Impersonating BERNARD ie: a pedant's whine.*) 'Can we play thirty-five overs with no limit on the bowlers because we've only got four bowlers?'.

SEAN: We've only got one bowler.

WILL: Can we bat first because we've got two players lost in South West London.

SEAN: So he wants us to field first in this heat? Oh yeah.

WILL: Sean, I don't think I can be nice to Bernard all day.

SEAN: I'll skipper.

CLIVE: I'll vice captain. I'll Gower to your Gooch. I didn't mean that as an insult. Sorry, I'm lying, I did.

SEAN: There's no way I'm letting them bat first. I'm not gonna gift them an advantage just cos they're a bunch of twats who can't read an A to Z. That's exactly what's wrong with this country. The more crap, desperate, and stupid you are the more you get given. Right, I'll go and do the toss. (*Beat.*) Haven't got a coin. You got a coin?

(*CLIVE gives him a fifty P piece. SEAN exits stage right.*)

WILL: Is he alright?

CLIVE: The usual.

WILL: How old are the kids now?

CLIVE: Three and five-ish.

(*REG offers the bat to someone else.*)

REG: I need a piss. What do I do?

THIZ: How old are you?

THEO: We go in the hedge. But try and avoid the walkers. We've had complaints.

THIZ: I've never had any complaints.

(*Over by the tea things.*)

WILL: 'Have you done vegetarian sandwiches?' 'Have you done any without butter?' One of them's strict vegan. Can't go within two yards of an animal product.

CLIVE: Won't be able to catch a leather ball then! And – have you done vegetarian sandwiches?

WILL: Course I have. We've been playing these pedants ten years.

CLIVE: Eleven years.

WILL: Don't you start.

CLIVE: It was my first game for this club. I drove down from Liverpool. Why Liverpool? Oh, it was that TIE show teaching school children that slavery is something that white people do to black people, instead of the unpalatable truth that it's what powerful people do, to vulnerable people. Entirely mendacious bollocks! But it was my first acting job! Hurrah! But what a great match that was, Sean scored eighty-three, and Thiz had to go to hospital to get his jaw wired up.

WILL: Did we win?

CLIVE: I can't remember. Didn't care. I was just so happy. I'd found a team.

(*CLIVE moves away, joins the group. Enter SEAN from stage right. Face set in a frown.*)

THEO: Here he comes Now! Has he won the toss? One can never tell with Sean's face can one?

CLIVE: Same face for everything. Whether he's having his cock sucked or his teeth drilled.

THIZ: How d'you know?

CLIVE: We share the same dentist.

(*They all look at SEAN.*)

SEAN: Nick! Keeper's pads!

(*The odd groan.*)

THEO: Fielding!

PAUL: You lost the toss then?

SEAN: No, I won the toss, and decided to field in this heat. Course I lost the friggin toss.

PAUL: Alright.

THIZ: Eh Theo, I've got this lump in my left bollock, like a gristly lump.

THEO: Can you feel it?

THIZ: Do you wanna feel it?

THEO: I haven't washed my hands since Asda.

CLIVE: Thiz hasn't washed his balls since Glastonbury.

THIZ: Didn't do Glastonbury this year. He wouldn't have us back. Said we eat too much. It's like a gristly hard thing, like a pen top. Go on, have a feel.

THEO: Is there any bruising?

178

THIZ: I'll have a look.

(*THIZ sits on the ground, pulls his pants down and inspects his balls.*)

REG: Are you a doctor mate?

THEO: GP, yes.

REG: Kaw! I bet everyone, you know, eh, all the time, all their –

THEO: – I don't mind. It's why God put me on this earth.

REG: I'm in telecoms. Big switches. Digital. Fibre ops. Yeah.

THEO: Excellent. I use the telephone a lot. Excuse me Reg, I haven't said hello to Len yet.

(*THEO goes over to LEN.*)

You need to cover your arms up Len. It's hot.

LEN: Who are you?

THEO: It's me, Theo. Roll these sleeves down. And drink some water.

(*THEO starts to roll his sleeves down for him.*)

LEN: If I drink any more water I'll need a piss.

THEO: Let us know and we'll carry you to the hedge.

LEN: You'd be too late. I played on this pitch you know.

THEO: You made a lot of runs against the Combined forces, didn't you?

LEN: Hundred and forty-three. Not out. No chances. We had a pavilion in them days. I blame central heating.

THEO: For what? For everything?

LEN: If they all had fires indoors the kids wun't be interested.

THEO: Mmm. We're fielding.

(*THEO goes back to the group.*)

THIZ: They look perfect. Kinda beautiful in their own way.

THEO: Let me have a feel then.

CLIVE: I'm after Theo.

NICK: I'm next after Clive.

(*THEO puts his hand in THIZ's whites and feels. The others groan and giggle. REG doesn't know what to do.*)

THEO: Is that it?

THIZ: No, that's always been there. Ow!

THEO: That?

THIZ: Yeah.

(*THEO removes his hand, and gets a wet wipe from his bag.*)

THEO: Go and see your GP.

THIZ: But he doesn't like me.

THEO: It's probably an epididymal cyst.

THIZ: What's that? Cancer?

THEO: It's a small fibrous lump of cartilage which has formed, surprisingly enough, as a spontaneous cure. Let me think of an analogy.

THIZ: I've got an analogy?

THEO: If someone was holding a wedding party in your testicular sack, understand?

THIZ: – er…yeah –

THEO: – it's all going well, sunny day, funny vicar, when suddenly BANG! A meteorite crashes into the garden, killing dozens of people. What would happen?

THIZ: Dunno.

THEO: The police would erect a crime scene tent, a protective carapace of cartilage, then if the police forgot to take the tent away you would then be left with an epididymal cyst. Your body has healed itself. Understand?

THIZ: I bloody love you.

THEO: But, your GP will want to check your pancreas and I'm not doing that for you.

THIZ: Where's my pancreas?

THEO: Beyond your arse.

CLIVE: And put a shirt on.

WILL: And stop playing with your nob.

OLLY: And tell the bees joke.

NICK: And lose some weight.

THIZ: Alright!

REG: Bananas.

THIZ: I thought you were.

REG: I don't have lunch at all. I just have one banana.

THIZ: (*Miming holding a huge banana.*) One huuuuuge banana. Banana and chips please. And a banana pie…and two crunchies.

(*They all laugh.*)

REG: I've lost twenty-seven pounds in less than a year.

ALAN: Easy to eat, bananas. Nature's fast food innit.

THIZ: Lobster's difficult to eat. The RAC do not recommend lobster as a driving snack. A banana, you just chuck it on the dashboard, but a lobster, you've got to keep it fresh in a bucket until that moment when you can't find the polos, and you've run out of crisps –

(At this point NICK grabs THIZ from behind and with his hand over his mouth wrestles him.)

NICK: Enough lobster!

PAUL: I've never eaten lobster.

REG: I've eaten dog. In Korea. Beautiful! They frighten it first. Frightened meat tastes better.

OLLY: How do they frighten it?

REG: Dunno.

THIZ: Every restaurant's got a sixteen stone ginger tom cat in a shed, and they take the dogs out now and then for a look. Miaow!

SEAN: Clive! Can you open the bowling please?

CLIVE: For you, anything.

SEAN: Which end do you want?

CLIVE: Let me ponder a while. Uphill, or downhill? Downhill.

SEAN: Olly! First over the far end please.

OLLY: Uphill? I don't think I can do it.

SEAN: Do you think Freddie Flintoff turns up at Lords with a blood system that is eighty-seven percent tequila?

CLIVE: Apparently!

THEO: Exactly!

THIZ: ⎫ Course he does!

ALAN: ⎬ Yeah.

NICK: ⎭ That's what I've heard!

WILL: By all accounts, yes.

SEAN: Bloody hell. Thiz! Open the bowling please, uphill.

THIZ: But I've got an epididymal cyst.

SEAN: Do you want to bowl or not? I want everyone wearing a cap in this sun.

(NICK picks up the scorebook and takes it over to LEN with a pencil. THEO follows quickly.)

NICK: There you go Len! Alright.

THEO: You don't want to be bothered with the book today do you Len?

LEN: I'll do it if you want me to son.

(*THEO ushers NICK and the book back to the huddle.*)

THEO: He's had a bit of a downward journey the last two weeks.

NICK: Shit. Yeah?

THEO: Yup. He's here. That's enough and we should celebrate that.

(*Enter BERNARD from the other team.*)

WILL: Yes Bernard?

BERNARD: Just hoping to have a sneak preview of the new ball. Ha, ha!

WILL: Supplying the new ball is the visiting team's responsibility Bernard.

BERNARD: Was it agreed that we would supply the new ball?

WILL: Yes, you rang me last year to check. Christmas Eve.

BERNARD: It's the only time you can be sure that people are going to be in.

WILL: Would you like to buy one of ours?

(*WILL goes to get the box of balls.*)

BERNARD: Are they proper quartered balls?

WILL: Yes. (*Aside.*) Hung, drawn and quartered.

(*BERNARD picks one out.*)

BERNARD: Ooh, they're good ones aren't they?

WILL: Yes, they're 'fifteen pounds each' ones.

BERNARD: We'll settle up in the pub.

(*To them all.*) Hot. Glad we won the toss.

(*To WILL.*) Shall we have two drinks breaks Will?

SEAN: Alright! Yeah, after fifteen overs and and twenty-five.

BERNARD: Eleven and twenty-two would be more equidistant spacing for a thirty-five over game.

SEAN: Yeah, it would, but I want fifteen and twenty-five.

BERNARD: OK.

ALAN: I'll show you how the new scoreboard works.

BERNARD: Lovely.

(*ALAN and BERNARD head upstage and take the scoreboard off stage right.*)

THIZ: She's happy enough in't she. Sunny day like this; husband; three kids; another one on the way; bag over her head.

PAUL: Actually, technically, that's a niqab.

THIZ: Maybe that's where I went wrong with Pammy. 'Oi! Pammy! You're not going to the Brits dressed like that! Everyone can see your tits! I got you a nice niqab for Christmas!? Wear that! Or else! I told her to do something once. Kaw! Never heard the end of it.

SEAN: Come on then!

NICK: Let's go boys!

(*REG heads for the middle directly out.*)

RUBEN: Reg!

REG: Yeah?

NICK: No.

WILL: Rule number one.

REG: Brain dead! Pavilion!

(*From the pitch.*)

SEAN: (*Off.*) Square leg Alan. Thiz. Thiz! Fine leg.

THIZ: (*Off.*) Where's that then?

SEAN: (*Off.*) Over there, on the line. Reg, midwicket please.

REG: (*Off.*) Aye, aye cap'n.

SEAN: (*Off.*) Er… Will, the usual please. First slip. Theo, mid off.

THEO: (*Off.*) Batsmen in!

BATSMAN: (*Off.*) Save your energy. You'll be clapping me out in a minute. Ha!

CLIVE: (*Off.*) We won't clap you out.

BATSMAN: (*Off.*) Which end are you opening?

CLIVE: (*Off.*) I'm opening.

NICK: (*Off.*) No bails!

BERNARD: (*Off.*) We've got bails! You can use ours!

WILL: (*Off.*) No thank you Bernard. Theo, use our bails. There are new bails in the bag!

(*THEO enters from stage right.*)

LEN: Forgot the bails?

THEO: Yes, Len the traditional run off the pitch to find the bails.

(*THEO finds the bails and starts to run straight out on to the pitch.*)

LEN: Pavilion!

THEO: Oopsadaisy!

(*THEO turns and exits stage right, down the steps.*)

NICK: (*Off.*) Come on The Nightwatchmen!

SEAN: (*Off.*) On your toes, walking in! Thiz! Hands out your pockets! Walking in please!

OLLY: Come on Clive!

BERNARD: (*Off.*) Play!

(*CLIVE bowls. It goes wide to the keeper.*)

BERNARD: (*Off.*) Wide ball!

SEAN: (*Off.*) That's OK! Don't worry about.

WILL: (*Off.*) Line OR length please Clive, one or the other!

(*Mild laughter. Enter the THIEF from stage left. He goes over to the pile of kit and personal belongings and sits. He then systematically and quite coolly goes through the trousers, jackets and finds the odd bits of cash and coins. LEN does not see him. Having taken a fair harvest he saunters off through the copse.*)

(*End of scene.*)

Act Two

(*The same, two and a half hours later. Still very sunny. The new scoreboard has fifty-three in the runs section; nothing at all in the wickets section; the overs section says twelve. It is pointing sideways, and not out to the players. The old scoreboard which is alongside the new scoreboard and is standing up has one hundred and eighty-one in the runs section; seven in the wickets section; and there is nothing in the overs section; the Last Man section reads eighty-four. WILL is organising the tea, specifically filling a twenty cupper teapot. The Nightwatchmen are sitting around their bags eating tea from paper plates. RUBEN is somewhat off the huddle to stage right playing a computer game on a hand held; THEO is sitting in a deckchair and eating an orange; THIZ is smoking a cigar, with his shirt off, and eating cakes; NICK is rolling a roll your own ciggie and eating sandwiches; CLIVE is reading PAUL's speech, somewhat surreptitiously, ie: hiding it from the others and OLLY in particular. PAUL is eating a cake; SEAN is eating sandwiches and sitting on a cricket pad; OLLY is drinking from a large bottle of water, texting on his mobile and smoking; REG is eating a banana and standing; ALAN is sat slightly off to stage left and eating sandwiches, and applying a plaster to a cut. LEN has a plate of sandwiches on his lap, untouched. He is asleep.*)

PAUL: Extraordinary! This tastes of almonds.

THEO: It's an almond slice.

THIZ: This bloke, right, he's a northerner –

VARIOUS: Hurrah!

SEAN: Ruben! Come over here! Quick!

(*RUBEN shuffles into the group.*)

THIZ: – goes back home, see his mum. Now he's done alright for himself in London. Got himself some shoes, and trousers, you know, he's done well. And he's walking down this street in his home town, and he sees this other bloke coming towards him, and he recognises him, and he wants to avoid this bloke cos he's a loser, and he's done well, our bloke, and he's a sensitive man is our man. But he's trapped and so he says 'hello' to the loser and the loser says 'hello' back. And the loser says 'nice shoes. Nice trousers. What are you doing nowadays?' and our bloke says 'oh you know, I'm in London, doing alright, bit of this

185

SEAN: Be quite nice for you to play in an all gay team wouldn't it?

NICK: No.

THIZ: All they talk about is cock.

NICK: All you talk about is women.

THIZ: What else is there?

(*At the tea table.*)

REG: The bees joke eh?

ALAN: I don't get it. Never have. Good catch.

REG: Ta. Just slapped in there, and stuck, like a firm little tit.

ALAN: You're next door to Gary, aren't you?

REG: Yeah.

ALAN: I'm in the next street. Laburnum. Yours is the one with the double garage yeah?

REG: That's the first double garage in Whitton Dean that is.

CLIVE: Reg eh?

THIZ: He's definitely gay.

REG: (*Beat.*) Nice scoreboard, are you a chippy?

ALAN: Plumber.

REG: I need a plumber. The enemy wants a sink up in the loft for her water colours. Be easy enough. There's a drain pipe comes down from the roof.

ALAN: It's illegal to plumb a soil waste into a rain water drain.

REG: No-one'll know. I'll pay cash.

ALAN: No.

(*ALAN walks over to the scoreboard and starts dismantling it and putting it back together. REG, somewhat puzzled, rejoins the main group.*)

PAUL: I'd like to play more matches in North London, and maybe tour France again. We could stay at your house Thiz.

THIZ: I told you. Pammy got the Lot.

THEO: And I don't think she'd appreciate eleven blokes turning up on her doorstep.

THIZ: She wouldn't mind that. It's me she doesn't like. If you go, take plenty of money.

PAUL: Mick Jagger's got his own team in the Loire valley. Maybe we could play them on the way down. Do you know Mick Jagger?

THIZ: He doesn't like me, Mick. I don't like him much. His own cricket team. Who does he think he is?

CLIVE: He thinks he's Mick Jagger.

THIZ: So? Yeah? And?

REG: I saw that Jerry Hall couple of years ago in...oh bugger, what's it called –

CLIVE: B and Q.

REG: Na! The one with that little Jewish bloke with the big hooter.

THIZ: Top Tiles on Stamford Hill.

REG: No, it's a bloody play, it was a film, she fucks the little bloke.

NICK: Snow White and the Seven Dwarfs.

CLIVE: The Graduate.

REG: That's it. Took all her kit off she did. Yeah.

(*ALAN is now dismantling the old score board and taking the numbers off the new one.*)

CLIVE: Did you see Ruben's catch Paul?

PAUL: What?

(*They giggle.*)

SEAN: You dropped two catches. The two openers. Their partnership was worth one hundred and twenty-seven.

PAUL: The sun was in my eyes.

SEAN: You didn't have a cap on.

PAUL: I don't like wearing a cap. I've got a sensitive scalp.

CLIVE: It's your hair. You're vain.

PAUL: I'm not vain.

CLIVE: You dye your hair!

PAUL: Actually, I thought this was a free country.

SEAN: What is the function of a cap on a cricket pitch? The brim keeps the sun out of your eyes so you can catch the opening batsman before he gets the chance to make seventy-three runs.

CLIVE: Whereas the function of your hair, your dyed hair –

PAUL: – my hair…it's about the ego ideal, which is er…
Freudian. It's a kind of externalised objectification of my
ideal self. Freud calls it the ego ideal. Everybody's got one.

CLIVE: So your ego ideal has got dyed hair?

PAUL: Oh, piss off.

SEAN: Clive's ego ideal is called Clive. Well bowled Theo.

NICK: Web of mystery.

THIZ: Did I bowl well?

SEAN: No. Neither did Olly.

THIZ: Oh, that's alright then.

OLLY: Thanks.

THIZ: Every other team we play, the West Indian bloke's
always good. Why have we got the only shit West Indian?

NICK: Yeah. Why's that man?

CLIVE: Why are you very average Olly?

OLLY: I'm in love aren't I.

THEO: Marvellous. Marriage?

OLLY: Next month.

THEO: Excellent! The world must be peopled!

SEAN: You'll have to move out of Paul's flat.

THIZ: Paul won't know what to do without you. Live off toast.

PAUL: I won an award once for my cauliflower cheese. Burton
Latimer Boys Brigade.

THIZ: Makes me fart.

THEO: This'll be the lovely Barbara then is it?

OLLY: Yup

THIZ: (*To OLLY.*) Barbara eh?

OLLY: Yeah, Barbara.

THIZ: Is the sex good?

OLLY: Fantastic.

THIZ: Is it?

OLLY: Yeah.

THIZ: Yeah?

OLLY: Yeah.

THIZ: I love sex.

CLIVE: Excuse me boys. Theo is here. Our lay preacher. He
may object to such a crude discussion of sex.

THEO: *Au contraire.* I take the gift of sex to be a compelling argument for the existence of my God. Through sex men discover love, and through love women discover sex.

THIZ: I went out with a Brenda once. She had a terrapin in a tank. Used to watch.

(*They laugh. REG goes over to the tea table. CLIVE watches him go.*)

CLIVE: Where did we find 'Reg'?

THEO: Gary's next door neighbour.

CLIVE: I didn't know Gary lived in a neolithic cave system.

THEO: That's a terrible thing to say Clive.

CLIVE: Concur. (*Shouted to REG.*) Sorry Reg!

REG: (*Halfway to the tea table.*) What?

CLIVE: Sorry!

REG: Alright.

(*At the tea table.*)

Good bunch of blokes.

WILL: They'll be talking about you now. Now you've come over here.

REG: Yeah?

WILL: Yup!

(*The group laugh at something. One of the group turns and looks at REG. He sees this.*)

Did I hear Thiz tell the bees joke?

REG: Yeah. Very funny. Great tea! The ladies done us proud! Say thank you to your wife from me. Smashing!

WILL: Rule number two Reg.

REG: Oh yeah, feminism, you made it yourself then, kaw! Well done mate! Look, if you're ever short give me a ring. For this I wouldn't bother asking the enemy, I'd just climb out the bog window and – (*Whistles.*)

WILL: Tea's ready. Sugar's there.

(*WILL walks over to LEN with a cup of tea. During the next WILL goes over to his dad and gets him to drink some tea using a straw. During the next REG goes through the hedge and into the copse where he throws up. THEO goes into the hedge for a pee.*)

SEAN: Len's had a bit of a dip then has he?

CLIVE: Yes. Sad, lovely man. Paul do you think you'll have any progeny to look after you? A son to make sure you're taking in enough liquids on a hot day.

PAUL: Actually, I've thought about this, and I've decided that I'm gonna shoot myself when I'm seventy. Like that American bloke.

CLIVE: Hemingway?

PAUL: Yeah, him.

CLIVE: He was sixty.

PAUL: Was he? Oh dear. Still I think the moment you become a burden on the people around you, yeah, well, knowhatimean.

CLIVE: Did anyone bring a gun?

NICK: So what are we gonna do about the scoreboard then?

THIZ: What's wrong with the scoreboard?

CLIVE: It's sensationally brilliant in every aspect of design, but it fails in its one and only imperative function - you can't read the bloody numbers when you're in the bloody middle.

SEAN: White reflects the sun, blinds you.

PAUL: It just needs painting matt black.

CLIVE: (*To PAUL.*) So you're gonna tell Alan are you?

PAUL: I don't mind telling him.

(*ALAN returns to the huddle and starts fiddling with his gear. He has a cup of tea and cakes.*)

Alan?

ALAN: What?

PAUL: Nothing.

ALAN: What?

PAUL: Good catch.

NICK: Yeah, inspirational catch man.

SEAN: This new scoreboard you've built Alan.

ALAN: Yeah?

SEAN: It's terrific. But one problem. On a sunny day like this, because it's black on white, not white on black, you can't read the numbers. Did you see they swapped to using the old scoreboard half way through the innings?

NICK: I'll paint it man. Matt black. White numbers.

(*ALAN goes over to the scoreboard which he starts to dismantle. REG returns to the huddle.*)

CLIVE: (*To SEAN.*) Have you ever considered a career as a bereavement counsellor?

NICK: If there's a war man, I wanna be on Sean's side.

THIZ: I think I'd get killed in a war cos I'd do something really brave but really stupid just so people would like me a bit more.

THEO: You're terribly insecure Thiz. That's what all the joke telling's about.

THIZ: Just want to be loved.

THEO: Enoch Powell's only regret about the second world war was that he came back. That he didn't die for his country.

REG: Bloody clever man. Kaw! Enoch Powell. What a brain!

SEAN: Len came back.

REG: What the old guy?

SEAN: He was at Pegasus Bridge.

REG: Pegasus Bridge? What? No!? British Sixth Airborne?

SEAN: Dunno about that.

REG: If there's one thing I do know, it's my British military history.

(*To LEN. Standing.*) I take my hat off to you sir!

THIZ: You're not wearing a hat.

(*Enter BERNARD for more cakes.*)

BERNARD: (*To WILL.*) Whose wife do we thank for a lovely tea?

WILL: Mr. Kipling's.

(*A mobile phone goes off. Two or three of them search.*)

It's mine. Don't panic boys.

SEAN: I think we had seven LBW shouts, and three were bloody plumb.

CLIVE: Four.

(*BERNARD slopes off, unwanted.*)

SEAN: No-one bats like that. You stick your front foot across middle stump and hit across the line. Miss and you're out.

CLIVE: What are you suggesting Sean?

SEAN: I don't think their umpires ever had any intention of giving either one of those two openers out. I bet you those two are top of their averages.

CLIVE: Four matches to the end of the season.

WILL: (*On phone.*) RAF Wittering? OK…we'll be finished about eight, if it doesn't rain…rain's forecast…where's the car?… they're my knees, I'll do what I like with them…Darling, don't you dare matronise me!…Goodbye!

(*He clicks the phone off. Enter ALAN to the huddle. He is in a sulk. He gathers his kit and puts it in his bag.*)

SEAN: What you doing Alan?

(*ALAN says nothing.*)

Oh bloody hell Alan?!

(*ALAN picks his kit up and walks over to the new scoreboard picks that up too, and walks off. REG rejoins the group.*)

Alan!

(*SEAN gets up and follows ALAN. WILL joins them.*)

THEO: Sean could start an argument in a ploughed field.

WILL: Where's Alan going?

CLIVE: Sean critiqued the new scoreboard by having a quiet word in his ear.

NICK: Which is why he's gone off for hospital treatment.

REG: My kinda cricketer, Sean. Look at the Aussies. Every last one of them's an evil bastard. This country's gone soft. Do you know what I blame? Pass the parcel.

NICK: Pass the parcel?

THIZ: Yeah! I agree. Pass the parcel. It's ruined this country.

REG: The parcel nowadays, if there's twelve kids, it's got twelve prizes in it. They wait their turn, they get a prize, no effort involved. When I was a kid, there was one prize, one magic bouncy ball! We used to tear at that parcel like starving dogs! Socialism.

NICK: (*As a retort.*) Thatcherism.

CLIVE: My go. Magnetism.

(*To THIZ.*) Thiz?

THIZ: Cannibalism. I've never played pass the parcel. Is it difficult?

CLIVE: You've never played pass the parcel?

THIZ: I went to boarding school didn't I. I was too busy wanking. Quite a few of them ended up playing professional sport.

CLIVE: Professional sport is an oxymoron. Sport is an activity taken up for pleasure or exercise, preferably both. The gods understand, and on a Sunday, on their day off, they knock a ball about with their mates.

PAUL: Gladiator. What a movie. Totally compelling.

REG: British!

CLIVE: I thought it was execrable nonsense.

THIZ: You weren't in it then?

(*They laugh.*)

PAUL: Actually Clive, have you ever had a part in a film?

CLIVE: Yes. Titanic.

REG: British!

OLLY: Hollywood surely.

REG: Yeah, but it was a British ship.

CLIVE: Which sank.

REG: Yeah, obviously.

PAUL: Actually, the Titanic didn't sink, it was its sister ship that sank.

THIZ: Oh fuck, here we go.

PAUL: They'd identified several design faults in the Titanic, so before the maiden voyage they switched name plates with the Olympic, which they were building right alongside.

NICK: So man, the Titanic was really the Olympic?

PAUL: Exactly.

OLLY: What happened to the Olympic then?

PAUL: On it's maiden voyage, it hit an iceberg and sank.

NICK: OK man, so…what happened to the Titanic?

PAUL: It was in service for twenty-four years, then decommissioned and all the fittings sold off at auction.

THIZ: (*To PAUL.*) I'd do almost anything to get away from you.

(*They laugh. THEO joins WILL at the tea table.*)

THEO: (*To WILL.*) So what's Harriet doing today?

WILL: RAF Wittering. She's handcuffed herself to the fence.

THEO: They've got a lovely day for it.

WILL: Yeah, they will all be singing now.

THEO: Will she get arrested?

WILL: Let's hope eh.

(*SEAN enters with their book. He is studying it.*)

PAUL: Lockerbie's another one. The bomb on flight 702 –

CLIVE: – oh no!

PAUL: – was put on that flight by the American Drugs Enforcement Agency.

REG: I can believe that. The Yanks, eh, they don't fuck about like we do.

PAUL: The theory is contained in a book called 'The Octopus Conspiracy' written by a CIA agent.

OLLY: So who put the suitcase on the plane?

THIZ: An octopus.

(*Some laugh.*)

He had eight suitcases. Got an upgrade to business class, said he didn't have enough leg room.

(*All laugh, including THIZ.*)

PAUL: It's important to retain a grip on the empirical truth in these difficult times when we are, technically, at war against an abstract noun, 'terrorrism' and er…yeah.

CLIVE: You wouldn't recognise the empirical truth if it jumped into bed with you and fucked you up the arse.

NICK: Boys!

SEAN: What did I tell you? Pilger and Begum are neck and neck for the averages. Forty-two point three versus thirty-eight point nine. They've got three matches left. Their umpires were never going to give them out.

THIZ: Which one's Pilger?

NICK: Pilger's the one who's not Begum.

SEAN: We're being shafted here.

CLIVE: Oh darling! Please! It's a friendly.

(*WILL arrives he listens. SEAN performs to him a little. Takes a sandwich.*)

SEAN: (*Not intense.*) You've got to play the game properly. As soon as you start tolerating bollocks, that's it. You might as well pack up and go home. (*With a mouthful of egg mayo.*) That is what it is to be moral, to be human. Surely? Brilliant egg mayonnaise Will.

WILL: Thank you.

REG: You godda a house in the south of France then Thiz?

THIZ: No. I said. She got the Lot.

THEO: (*To REG.*) Thiz is divorced. As part of the settlement his wife, Pammy, was given the house in France in the 'departement' known as 'the Lot and Garonne', which Thiz abbreviates to 'the Lot', as in 'she got the lot', which suggests that Pammy fleeced him which is untrue, and ignores the fact that she gave him three beautiful children, whilst he was bedding teenage girls from Helsinki to Hartlepool.

THIZ: Where's Hartlepool?

REG: We go to France every year. Caravan. What a beautiful country. Kaw! It's wasted on those bastards!

WILL: So, what's it like living next door to Gary, Reg?

REG: Bidda of a nutter eh?!

THEO: A saint, would be my assessment, given all that he's had to cope with.

REG: Yeah, he's got his hands full with her.

THEO: I meant Jack, the autistic child.

REG: Oh yeah! That little bugger! I've had to get a new fence. The ship lap wasn't up to it. Another cup of tea I think.
(*REG goes over to the tea table. THIZ is inspecting his sandwich.*)

THIZ: Eh Will, is this butter?

WILL: No. It's 'I can't believe it's not butter'.

THIZ: Fuck me, it's marge!?

CLIVE: Now that would be a good brand name. 'Fuck me, it's marge!' Excuse me miss, do you work here, in which aisle would I find the 'Fuck me it's Marge'?'
(*Some giggle.*)

WILL: If you had ever 'made' a cricket tea Thiz, as opposed to subcontracting the task to Harrods, you'd know that butter is difficult to spread.

THIZ: It's not my fault I'm bloody loaded.
(*At the tea table. THEO is clearing away and REG comes up. He is eating a banana.*)

REG: Well bowled matey.

THEO: Thank you Reg.

REG: You know, as a doctor, well, I've got four kids, teenagers. How can you tell if they're on drugs?

THEO: Social withdrawal, confusion, memory loss, staying in bed all day.

REG: Bloody hell, the wife's on 'em an'all!

THEO: The best way is to talk to them.

(*Silence, as REG considers the horror of talking to his kids.*)

We looked at the houses in your street.

REG: It's good for the schools, you don't get any, you know… they're all down the road. It's a good Catholic school, you know what I mean. You have to get 'em all Christened like, but you know, I'm not a racialist, but at the end of the day 'is the Pope a Paki?' Knowhatimean?

THEO: Yours must be the one with the double garage?

REG: Yeah, that's the first double garage in Whitton Dean that.

THEO: The houses are a bit big for us to be honest. No kids.

REG: Think of the money you've saved. I haven't been skiing for bloody years.

THEO: I saw you vomit earlier. In the copse. I was having a pee.

REG: Food after a bit of a work out, upsets the plumbing.

THEO: But not bananas?

REG: No. I used to be fifteen stone. I play squash three times a week. Never felt better. Apart from the odd chunder.

(*REG rejoins the huddle. SEAN is writing out the batting order.*)

WILL: (*To SEAN.*) I'll bat eleven Sean. Knees.

SEAN: No. Ten.

CLIVE: You've been told.

SEAN: Alan's disappeared.

WILL: You mean – gone home?

SEAN: Yeah. Paul – pad up. Me and you can open.

THIZ: Thiz three.

SEAN: Nick, three. Pad up.

THIZ: Thiz four.

SEAN: Clive, four.

THIZ: Thiz five.

SEAN: Olly five.

THIZ: Thiz six.

SEAN: Reg!? Do you bat?

REG: Give it a go.

WILL: You'll have to.

NICK: Who do you bat like man? Geoff Boycott? Viv Richards?

THIZ: Amy Winehouse.

REG: Boycott. Slow but sure. I completed my first hundred when I was fifteen.

CLIVE: How old were you when you started it?

(*They laugh.*)

REG: Fifteen.

THIZ: Thiz seven.

SEAN: Thiz, seven.

THIZ: Yes!!!!

SEAN: Theo, eight; Rubes, nine; Will ten.

(*Those who need to pad up, pad up.*)

THEO: I'll umpire the first ten Sean.

(*THEO heads over to the tea table.*)

SEAN: Ta. Er…Thiz, can you umpire for me? Ten overs.

PAUL: I'm not batting if Thiz is umpiring.

WILL: I'll do it.

SEAN: Ta. I'm gonna have a word with Bernard.

(*SEAN exits stage right passing the tea table as he goes.*)

THEO: Sean!

SEAN: Yeah?

THEO: Relax.

SEAN: Yeah. Have you got a tea there?

(*THEO pours.*)

THEO: How's Cath?

SEAN: I can't afford to move out. But I can't afford not to.

THEO: It's that bad is it?

SEAN: I go to bed every night thinking about killing myself.

THEO: You wouldn't kill yourself.

SEAN: I'm the type apparently. Like farmers.

THEO: You work in adverstising.

SEAN: I just want my life back Theo. I spend the whole of my life doing things I don't want to do.

THEO: It's become very difficult for your generation. You marry too late.

SEAN: She hasn't spoken to me today, because I'm coming here. It is a deliberate attempt by her to destroy the only source of joy left in my life. You know, I mean, apart from the kids.

WILL: Has she told you to give up cricket?

SEAN: I can't give it up. It's who I am.

THEO: It's a long day, a cricket match. Seven, eight hours.

SEAN: I did all the shopping yesterday and took them both to the Natural History museum. I sanded down one of her fucking pine doors. Every Saturday is me working to buy a pass for myself for Sunday.

THEO: That's how marriages work.

SEAN: I rang the Samaritans one night Theo.

THEO: Did that help?

SEAN: Not a lot.

THEO: I'm sceptical about the Samaritans. If they really cared they'd ring you.

(*THEO walks off.*)

THIZ: (*To WILL.*) What's your Ellen doing now?

WILL: It's Beth you fancy.

THIZ: Who said anything about fancying anyone?

WILL: Ellen is 'reading' media studies at Loughborough. Beth is at Sheffield Hallam – Applied Modern Languages. And Daniel, not that you're interested in him, is doing an MBA in Newcastle – I think. None of them have been taught how to think, and consequently all three of them are morally illiterate. The only thing any of them will be able to do is get a job.

NICK: They're students. Sex and drugs and rock and roll.

WILL: I hope they are doing sex and drugs and rock and roll. It's the way my children seem to accept, unquestioningly, that all Israelis are Nazis; America is evil, obviously; Hamas are, without question, cuddly Teddy Bears, cruelly wronged –

CLIVE: – should I be taking notes or is there a hand out at the end?

WILL: I don't mind if they do crack, get pregnant, drop out, but to end up terminally credulous – breaks my heart.

CLIVE: I posit this, your children take these positions because of who you are, what you once were, and what you now say publicly. In 1972 you were the Johnny Depp lookalike – I've seen the pictures – 'pain in the arse' psychologist who wrote 'Motivation, Madness and the Molotov Cocktail'. Compare – your latest book – 'In Defence of England'.

WILL: OK, don't rub it in.

RUBEN: I'm not stupid.

CLIVE: No Rubes! You are Hope!

THIZ: (*To WILL.*) Have you finished?

WILL: Yes. Sorry.

THIZ: Good. I'm gonna get on with this sandwich now, alright?
(*Some giggles.*
Silence.)

NICK: Fifty today boys. Fifty.

PAUL: I don't actually see what a coach could teach me.

CLIVE: Grace.

PAUL: You what?

CLIVE: Fucking grace!
(*CLIVE gets up and goes over to the tea table. OLLY sees this and follows. WILL goes to LEN.*)

WILL: We're batting now, Dad.

LEN: William?

WILL: Yes, it's me.

LEN: I don't like Paul. He'll kill this club.

WILL: Yes, I know he will. Do you need anything?

LEN: (*Barely audible.*) Son. Can you tell your mother all about it.

WILL: She knows 'all about it'.

LEN: Who told her?

WILL: You did. Yesterday.

LEN: How did she tek it?

WILL: Very badly. She's not talking to you.

LEN: You'd better not tell her then. I'd like a ciggie. Olly's got some Marlborough Lites.
(*Over at the tea table. Somewhat surreptitious from OLLY.*)

OLLY: I'm glad you can make the wedding.

CLIVE: I wouldn't miss it for the world.

OLLY: Her parents are…they're really bloody difficult, her dad was in the Army for twenty-five years you know. I wondered, if you could do the speech, the best man speech? I was gonna ask Paul to be best man, but can you imagine what kind of a speech he would make?

CLIVE: Yes I can.

OLLY: You wouldn't have to do any planning or anything it's just the speech.

CLIVE: Olly, I would consider it an honour, but –

OLLY: – and if you could look at my speech for me, please, just have a read, tell me what you think, I'd appreciate that.

(*OLLY gives him his speech which is two pages of A4 stapled together.*)

CLIVE: It would be a pleasure. I'd love to. Does Paul know he's not going to be best man?

OLLY: I'd better tell him eh?

CLIVE: Ya. He'll presume.

OLLY: Right.

(*REG gets his blackberry out of his bag and fiddles with it.*)

THIZ: What's that?

REG: It's a blackberry. Couldn't live without it matey. Wupse! Fuck, pressed the wrong tit.

THIZ: I'm gonna get one of them. Do they do really big ones?

REG: Smaller the better innit.

THIZ: Since when?

(*WILL goes over to OLLY.*)

WILL: Len really wants a cigarette.

OLLY: That's alright.

(*OLLY stands and goes over to LEN.*)

LEN: Ta son. Light it for us will yer.

(*OLLY takes the cigarette and lights it for LEN. He gives it to him.*)

Getting married eh, Olly?

OLLY: Yeah.

LEN: You know you're making a terrible mistake don't you.

OLLY: Yeah.

LEN: We had a lad from Saint Lucia in the team…must've been the seventies. Rennie Greaves. Nice lad. Do you know him?

OLLY: (*He's answered this many times before.*) No, I don't know him Len.

(*Silence.*)

LEN: Ta.

OLLY: If you want another one. Just give me a shout. Alright?

(*OLLY returns to the huddle.*)

WILL: Thanks.

REG: Where are you from then Olly?

OLLY: Crouch End.

REG: I mean originally.

OLLY: Bury St Edmunds.

REG: Constable country.

OLLY: Yeah.

REG: Yeah, he wouldn't get his brushes out for this would he?

OLLY: I like the city. I don't like the country. If you're black, they look at you funny.

REG: What's your line of work then?

OLLY: I work for the British Council.

REG: Right. What's that kinda race relations?

OLLY: No. It's cultural imperialism. I'm taking the Tate Modern's Death and Sex Exhibition out to Uzbekistan next month.

REG: Right.

OLLY: Did you see it?

REG: Death and Sex? No, I must've missed that one.

(*Enter SEAN.*)

SEAN: Alright! Team talk! Come on!

CLIVE: We never have team talks.

SEAN: Today's different. Nick! Paul! Come on!

(*They form a half circle around SEAN.*)

I've spoken to Bernard. I told him I was unhappy with their umpiring, specifically the decisions on the LBWs. I said I thought his umpires were protecting his openers on account of the fact that they are neck and neck in the averages. Absolutely incredible…

CLIVE: – he admitted it?

SEAN: Yeah. He said he'd be happy if we play the rest of the
game without LBs.

THIZ: Great!

SEAN: No! It is not great! It's the polar opposite of great.
It's shit. The essence of any game is its rules. This is not
tiddlewinks. Our umpires, we, are gonna apply the laws
of the game to the letter. Anyone out there umpiring, if
anyone is out LBW you give them. And if you're batting
and get an edge to the keeper – you walk. We're gonna
play this game how it's supposed to be bloody played.
OK. Hundred and eighty is not an easy score in thirty-
five overs, but we've done it before. Remember Osterley
last year. The first target I want anyone to worry about is
the first hundred. If we get that in twenty-five overs we're
alright. They've tried to cheat us out of this game, they've
admitted it, so whatever happens we've won already,
morally. But that's not enough for me, and it shouldn't
be enough for you. I want to teach them a lesson, so
they'll think twice before they try this again. Go out there,
concentrate, and we'll beat these fucking cheats.

(*SEAN breaks away from the group. The others stand, somewhat
stunned.*)

OLLY: Yo!

NICK: Woo!

THIZ: Kaw! Look! I've got a hard on!

(*To black.*)

(*Interval.*)

Act Three

(*Ten minutes later. The cuckoo again. RUBEN looks after the old scoreboard. The total needed score is set at the bottom and reads 181. WILL is knelt down, near the tea things, tying his shoe laces. THEO is stage right clearing up tea things. SEAN and PAUL are getting ready to bat ie: strapping on pads etc. Birdsong and almost idyllic.*)

WILL: (*To THEO.*) I'm getting old. When I was tying my shoe laces just then, I said to myself, 'Is there anything else I can do whilst I'm down here'.

THEO: I can hear a cuckoo! Bird song in the city – beautiful! Can you hear it?

(*WILL shuts his eyes, listening. There is birdsong. The electronic beep of REG's blackberry.*)

REG: (*On the blackberry.*) Train crash in the Philippines. Two hundred dead.

(*Enter BERNARD carrying some used paper plates. He puts these down on the table.*)

BERNARD: I worked out what the problem is with your new scoreboard. All objects have an inherent spectroscopy. White, specifically gloss white, reflects the sun, creating glare.

(*BERNARD leaves.*)

THEO: Deborah has been offered a sabbatical from work. She's suggesting we live in the Perigord for six months, a kind of trial, to see if we could live there permanently, and to discover what we miss.

WILL: Six months, across the cricket season?

THEO: You guessed. How's Harriet?

WILL: We haven't had made love since 9/11.

THEO: Mmm. I heard you on The Moral Maze last week. I really think you should be careful Will.

(*THEO holds up a beautiful white stone.*)

WILL: What beautiful stones.

THEO: Yes. The Sunday of the Beamers match, I was on Eastbourne beach with Deborah. I'd wanted to play, couldn't, and so did the next best thing – scoured the beach for umpiring stones.

WILL: I've wasted the whole of my life playing this game. It's claimed my knees, and it fills every spare synapse in my brain. Not even sure I like it anymore.

(*WILL goes over to LEN.*)

SEAN: (*To PAUL.*) Are you ready?

(*PAUL is in a world of his own, and doesn't hear.*)

CLIVE: Communication. The key to an effective opening partnership.

PAUL: What?

WILL: Alright Dad? I'm umpiring, for the first ten.

LEN: (*Very weak.*) I think I'm going.

WILL: Well, no-one's stopping you.

LEN: The best moments of my life have happened on this pitch.

WILL: I won't tell my mother you said that.

(*THEO joins WILL.*)

THEO: Ready? You and Harriet must come round for dinner sometime –

(*WILL and THEO walk off to the centre. PAUL has picked up OLLY's bat.*)

NICK: Go on lads!

OLLY: (*To PAUL.*) Are you going to borrow my bat?

PAUL: Yeah. My bat's split. I told you.

(*PAUL sets off on his own to the middle.*)

SEAN: Paul! I'd like us to walk out together, like members of the same team.

(*PAUL tuts and waits.*)

Call OK. Shout loud. 'WAIT' or 'YES'. No 'NOs'. OK?

PAUL: What's wrong with 'NO'.

SEAN: It sounds like 'GO'.

PAUL: No it doesn't. Go's got a Gu in it.

SEAN: Oh piss off.

(*PAUL turns and heads off.*)

NICK: Play your natural game Sean!

WILL: (*Off.*) No bails! Bernard!? Have you got our bails?

BERNARD: (*Off.*) They should be in the umpires' coats.

WILL: (*Off.*) Yes, but whose umpire's coat?

BERNARD: (*Off.*) Whose coats are those? They look like ours.

WILL: (*Off.*) These coats are ours Bernard.
(*The huddle is now giggling somewhat.*)

CLIVE: Bernard. He's the human equivalent of spam email isn't he?

NICK: Somebody somewhere loves him I bet.

THIZ: She's over there, lime green shorts.

CLIVE: Forget nature's beauty, birdsong, flowers – the fact that even Bernard has found love is the best argument there is for the existence of God.
(*NICK laughs. THIZ sits up. Enter WILL. He goes to the kit bag.*)

WILL: They've lost our bloody new bails.

NICK: Hurry up Skip, rain's forecast.
(*WILL picks up a pair of old bails and runs back out to the middle.*)

OLLY: (*Reading from the Sundays.*) What did Reg Varney do on June twenty-seventh nineteen sixty-seven that no-one had ever done before?

THIZ: He fucked a polar bear.
(*Some laughter.*)

OLLY: He was the first man to use a hole in the wall cash machine.

REG: First ATM! Course. Obvious!

CLIVE: Reg Varney might have been the first 'celebrated individual' to use an ATM, but they would have been testing that ATM in a live situation for a whole month before they let him anywhere near it. The only certain truth here is that Reg Varney was not the first person to use an ATM.

NICK: You're questioning the nature of truth again.

CLIVE: That's why we're here isn't it?

THIZ: Is that what we're here for?

CLIVE: Why do you think you're on this earth Thiz?

THIZ: Play the bass, don't stand in front of the drummer, look gorgeous.

NICK: You're a simple man.

OLLY: A rock and roll artisan.

THIZ: Eh! That's quite good that. Ruben, giss your pencil.

(*RUBEN, who is doing the book, gives THIZ a pencil from the scorer's tin.*)

What was it again!?

OLLY: Baby, I'm a simple man –

NICK: – baby, I'm a rock and roll artisan.

REG: That's why we're here. Babies.

CLIVE: Urge, and urge, and urge! Always the procreant urge of the world!

REG: Done my bit mate. I've had four of them. Kaw! Never again.

WILL: (*Off.*) Play!

SOME OF THEM: (*Off.*) Bowling Rami!/ Good start!/ Line and length.

OLLY: Quickish.

RUBEN: Bowler's name?

NICK: (*Shouted.*) Bowler's name please!

BERNARD: (*Off.*) Parameswaram!

(*OLLY mimes not hearing and sticks his hand behind his ear.*)

P.A.R.A.M.E.S.W.A.R.A.M.

REG: That's not a name, it's a bloody anagram!

NICK: Steady Paul! Plenty of time!

OLLY: I caught Paul on the internet last week.

THIZ: Wanking?

OLLY: No. He watched the beheading of that American on Al Jazeera.

CLIVE: Oh no! That boy is sick.

OLLY: He said he wanted to feel something.

REG: Islam? It's a fucking death cult mate!

CLIVE: I know a way of getting rid of Osama Bin Laden. We'd never hear from him again.

NICK: Yeah? What?

CLIVE: Get my agent to represent him.

(*OLLY AND NICK laugh.*)

Good shot big fellah!

(*Applause.*)

REG: My daughter had a couple of Muslim friends, at primary school, and every year she invited them to her birthday party. Did they come? Never.

NICK: Two there boys! Come on!

REG: I took it up with their dads, in the playground, they both had the same excuse, grandma was ill. Huh! Do I look stupid?

CLIVE: Reg, you'd be offering ham sandwiches, vodka, competitive pass the parcel.

REG: I invited them into my house, and they wouldn't come. How do you explain that to a five year old?

(*Silence.*)

NICK: How's the song going man?

THIZ: I'm stuck.

OLLY: Oi! Paul! You watch the edge of that bat!

(*Some giggle.*)

NICK: Four off the over Rubes.

OLLY: Good start.

BERNARD: (*Off.*) Bowler's name is Begum! Like Begun but with an M! M for mother.

OLLY: We can spell Begum Bernard.

NICK: Olly, how about getting married in September or October. You know, outside of the cricket season. We're gonna miss a game.

OLLY: She wants an August wedding, in Cornwall, by the sea. Don't ask me why.

CLIVE: Thiz! Have you got any advice to Olly about marriage.

THIZ: If you tour Denmark, don't take her with you.

OLLY: Have you got a girlfriend Thiz?

THIZ: Yeah. Sasha.

CLIVE: And what does she do?

THIZ: Anything. You've only got to ask nicely.

SEAN: (*To CLIVE.*) Why don't you and Sian get married?

CLIVE: If it ain't bust don't fix it.

SEAN: Yeah. Must be ten years.

CLIVE: Thirteen.

OLLY: And you love each other?

CLIVE: What the fuck is this? A soap opera? I refuse to talk to you lot about my emotional life.

NICK: Beamer!

(*Sound of ball on skull. NICK and OLLY jump to their feet.*)

OLLY: Top edge! He's got it in the eye. Shit!

CLIVE: Where's the first aid box!?

NICK: Oh God!

OLLY: We don't have one.

WILL: (*Off.*) There's a first aid kit in my campervan!

CLIVE: Water.

NICK: Has anyone got water?

WILL: (*To RUBEN.*) Ruben! The keys to the van are in the
valuables bag!

(*NICK picks up the valuables bag. He picks out the keys and
exits to the van. CLIVE exits to inspect SEAN. Sound of camper
van door opening.*)

THIZ: What rhymes with artisan?

OLLY: Parmesan.

RUBEN: Anything with 'man' at the end.

THIZ: Fireman. Elephantman. Bedpan. Bedpanman. Not much
of a song is it?

(*Enter from stage left THEO, CLIVE, and SEAN. CLIVE holding
SEAN's bat and gloves. His whites are blood stained from a
bad cut under his eye. NICK has the first aid box. BERNARD
accompanies.*)

SEAN: I'm alright. It's alright.

OLLY: That was a beamer.

NICK: Was it deliberate?

THEO: Nick, please! I can't imagine that he meant it. Now,
Sean, listen to me, I want you to close your eye, I'm just
going to have a look.

(*THEO inspects the cut. WILL goes to the van and returns with
a green first aid box.*)

NICK: Three stitches there man.

BERNARD: Sutures. Now, I recommend that we wash the
conjunctiva with clean water.

THEO: Bernard! I'm a doctor, the very worst thing one can
do when there is bleeding from a cut on the supra orbital
bridge is to wash the conjunctiva.

BERNARD: Well, that's what I'd do.

(*BERNARD leaves.*)

THIZ: Why is there never a sniper when you really need one?

THEO: You'll have to go to A and E.

SEAN: No, I'm not going. Just patch it up Theo.

THEO: No! You're going to need stitches.

THIZ: Sutures.

SEAN: I'm not going! Alright. Just patch me up. Nick, stick a laggy plast on here will you.

NICK: With that, you godda go hospital man.

SEAN: I can still see.

THEO: Sean, I'm a doctor and I'm telling you to go to –

SEAN: – I'm not going Theo! I've just got me eye in out there. (*THEO storms off in a huff.*) Nick, patch me up. Hurry up! (*NICK and CLIVE patch up the cut.*)

THIZ: We had a teacher at my school just like Bernard. They said he was a paedophile.

OLLY: Did he abuse you?

THIZ: Never touched me. But, what he did do, he used to pay me ten bob to wank him off. (*They laugh.*)

SEAN: Will you shut up Thiz, you're making me laugh.

OLLY: That's child abuse! Him – getting you – to wank him off – that is him abusing you. (*REG is miming that OLLY and THIZ should care about RUBEN listening.*)

THIZ: He never touched me! And, it was my idea in the first place. I needed the money. I said to him, if you give me ten bob, I'll wank you off. They say all the best ideas are simple, don't they.

CLIVE: There you go big fellah!

NICK: Come on Sean man! Give 'em hell! (*SEAN heads back out. He heads straight out.*) Steps!

OLLY: Pavilion! (*SEAN changes direction without comment and exits stage right, and down the steps.*)

THIZ: (*Writing.*) Lollipopman.

NICK: What would you have done if you hadn't become a rock and roll legend?

THIZ: Dunno. Job where you don't have to do much; girls; drugs; loads of money; no lifting. I wouldn't mind being information officer at Stonehenge, cos they don't know anything about it, so if anyone asks anything you just say 'dunno'.

NICK: Excuse me sir, who built this stone circle?

THIZ: Dunno.

OLLY: When was it built?

THIZ: Dunno.

CLIVE: *S'il vous plait, Monsieur, est-ce que ce monument megalithique circulaire represente un temple au soleil?*

THIZ: (*Beat.*) Dunno. Get off the fucking grass! Next!
    (*THIZ/NICK/OLLY/CLIVE Laugh.*)

OLLY: Oh Paul! You dickhead!
    (*Owzats etc. Cheers off.*)

CLIVE: That was possibly the ugliest shot I have ever seen.

OLLY: Come on Nick! Fifty today!

CLIVE: Coaching!
    (*PAUL walks off the pitch, and NICK walks on. They cross. RUBEN is writing in the book and then puts up forty-two for two on the scoreboard.*)

PAUL: I think there's something wrong with the pick up on your bat Olly.

CLIVE: Oh dear Olly, Paul was out because there's something wrong with the pick up on your bat.

PAUL: Gimme a cigarette.
    (*OLLY chucks his cigarettes over. PAUL lights one.*)

OLLY: What's the pick up like on that ciggie?

PAUL: Alright. I find the first three minutes after you're out, really existentially threatening. It's a Joy Division, Ian Curtis interlude. When I got that duck against East Sheen, I came within a whisker of self harming.

OLLY: Bowled him!
    (*Laughter off.*)

CLIVE: Oh no! Who?
    (*Cheering off. Mixed with impolite laughter.*)

OLLY: Sean.

RUBEN: Bowled Begum.

REG: They're a mouthy bunch aren't they.

OLLY: They're laughing at us. They think we're useless.

CLIVE: It's a situation peculiar to this level of cricket. An ordinary team get a big score and then, fielding second, pick up two quick wickets. They are then inexorably sucked into the delusion that they might be, after all, gods. What is required now is a hero – late thirties, handsome, and ostentatiously well educated. Said hero goes out there tonks two fours in quick succession and it all goes fucking quiet!

OLLY: – yo!

CLIVE: It's not the two fours that shut them up, it's the collective smack of epiphany. The realisation that they're not gods after all, but overweight, middle-aged men stuck in loveless marriages. Goodbye gentlemen! I may be some time!

(*CLIVE strides out to the middle with utter confidence.*)

REG: Go on Clive matey!

THIZ: I love him.

OLLY: Brilliant man!

RUBEN: Good luck Clive.

REG: I wish I'd learnt to talk. At my school they just wanted you to shut up.

(*Enter SEAN. RUBEN changes the scoreboard to read two wicket down for eleven runs.*)

OLLY: Bad luck Sean.

SEAN: Sorry boys.

THIZ: Shoulda swiped it out the ground mate. That's what I'm gonna do. With my new bat. Two hundred and forty quid. Oh yes.

OLLY: Shot Nick!

RUBEN: I love that shot of Nick's.

OLLY: I did a cover drive for four last year.

RUBEN: I remember. Wandsworth Cowboys.

SEAN: How many did you get that day?

OLLY: Four.

(*They laugh.*)

OLLY: Christmas Eve. First time I'd met her parents, and she hadn't told them.

THIZ: What?! She hadn't told them you can't bat!

SEAN: (*Laughs.*) Mad Christmas present. A black son-in-law. Sorry.

OLLY: I couldn't sleep. I was staring at the ceiling getting really angry. But I forced myself to think about that shot against Cowboys, next thing I knew it was Christmas morning.

SEAN: Shot Clive!

OLLY: There's one of them.

(*SEAN paces, and looks over RUBEN's shoulder at the book.*)

SEAN: Twenty-three for two off five.

(*RUBEN changes the scoreboard. SEAN goes over to the tea things and mixes himself an orange squash.*)

PAUL: If we lose this game, which looks likely, I'd blame Sean's field placing.

OLLY: Nick's not here. Why don't you slag him off while you can?

SEAN: Shot!

OLLY: Shot Clive!

(*THIZ stands, a rare event in itself, and shouts out to the pitch.*)

THIZ: Oi Bernard! Go and look for the ball! Ha, ha, ha!

REG: Get a ton off the first twennie, then go nuts with the bat.

OLLY: Piece of piss.

SEAN: 'cept we're playing with ten men, and we've already lost two wickets.

OLLY: We're gonna need Alan?

(*RUBEN adjusts the scoreboard. SEAN finds his phone in the valuables bag, dials a number and goes walkabout.*)

Can you throw a couple of balls at me Ruben.

RUBEN: I'm doing the book.

OLLY: Paul. Do the book can you? I want to try and get my eye in.

RUBEN: This is Paramaswaram.

(*PAUL takes the book. SEAN is on the phone to ALAN. OLLY and RUBEN go upstage and RUBEN bowls at OLLY and OLLY pats it*) *back and in between patting it back mimes some extraordinary shots which Brian Lara might find a tad extravagant.)*

REG: Nice bunch of lads.

PAUL: Most of them are resistant to change.

REG: Yeah?

PAUL: I'd like to play more games in North London. But they've always played here.

REG: It's a bit skuzzy here innit.

PAUL: Here is the official epicentre of skuzz.

SEAN: Shot Clive! Run 'em up. Three there! One for the throw, come on!

PAUL: I'm gonna go for the captaincy at the AGM. That's a no ball. You see, no signal. I can't put it in the book. Over shoulder height. If we lose by one run. You see no-one in this club knows how to umpire – properly. I'm taking a course at the moment.

REG: I hate umpiring.

PAUL: That's because you don't know the rules.

REG: It's not that, I know the rules.

PAUL: If you're playing a shot and the ball hits your pad outside the line of off stump, and the ball looks like it would hit middle stump. Is that out?

REG: Isn't it?

PAUL: No.

REG: Why not?

PAUL: The rules innit. (*Beat.*) Pitches outside leg?

REG: Not out. I know that.

SEAN: (*On the phone.*) – it reflects the sun... Look, I want you back here to bat, to win this match for me...yeah.
(*To WILL/THEO indicating umpires change.*) Will! Theo! Umpires! Paul, can you umpire for me please. Ten overs Reg? How do you feel about umpiring?

REG: I'm a bit rusty on the rules skip.

SEAN: Alright, I'll go. Shot Nick!

OLLY: What's he on now?

PAUL: Twennie odd.

(*PAUL pulls himself to his feet. WILL and THEO enter from the centre. They are both holding umpires coats. They help SEAN and*

215

WILL: (*To THEO.*) I think Reg wants to talk to you. Go on!
You're a doctor and a Christian. Get over there and do
your stuff.

(*THEO goes over to the tea table.*)

THEO: Alright Reg! Drinks at twenty overs. Might as well get
them ready now.

(*THEO starts to organise the drinks for the interval.*)

REG: Think I might have a bidda sunstroke.

THEO: If you live in Whitton Dean why aren't you with me?

REG: I haven't been to the doctor for twennie years.

THEO: How old are you?

REG: Fifty er, bloody hell, er fifty-nine.

THEO: A fifty-nine year-old man does not lose two stone in
eight months by eating bananas. I would recommend that
you have some tests, so tomorrow, register with a GP. But
for now, get your pads on – you're in next.

OLLY: (*Off.*) Yes!

NICK: (*Off.*) No! Go back!

RUBEN: This is a run out!

THIZ: It's comedy cricket.

VOICES: (*Off.*) Owzat! / How is that!

CLIVE: He's given it.

WILL: You're in Reg.

REG: Sorry boys! I'm not padded up. Can –

WILL: – Thiz! Get out there.

THIZ: Eh?

WILL: Reg isn't ready yet. You're in now.

THIZ: But I'm not dressed.

(*THIZ puts his helmet.*)

WILL: Just get out there you big wuss!

(*THIZ wanders towards the wicket without a bat, then turns
and comes back.*)

THIZ: Forgot my bat. Haven't got my box on. Does anyone
want a list of the ways in which I'm not prepared? Put that
song in my bag, and don't read it. Giss it here. I don't trust
you lot!

(*CLIVE gives him the song, and he puts it in his pocket. He roots
around in his bag for his box. OLLY enters from the field. He*

*throws his bat down, goes for a therapeutic wander around the
grass upstage.)*

WILL: Come on Thiz! Bernard'll time you out, you know
he will.

*(THIZ picks up his bat, finds his box and then puts his
helmet on.)*

THIZ: I'm scared.

(THIZ walks out to the wicket, putting his box in as he goes.)

WILL: Ruben. Get your grandad to drink some water. He's sick
of me.

*(RUBEN gives his dad the book, goes to the tea table to get some
water and goes to LEN.)*

RUBEN: Some water here grandad.

LEN: Get a job.

RUBEN: What?

(He grabs RUBEN's wrist. RUBEN is alerted, focussed.)

LEN: A job you like. And a hobby. And a wife. You can't live
your life without giving yourself to a woman. You got that?

RUBEN: Job, hobby, wife.

LEN: Aye. Now. I want to tell you, Pegasus Bridge. I was a
coward.

RUBEN: But you went. *(Beat.)* You were there.

LEN: I was no fucking use to anyone. That's all, go on. Get
back to the lads.

RUBEN: You've got hold of my arm.

LEN: Aye.

(LEN lets go of his arm. RUBEN goes back to the group.)

WILL: I've heard you're very good in this new thing at the
Gate.

THEO: Is it in French? Just that I'm working on my French.

CLIVE: It's a translation.

WILL: You've got ten years before you retire to France.

THEO: Yes, but when we do go to live there, permanently,
we're determined not to do that ex-pat thing of whist
drives, and –

WILL: – Cricket?

THEO: There are cricket teams in the Perigord but I'm
determined not to play.

CLIVE: You should play it on their village greens! Under their noses!

WILL: Every immigrant community that comes into this country – we bend over backwards to encourage them to keep their lousy cultures ticking over –

THEO: – lousy cultures? Will!

WILL: Not just ticking over, flourishing, expanding and yet you, with the most beautiful gift on earth –

CLIVE: – cricket.

WILL: – daren't play it in France for fear of offending the locals.

THEO: I didn't say 'daren't'.

WILL: Self-hatred is the cancer at the heart of our nation. If we're not gnawing away at our own back legs in an orgy of self-repudiation, we're not happy.

THEO: Yes, but we want to fit in. To be at least Frenchish. (*Blackberry beeps.*)

REG: (*On his blackberry.*) Oh bloody hell! One of them London bombers has left hundred and fifty-seven thousand pounds in his will.

WILL: I hope they confiscate that money and build a bloody synagogue.

THEO: Will!?

WILL: They nearly killed me that day. They're racists, they're fascists, and they're bastards.

THEO: Oh come on! If we hadn't got ourselves involved in an illegal war in Iraq –

WILL: – I've got a plan which would make this country completely safe from sexually frustrated Yorkshiremen of a Wahabi Sunni persuasion.

THEO: Oh good heavens!

WILL: It's based on your theory, that we should try not to upset them. So I propose that – one – we should execute all our gay men –

THEO: – oh Will!

WILL: – two – no women can go shopping unless they're wearing a tent.

THEO: – this is silly! –

WILL: – three – kill all infidels, that's basically everybody.

THEO: – Will, Will, Will!

(*Some laughter.*)

What's happened to tolerance?

WILL: You're the one leaving the country.

THEO: I'm upset. I'm very very upset.

WILL: Do you know what upsets me? They look at you, you Theo, possibly the kindest, most soulful individual I have ever met in my entire life and their book tells them that you're nothing, you're going to hell, you're a kaffur.

(*THEO stands and walks off stage left.*)

RUBEN: You don't win those arguments with mom.

WILL: Shutup.

(*Laughter. LEN dies. Nothing noticeable, but this is the moment he stops breathing. Big appeal of Owzat! from off.*)

OLLY: Oh no!

CLIVE: Sean's given it.

WILL: Who's out?

CLIVE: Nick.

WILL: Shit. What was he on?

RUBEN: Forty-eight.

CLIVE: Nick's not happy.

WILL: You're in Reg.

REG: Any instructions?

CLIVE: Yes! Could you score a quick, stylish century please!

REG: Do me best.

(*REG exits stage left and on to the field via the steps. NICK comes back off the pitch to a big round of applause and 'well batted' from the opposition.*)

WILL: Well batted Niranjan!

CLIVE: Bad luck Nick! Brilliant.

OLLY: Great stuff Nick.

NICK: That wasn't out man. It pitched outside off, I was playing a shot, not out. That was Sean doing his bloody moral…whatever…thing.

CLIVE: Sorry, explain.

NICK: What Sean said about LBWs at tea man. He's given me out man, cos he has to give someone out LBW, to show that he's a man of his word.

(*Beat.*) How many did I get?

RUBEN: Forty-eight.

NICK: Shit! Forty-eight?

CLIVE: Pad up Rubes!

RUBEN: I'm not next. It's Theo.

CLIVE: Exactly. Give me the book.

(*RUBEN hands the book over to CLIVE and RUBEN, during the next, gets padded up.*)

WILL: Get Sean back here. We're losing more wickets on the boundary than we are out there on the pitch.

CLIVE: (*Standing and walking forward.*) Sean! Sean!

WILL: Who's going out?

OLLY: I'll go.

WILL: Bloody hell! Heads!

CLIVE: Watch out!

WILL: Reg! Shot Reg!

(*RUBEN retrieves the ball from the copse. Enter SEAN.*)

SEAN: What's occurring?

WILL: Theo's gone off in a huff.

SEAN: Eh?

CLIVE: Will suggested that this country's pusillanimous liberal left political elite have established the orthodoxy of multiculturalism to such an extent that the nation is sleep walking towards the establishment of a European Islamic caliphate.

SEAN: Who's in next?

WILL: Theo!

CLIVE: Ruben's padded up.

SEAN: So we're down to nine men. Brilliant.

(*Enter ALAN. He is acknowledged by SEAN. No-one else says anything.*)

WILL: Heads!

SEAN: Shot Reg!

(*NICK retrieves the ball and throws it back. RUBEN indicates six runs.*)

CLIVE: Hundred up.

(*All on the boundary clap.*)

NICK: Well done lads!

SEAN: Keep it up Thiz!

WILL: Thiz is playing well.

(*Laughter off.*)

What's he done?

CLIVE: He's coming off. He's not out, what is it?

(*Enter THIZ with broken bat, in two parts.*)

THIZ: Two hundred and forty quid. I'll get a Toyota next time.

WILL: You hadn't knocked it in. I told you!

SEAN: You're doing well Thiz, keep your head down, listen to Reg.

THIZ: I'm not listening to him. He's a nutter.

SEAN: Running, I'm talking about.

(*THIZ walks out.*)

(*To ALAN.*) Come over here.

(*SEAN drags ALAN over to the tea table.*)

Are you gonna bat for me?

ALAN: I only came back for my watch.

SEAN: No! You're batting. The only way I'll exclude you from batting today is if you supply me with a death certificate.

ALAN: I don't know why you get so excited, it's a Sunday game, a friendly.

SEAN: Saturday, Sunday, Monday! What are you telling me? That's there's a time when you don't have to do the right thing?

ALAN: Who? Me?

SEAN: You don't need to prove your worth to us by building score boards. Thiz is not a great cricketer, and he's not in the team cos he's famous or cos he tells jokes, he's in the team cos he rings up and says he's available. You're in the team, you're wanted. It might not be love mate, but it's as near as we're gonna get alright?! So, are you gonna bat for me or not?

ALAN: I'm not batting at eleven.

SEAN: I'll sort that. I'm gonna go get a cigarette.

ALAN: Here.

(*ALAN produces a packet of twenty. SEAN takes one.*)

Don't tell anyone.

(*ALAN lights SEAN's cigarette for him.*)

How old are your kids now?

SEAN: Three and five.

ALAN: And you're still together?

SEAN: Just.

ALAN: Difficult yeah?

SEAN: My life's fucked mate.

ALAN: At the end of the day, when all's said and done, if you've godda go you've godda go. I've been divorced twice.

SEAN: I didn't know you'd been married twice.

ALAN: Been married three times. I've got five kids. My eldest, he's sixteen.

SEAN: Does he play?

ALAN: I don't know.

SEAN: We need a bit of new blood.

ALAN: I'll ask.

SEAN: Go and get your pads on.

(*ALAN goes over to the group. SEAN follows a couple of moments later.*)

NICK: Shot Thiz! (*Beat.*) So where did that ball pitch Sean?

SEAN: What ball?

NICK: You know man, you know what you did.

SEAN: What are you on about?

NICK: I wasn't out.

WILL: Come on lads! Forget it.

NICK: Sean said at tea, didn't you man, you said they offered no LBWs for our innings and yeah, –

SEAN: – the rules –

NICK: – listen to me yeah – you made this big deal out of playing the rules properly, well what I'm saying is that you gave me out cos –

SEAN: – you were out.

NICK: It pitched outside the line, I was playing a shot!

SEAN: It doesn't matter where it pitches on the off side, it's where your leg is that matters…

NICK: Alright, well, my leg was outside the line –

SEAN: – make your mind up. Was the ball outside the line or your leg?

NICK: My leg!? And that's not out unless the umpire's actually itching –

SEAN: – itching?

NICK: – yeah itching to give someone out LBW – because of –

SEAN: – because he wants his team to lose?

NICK: – cos of what he said.

SEAN: You were plumb Nick.

WILL: Come on lads. We're a team.

NICK: I was on forty-eight.

SEAN: You were on forty-eight when you got hit on the pads in front of the wicket.

NICK: I know you Sean. There are two things, yeah, you enjoy most in this beautiful brilliant game. One is scoring a century and winning the match, and the other is walking, when you've nicked one to the keeper, and only you and the keeper know, you walk, yeah, you get a lot of pleasure from that, yeah. You love walking. You love showing everyone that you play the game properly, fairly, it's like sex for you.

SEAN: Ooooh!

WILL: Eh, come on boys. Forget it.

SEAN: I walk, yes. And I hope that if you're on forty-nine and you nick it to the keeper and no-one hears it, I hope that you walk. Cos I for one don't want to know you if you don't walk.

NICK: (*Quietly.*) I wasn't out was I?

(*Beat.*) You gave me out to prove a point about playing the game fairly when in fact, all you're doing man, is putting yourself at the middle of everything.

(*Beat.*) It's just selfish actually.

(*Beat.*) Was I out?

(*Beat.*) Answer me. You know I wasn't out.

(*Beat.*) I want an answer, man. I know I'm right. Was I out?

(*SEAN starts sobbing. No-one moves. No-one says anything.*)

CLIVE: Come on, come on, big fellah. It's alright Sean. You're alright.

SEAN: I can't stand it…I can't stand it….

(*WILL stands. RUBEN is amazed and stares at SEAN.*)

WILL: Ruben, come on, I'll throw a few balls at you. Nick can you do the book.

NICK: Yeah, man, giss it here.

(*WILL and RUBEN go upstage to practice, handing the book over to NICK.*)

(*Struggling with the book.*) Who's this bowling Rubes?

RUBES: Thomas. Pilger is the spin bowler from the other end.

NICK: Got it. Ta, man.

CLIVE: Have we got some water?

NICK: Here.

(*NICK goes in his own bag and brings out a bottle of water and hands it over.*)

SEAN: Sorry.

NICK: I'm sorry, actually. Yeah?

SEAN: Alright.

NICK: Cool.

(*SEAN swigs the water – still sobbing.*)

BERNARD: (*Off.*) Can you keep the overs up to date please!?

CLIVE: What's the score?

NICK: Hundred and twennie one. Eleven overs left.

BERNARD: (*Off.*) Telegraph!

CLIVE: (*In clear, loud actor's voice.*) The score is One hundred and twenty-one for five off twenty-four overs! And you're holding up play Bernard. They're waiting for you.

NICK: Reg is batting like a train man!

(*Howzat! Off.*)

What's Thiz doing?

CLIVE: Hit wicket.

NICK: Rubes! You're in.

(*WILL and RUBEN come down and rejoin the huddle. RUBEN walks out, with a quick look to LEN – who of course is dead.*)

CLIVE: Concentrate Ruben! Backing up! Think! Cricket brain!

(*THIZ walks off, not too bothered.*)

NICK: Batted Thiz. Good stuff man.

THIZ: Hit me own wicket. That bat's a bit longer than I
    thought.

WILL: Sean, do you want me to pad up or are you going to let
    Alan go number nine?

SEAN: Er…yeah. Alan nine, Will, ten. Yeah. Sorry.

WILL: No, it's alright. The knees.

    (*THIZ sits back in WILL's chair.*)

NICK: Full toss. They're bowling bloody beamers at a
    twelve-year-old.

WILL: Thirteen.

CLIVE: He's got a helmet on.

    (*ALAN scratches a bit of bare leg.*)

ALAN: I got really badly bitten last week.

THIZ: What was her name?

ALAN: Midges.

THIZ: Never heard of her.

NICK: Another beamer!

CLIVE: (*Stands.*) Excuse me! We've paid for this pitch, do you
    mind using it!

    (*They laugh.*)

NICK: Reg is on forty already.

THIZ: I don't like him.

WILL: I don't like him.

NICK: Alan?

ALAN: What?

NICK: Do you like Reg?

ALAN: No.

CLIVE: He's brilliant. I love him!

NICK: That's cos you're an actor, man, you can see it's a part
    you could play.

CLIVE: Most actors would play Reg ironically, and that
    would be a disgrace. I'd do it with beauty, commitment,
    emphasise the heroic. I would deliver a celebration of
    England.

SEAN: Lovely shot Ruben!

THIZ: Bloody hell, Sean! Are you here?

SEAN: Yeah.

THIZ: Bit quiet. You're usually biting someone's head off. What's going on?

NICK: Five off the over. Going well?

(*WILL goes over to LEN with a glass of water. He is intending to tell LEN that RUBEN's batting and give him some water. WILL realises LEN is dead.*)

WILL: Dad? Jesus. Oh hell, what do I do? Dad!

VARIOUS: Shot Reg! / Heads / Six!

(*The ball goes flying over the copse into the field beyond. Several of the group on the boundary go after the ball disappearing through the hedge WILL checks LEN's breath and pulse and accepts that he's dead.*)

SEAN: (*Off.*) Lost ball! Bring a bat someone please!

(*BERNARD is heard coming off the field via the steps. He appears holding a bat. This he gives to those looking for the ball. He then turns and approaches WILL having looked at the scoreboard.*)

BERNARD: Will! I think the overs must be wrong. It's twenty-five gone by my calculations. The first over was bowled from the far end, so any over bowled from that end has to be an odd number, but you've got twenty-four on the board. Twenty-four is an even number.

WILL: Fuck off Bernard!

(*BERNARD stands still but assesses the situation correctly (ish.) and moves off into the copse to help look for the ball.*)

SEAN: (*Off.*) Found it!

(*NICK gives the ball to BERNARD. WILL adjusts LEN's hat and rejoins the others.*)

NICK: Fifty up Reg!

(*Applause.*)

VARIOUS: Keep going Reg! / Come on boys! Another fifty Reg!

WILL: Does anyone have a cigarette?

NICK: Olly.

CLIVE: No they're all gone.

(*SEAN looks to ALAN. ALAN offers a cigarette to WILL.*)

NICK: Alan!?

SEAN: Bowled him!

NICK: (*Quietly ie: not to RUBEN.*) Oh bad luck Rubes.

CLIVE: Run those singles Alan!

(*ALAN walks out. RUBEN comes in to a round of applause from all. He chucks his bat aggressively down, partly from natural frustration but it is also, clearly, learned behaviour.*)

You'd better get padded up Will.

NICK: Two more runs man. The champagne is on ice.

WILL: There is champagne actually, in the van. In the fridge. If required.

RUBEN: You're smoking.

WILL: No, I'm looking after this for Thiz.

(*He hands it to THIZ, who takes it.*)

THIZ: Have you ever tried ciggies Ruben?

RUBEN: Yeah.

THIZ: Waste of money, make you stink, gives you cancer. Don't start, don't be a fool. If you need a high, bit of a rush, you can't beat heroin.

NICK: Lovely shot Reg!

THIZ: It gets a bad press, I know that, but –

WILL: – Thiz!

CLIVE: Good lord! Reg certainly hits that ball hard.

SEAN: Ten off the over! We could win this you know.

NICK: Three overs left, twenty-two required. Bowler's name please!?

BERNARD: (*Off.*) Mohammad!

WILL: (*Quietly.*) Like the prophet.

BERNARD: (*Off.*) Like the Prophet! M. O. –

NICK: We can spell Mohammad!

THIZ: If you can't spell it just draw a picture.

(*They laugh.*)

NICK: Can we just have a day off Islam please!? I'm fucking sick of it man, alright?

CLIVE: There's a single there.

SEAN: Two there! Run 'em up Alan!

WILL: Alan doesn't know what he's doing but he's quick between the wickets.

NICK: Come on Reggie!

CLIVE: Oh. 'Reggie' now is it?

NICK: Yeah, it's Reggie.

THIZ: Big one!

WILL: Heads!

(*A ball comes sailing over them into the copse. RUBEN goes for the ball and throws it back.*)

NICK: End of the over. One hundred and seventy for eight. Two overs left.

THIZ: (*Standing.*) Come on boys!

(*SEAN goes over to the scoreboard and puts the runs up. One hundred and seventy for eight.*)

RUBEN: Is grandad alright?

WILL: Yeah.

(*RUBEN stands as if to go over to LEN. WILL grabs his arm.*)
He's alright.

(*RUBEN sits. Enter THEO.*)

SEAN: You're back.

THEO: How are we doing?

SEAN: Put your pads on. Will's in next, but you know, with his knees.

CLIVE: Bowled him!

SEAN: Who's out?

WILL: Alan.

SEAN: Good! As long as Reg is out there we're alright.

WILL: Sean! Do you want me to go out now, or are we going to wait for Theo?

SEAN: Yeah, yeah, go out now Will. Good luck.

(*WILL walks out to the wicket passing ALAN as he comes in to applause.*)
Thank you Alan.

WILL: Played Alan.

NICK: Good work man.

ALAN: Inside edge. I should've left it alone.

CLIVE: Bowled by one you should've left alone. The ultimate tragedy.

(*SEAN changes the wickets on the scoreboard to eight. RUBEN goes over to LEN.*)

RUBEN: Grandad? Grandad?

NICK: Shot Will!

CLIVE: Three there. Not.

NICK: Go on Will!

(*They laugh.* CLIVE *takes rests some paper on his Homer and writes something down.*)

SEAN: Oh God it's embarrassing.

CLIVE: He should have a runner.

SEAN: That's two runs gone begging there. That's pride. If we lose this game –

CLIVE: – Calm down Sean. He's done the important thing. He's got Reg on strike.

SEAN: What was that, you wrote down?

CLIVE: I took a note of something Reg said earlier. I am now a writer.

SEAN: Why haven't you ever written anything?

CLIVE: Because Reg came into my life for the first time today.

RUBEN: Grandad?

(RUBEN *walks back to the group. He realises that* LEN's *dead.*)

SEAN: We're an ageing team.

CLIVE: What we need is a six foot seven inch sixteen-year-old fast bowler, with four foot long arms, no brains –

SEAN: – big fast bowler's arse.

THIZ: Big tits.

SEAN: Alan has a teenage son.

ALAN: I'll ask.

NICK: Shot Reggie!

SEAN: (*With arms in the air like a fan.*) Six!

NICK: End of the over. One seven seven. For nine. One over left. And Will is on Nine thousand nine hundred and ninety-nine runs for the club.

CLIVE: Thank you Bearders.

NICK: He needed eleven at the beginning of the season. Fifteen matches later he needs one. It's a mini series.

SEAN: Is that more runs than Len?

RUBEN: Grandad is twelve thousand two hundred and eleven runs.

(*They all look across to* LEN.)

CLIVE: Round of applause gentlemen.

(*They clap.*)

NICK: Well done Len!

THEO: Is he alright?

RUBEN: He's sleeping.

NICK: Come on Will! One run!

RUBEN: I'll get the champagne.

(*RUBEN goes to the van.*)

FARRINGDEN: (*Off.*) How is that! Owzat!

CLIVE: That's not a stumping. His bat's down.

SEAN: Stop begging!

CLIVE: I know Paul, he'll give that, because he wasn't looking.

FARRINGDEN: (*Off.*) Yeah! / Yes! / Woo! / Woo!

SEAN: How can he give that, he didn't see it?

(*RUBEN arrives with champagne.*)

CLIVE: Back in the fridge Ruben.

(*They laugh.*)

SEAN: Theo. Try and get a single. Get Reggie down that end.

THEO: Yes. Of course. Reggie.

(*THEO strides out. WILL hobbles back in.*)

NICK: Bad luck Will!

WILL: Three more games this season.

(*SEAN changes the scoreboard. Stays beside it now, putting up the score one by one.*)

SEAN: Five balls left. Five to win.

(*They're all on their feet and even edge forwards on to the pitch.*)

NICK: Shot Theo.

THIZ: Two there!

SEAN: No! We want Reg on strike. Stay for one. Oh no! You idiot!

CLIVE: Sean, that's Theo. That's not an idiot.

(*SEAN puts two more runs up. The board reads one hundred and seventy-nine.*)

ALAN: What do we need?

CLIVE: Three to win.

SEAN: Four balls left.

VARIOUS: Oooh! OH!

SEAN: Bloody hell, come on. Just get a Nick on it.

NICK: Three balls to go.

CLIVE: Come on Theo love.

VARIOUS: Oh! / Fuck. / Groans.

SEAN: We need the ball to hit him and run off for leg byes.

NICK: Two balls to go. Runs required. Three.

SEAN: Get some wood on it!

NICK: Shot Theo!

CLIVE: Four!

VARIOUS: (*Within laughter.*) Yes! / Yo! / Yeah!

> (*They hug, and jump, and cheer, shake hands etc. It clouds over.*)

CLIVE: What a beautiful shot.

SEAN: Fantastic! Yes!

CLIVE: Well done Sean.

SEAN: Well done guys. Brilliant. Thank you!

VARIOUS: Well done Sean/brilliant Seanie/well skippered/ cheers big fellah.

> (*REG and THEO walk off the field together to applause.*)

SEAN: Thank you guys. Well batted Reg.

NICK: Brilliant shot man!

SEAN: Guys! Please, clap the fielding team, shake hands.

> (*BERNARD approaches shaking hands with everyone.*)

Bad luck skip.

> (*The others of Farringden walk off the field and shake hands with everyone, with lots of 'thank yous', 'well bowleds', 'well batteds' etc as appropriate.*)

WILL: Alan, Ruben, can you get the boundary markers please. Thank you.

> (*WILL starts to pack the bag. REG takes a swig of water. THEO is still having his back slapped. Some individuals get changed back into civvies – these are CLIVE, OLLY, PAUL. The others keep their cricket gear on and pack their civvies into their bags.*)

REG: What did I get?

NICK: Eighty-four.

THIZ: I got eleven.

REG: Bloody hell! I enjoyed that! That first pint ain't even gonna touch the sides.

CLIVE: I'm available next week. Who's match managing?

WILL: Alan.

ALAN: Anyone else.

SEAN: Yeah.

ALAN: Paul?

PAUL: Yeah.

ALAN: Theo?

THEO: Sorry, not Hampstead Heath. It's two hours for me.

REG: You can put me down Alan.

SEAN: Er… Give Alan your number Reg, and if we don't have eleven from members, you know, people who've paid their annual subs, then we'll give you a ring. Alright?

REG: What's the subs?

SEAN: The amount of the subs is set each year at the annual general meeting.

REG: I'll pay now.

SEAN: Give Alan your number. OK.

REG: OK.

ALAN: I've only got four for next week.

WILL: Ring Gary.

SEAN: Match fees please! Five pounds. Anyone not going to the pub don't leave without paying.

(SEAN goes for his money in his cricket trousers in notes and so separates one five pound note out and puts it in a separate pocket.)

THIZ: I haven't got any money.

CLIVE: Impossible. Thiz Carlisle, no money?

THIZ: I had a lot of money in here this morning.

OLLY: We've been done. My cash has gone.

CLIVE: Oh fuck! I had forty pound. Bloody hell!

SEAN: I keep notes in my pocket.

WILL: I did organise a valuables bag. You ignore your elders and betters every week.

THIZ: That little chav, do you remember. It'll be him.

REG: Bastard! Fifty fucking quid! Bastard! I don't believe it. I do not fucking believe it.

NICK: My cash has gone but he didn't take my cards.

THIZ: I got me cards still. Oh alright then, dunt matter, I'll go and get some more.

WILL: Has anyone had cards stolen?

NICK: I'm alright.

CLIVE: No.

OLLY: Just the cash.

ALAN: Got mine.

SEAN: Will, better have a word with Bernard. He might have done them over as well.

WILL: I'll ring the police.

THIZ: Na! It's only cash.

WILL: That's why he didn't take your cards. Hoping we wouldn't phone the police.

THIZ: I'm gonna the pub. I'm not hanging around here waiting for the Old Bill to turn up. I got platinum.

(*WILL makes the phone call. NICK goes around with a carrier bag picking up litter. Enter BERNARD.*)

BERNARD: Which pub is it William?

WILL: It's the first one you come to.

BERNARD: Yes, but what is it called?

WILL: The Samuel Beckett.

BERNARD: That's it! I knew it was an Irish playwright who believed in the folly of all human endeavour. Ha, ha!

WILL: We've had cash stolen from our wallets.

BERNARD: Oh dear me.

WILL: Did you see anyone? When we were fielding?

SEAN: Young chavvie looking kid, white track suit bottoms.

BERNARD: I was umpiring.

WILL: When I say you, I mean your team, collectively.

BERNARD: I'll ask. Bad luck chaps. Here, we always use a valuables bag.

(*BERNARD walks off.*)

SEAN: Ask them why they didn't stop the guy going through our bags. Why they didn't physically challenge him, and restrain him.

NICK: See you in the pub.

WILL: I'm not going to the pub. I'll see you next week Nick.

(*NICK leaves. WILL is packing the kit bag, tea things etc and doing a reverse of the opening scene ie: carrying them back to the van. He is given a helping hand by THEO when lifting the kit bag to the van. Having done that they come straight back on.*)

THIZ: See you Len!

(*THIZ walks off.*)

PAUL: Are you staying at the flat tonight?

OLLY: I'm waiting for a text.

PAUL: I've got to show you my speech at some point haven't I.

OLLY: What speech?

PAUL: The best man speech. I'm worried that…well, her parents are snobby aren't they. Are you gonna the pub? I'll talk you through it then.

OLLY: Yeah.

PAUL: Alright.

(*PAUL walks off.*)

WILL: Goodbye Paul!

PAUL: What?

WILL: Goodbye.

PAUL: Yeah, see you. What?

(*WILL collects the old scoreboard and puts it in the van. SEAN leaves.*)

SEAN: Are you gonna the pub Theo?

THEO: *Bien sur*! I'll see you in the garden?

SEAN: Yeah.

CLIVE: Sun's gone in.

THEO: Timing. Brilliant.

OLLY: Are you gonna the pub?

CLIVE: Indeed.

OLLY: My lot are a bit arty, you know, but Barbara's.

CLIVE: Let's find five minutes in the pub. OK See you chaps!

(*OLLY and CLIVE leave. REG goes over to ALAN who is writing names down for the next week and packing his kit.*)

REG: Kaw! I won't need rocking to sleep tonight. Let me give you my number mate.

(*ALAN offers him the pen and paper he's been using to write next week's team on. REG starts writing down his number on.*)

About the sink. I'll pay you to do it properly.

ALAN: Here's my card.

(*ALAN gives him a business card.*)

REG: Ta.

ALAN: I've got a car and a van. The council wouldn't give me planning permission for a double garage. They said it's a policy across the borough. (*Beat.*) It's only a matter of time before you're gonna have to knock that double garage down. See you.

(*ALAN leaves. THEO and WILL return from the van.*)

REG: (*Offering his hand to shake.*) Thanks for the game Will. Been really bloody marvellous.

(*Shaking hands with THEO.*) And –

THEO: Theo.

REG: Theo. Ta pal! I'll get down the doctor's tomorrow.

THEO: I hope you do, but I don't think you will.

REG: No. I will. Something's wrong. I know. Something's…not right. See you in the pub.

(*REG leaves. WILL and THEO go over to LEN, and wait until everyone else is gone.*)

WILL: What do I do I have to do now?

THEO: One is supposed to call an ambulance and the police. Paramedics can declare a death. But so can doctors. And I'm a doctor and he's dead. Take him home, put him in his chair, and call his doctor.

WILL: Why would I need to ring the police?

THEO: They get involved if there are any suspicious circumstances. But there aren't. I suspect Len died exactly where he wanted to die.

WILL: Exactly where he wanted to die would be out there on the wicket with a bat in his hand.

THEO: Does Ruben know?

WILL: Ruben!

RUBEN: What?

WILL: Come over here.

(*RUBEN joins them.*)

RUBEN: What?

WILL: Grandad's died.

RUBEN: Yeah. I know.

WILL: You know?

RUBEN: I spoke to him, after I was out. He was already dead then.

THEO: How did you know he was dead?

RUBEN: I watched his stomach. It didn't move, you know, with his breathing. He's always asleep at home, and his stomach always moves up and down, not his chest.

THEO: (*Looking at the scorebook.*) So, time of death five past six.

WILL: So I can move the body, I don't have to ring the police?

THEO: Tell his doctor exactly what happened, give him my number.

WILL: I'm feeling guilty now. But I didn't want the lads to know. There'd be a fuss, and…but now it's beginning to feel, wrong.

THEO: Let's get him in the van.

(*THEO and WILL pick up LEN and carry him to the van.*)

WILL: Ruben! Open the sliding door please.

(*They carry him off. Doors are heard to open and close. They come back for other bits and pieces including RUBEN's bike.*)

Are you cycling back?

RUBEN: Yeah.

WILL: Do you mind son? I'd like someone in the van with me.

RUBEN: Alright.

(*RUBEN puts his bike in the van.*)

THEO: He was a lovely man. A great man as well. A soldier. My father was a conscientious objector. Will the funeral be Yorkshire?

WILL: No. Cremation.

THEO: And the ashes?

WILL: Where do you think?

(*THEO looks out to the middle.*)

THEO: Pegasus Bridge, or out there.

WILL: Out there.

THEO: I'll come in the van with you if you want.

WILL: No, I'll manage. You go to the pub.

(*WILL and THEO shake hands.*)

THEO: You must come to stay with us in France.

WILL: France?

THEO: I'm not sure I'll play again. I was very upset today.

(*THEO starts to walk off.*)

(*Off.*) Well batted Rubes!

RUBEN: (*Off.*) Ta.

(*WILL picks up the deck chair and starts to walk off. He has a glance around and sees an empty cigarette packet which he picks up. He walks off. Sound of Camper van door opening. Then Van Morrison kicks in half way through 'And the Healing has begun'. The engine starts, and the van drives off. There is a distant flash of lightning and then seven seconds later, thunder. Then the rain – an exuberant summer shower, the kind which feels like a celebration.*)
(*To black.*)

UP ON ROOF

This play was a commission for Hull Truck Theatre company, written for the theatre at Spring Street, Hull, with the intention of revisiting the Hull Prison riot of 1976 which wrecked the prison and closed it down for over a year.

Characters

SINGE   40's

YEBSLEY   20's

KATH   20's

MAD HATCHET JACK   40's

DECLAN   30's

CHRISTOPHER   30's

SET

The roof of A wing, Hull prison. 31 August 1976. As the audience take their seats the roof is undamaged. The lighting suggests night time and moonlight. The stage area consists of a flat leaded roof downstage edged by a lip of coping stones. A tiled sloping roof rises from the flat roof stage right. Stage left is a brick built 'broom cupboard' with a steel door facing down stage. The balconies of Newtown Court flats overlook the roof.

Up on Roof was first performed at Hull Truck Theatre on 5 March 2006 with the following cast:

SINGE, 40's   Martin Barrass

YEBSLEY, 20's   Matt Sutton

KATH, 20's   Rachel Helen

MAD HATCHET JACK, 40's   Chris Connell

DECLAN, 30's   Michael Glenn Murphy

CHRISTOPHER, 30's   James Weaver

Director   Gareth Tudor Price

Designer   Richard Foxton

Act One

SCENE ONE

(*To black. Strobe lighting. Sounds of rioting, sirens, smashing of glass, smashing of tiles. 'White Riot' by The Clash plays.*

The riot moves on and the strobe lighting ends. It's just before dawn on Wednesday 1 September . The roof area is transformed, tiles have been torn from the roof leaving holes, the chimney pots have gone, coping stones are torn from the roof edge. Distant sounds of traffic.

Enter MAD HATCHET JACK from stage right, ie; the roof that would connect to the Centre. He is bare chested, covered in tattoos. He has a full face spider web tattoo. He carries a home-made spear made out of a bit of two by two and a pair of scissors. His body shows the results of body building and self mutilation.

JACK goes downstage and stares up at the moon. He is relatively calm in this speech.)

JACK: In the beginning God created the 'eaven and the earf. And the earf was f f f f f facking formless. And darkness was over the deep, and God's spirit was hovering over the surface of the water. And God said 'Let there be light' and there was light. And God called the light 'facking day', and the darkness he called 'night'. And the evening and the morning were the f f f f facking first day.

(*Exit JACK stage left along the roof and off towards the Centre. The sun comes up. Sound of traffic on Hedon Road. It's very sunny. SINGE is standing on the chimney stack looking into the distance down the river to the sea. YEBSLEY is standing on the edge of the roof holding a TV over his head about to chuck it down. SINGE, a middle aged man, is wearing prison issue trousers, prison issue shirt which is open to let the sun on his chest. He has placed his various pets and his prison potty which is full of urine downstage. A budgie in a cage, a bag with a corn snake in it and a goldfish bowl with goldfish. His slop potty is also on the roof. YEBSLEY is a young man wearing a prison officer's peaked cap, prison issue trousers adorned with random yellow patches.*

He is wearing a Che Guevara T shirt and a balaclava with eye holes cut out. He has a ring of stolen keys around his belt.)

SINGE: Yebsley!!

YEBSLEY: What?

SINGE: Why are yer chucking a perfectly good telly off the roof?

YEBSLEY: It's political, innit. Destroying consumer goods is a legitimate revolutionary act for the disempowered working class.

SINGE: You are not a member of the 'disempowered working class' Yebsley. The technical term sociologists use for people like you is 'wanker'. Or, if they've met yer, 'total and complete fucking wanker'. Now put that telly down. Even them Irish lads over in C wing, they're not gonna be thick enough to chuck their telly off the roof.

YEBSLEY: That's racist that is.

SINGE: I said they are not thick enough to chuck their telly off the roof. There's a full card at Haydock. As A wing bookie I've got responsibilities.

(YEBSLEY puts the telly down. YEBSLEY takes his mask off.)

YEBSLEY: Hot innit?

SINGE: Yeah. I'm sweating like a Scouser in a personality test.
(SINGE comes down off the stack. During the next he unfurls a sheet and starts writing out a slogan on the sheet. He's using a paint brush and black paint. The slogan reads 336 CALVERT NOT INVOLVED IN RIAT.)

YEBSLEY: What yer doing?

SINGE: I'm out in two months. That's cos of me three years remission for arse licking. I've done six and half year. I can't do another three. It'd kill our lass. What's more important is, it'd kill me. I'm staying put, here, up on roof, my roof, while this is ovver. Where the whole fucking world can see it in't me smashing the place up, bonning up the offices, and what have yer.

YEBSLEY: Why've yer brought yer pets up?

SINGE: Cos six month back Mad Hatchet Jack said he'd eat them. I owe him fifty quid don't forget.

YEBSLEY: They wunt let Jack out.

SINGE: Them IRA boys are letting everybody out.

YEBSLEY: Yeah but yer gorra be mad to let Jack out.

SINGE: The IRA are mad. Blow up a pub, killing twennie Brummies and blame it all on Oliver Cromwell. What's that if it in't fucking mad?

YEBSLEY: They're political prisoners.

SINGE: My arse.

YEBSLEY: Give Edna some sun then.

(*He pulls the shade off the budgie.*)

SINGE: Put that cover back on!

(*YEBSLEY complies.*)

YEBSLEY: They love the sun, budgies. They come from Brazil.

SINGE: Not that one. She's from Whitesides on Hessle Road. She's allergic to sunshine. If she weren't in a cage, she'd be up and off, migrating in search of drizzle.

YEBSLEY: How d'yer know she's a she?

SINGE: She must be a she. Cos nothing I ever do is good enough.

YEBSLEY: That's a sexist er…patriarchal narrative you've got running in yer head.

SINGE: Good. It's not full of shit then like yours?

YEBSLEY: 'Woman is the nigger of the world'. John Lennon.

SINGE: 'Bollocks'. Singe Calvert. You wait until you live with a woman, then you'll find out who's really in charge. You'll be singing a different tune after four or five years of leaving yer dick in the fridge every time yer go down the pub.

YEBSLEY: You know what Singe? This riot…this has gorra be a good time to escape.

SINGE: You? Escape? Yer couldn't break out of Boys's.

YEBSLEY: Declan told me they're gonna give it a go.

SINGE: The whole of Britain's watching this prison expecting a break out. Every spare screw in Yorkshire is camped on Hedon Road waiting. Yer on telly right now. News at Ten. Over there. Look North over there. Wave. Go on!

(*YEBSLEY waves.*)

YEBSLEY: Them cameras are pointed at C wing roof.

SINGE: Aye, and that's the way I wannit to stay. If yer wanna riot go over there. If yer on my roof, tek that fucking hat off and behave.

(*YEBSLEY complies and takes off the hat.*)

YEBSLEY: (*Showing him the ring of keys.*) Got a set of keys.

SINGE: Whose are them?

YEBSLEY: Found 'em in the A wing office.

SINGE: Giss 'em.

(*SINGE takes the keys and starts to try them on the padlock on the broom cupboard.*)

(*Reading a label.*) Roof store.

YEBSLEY: Wanna panatella. We broke into the shop.

SINGE: An't you bin listening!? I've been well behaved for too long, it's doing my head in. I'm not used to being this good. But I'm not gonna fuck up now by smoking a stolen panatella.

(*YEBSLEY lights up.*)

YEBSLEY: Why've yer brought yer slop up on roof?

SINGE: Mind yer own business.

(*SINGE opens the padlock and the door to the broom cupboard.*)

Here we go!

YEBSLEY: What is it?

SINGE: Looks like the top of a set of stairs but they've closed it off and concreted it up. Just a broom cupboard now.

YEBSLEY: (*Beat.*) Wow! Beautiful view from up here.

SINGE: What? Saltend? You should get out more.

YEBSLEY: What I mean is yer can see for miles.

SINGE: True. That's Paull that is.

YEBSLEY: Do you know everyone in East Hull then?

SINGE: Paull. That village there, past Saltend, this side of them two lighthouses, that's called Paull. I thought you were a bloody Hull kid.

YEBSLEY: I'm West Hull aren't I. What would I wanna go to fucking Paull for.

SINGE: I had a week's holiday there once. Passed the time by crying and shitting me pants.

YEBSLEY: Just a bain were yer?

SINGE: I was twennie three. Back in them days you had to mek yer own entertainment. I got a brother out there. He's gorr an allotment.

YEBSLEY: They've all got their curtains drawn.

SINGE: If you lived in a block of flats what overlooked a prison you'd have yer curtains drawn.

YEBSLEY: Seen any birds?

SINGE: There will be members of the enemy living in them flats aye, on account of it being the free world and not a maximum security prison.

YEBSLEY: Wakey wakey! Rise and shine! Come on girls! Let's be having you.

SINGE: Have you always had the gift of the gab?

YEBSLEY: What's that there then?

SINGE: Lavers Wood yard.

YEBSLEY: You've only gorra get out the fence at the back there and yer in their yard, and yer can get into the cemetery.

SINGE: Lavers have got dogs. Dogs they don't feed.

(*The sound of a French windows opening.* YEBSLEY *runs behind the chimney stack.*)

YEBSLEY: (*Retreating to behind the chimney.*) Eh! Eh! Eh! Look! The flat above. Phwoargh. She's fucking gorgeous.

(*KATH comes on to the balcony. She's about twenty-two and with a punk demeanor.*)

KATH: Calmed down a bit after last night then?

SINGE: Weren't me love.

KATH: If you're gonna have a party, you should invite your neighbours.

(*YEBSLEY comes into view.*)

YEBSLEY: Hiya.

KATH: Hi.

YEBSLEY: What's them flats of yours there?

KATH: Newtown Court. There's more villains in here than you got in there. You've been lucky with the weather.

SINGE: What's yer name love?

KATH: Kath. What's yours?

SINGE: St John as in Saint John.

KATH: Posh.

SINGE: Aye, me mam thought we was a bit better than everyone else cos she'd married a crane driver. They call me Singe.

KATH: And what's your name?

YEBSLEY: Alan. But everyone calls me Yebsley.

KATH: How do you gerr a mad name like that?

YEBSLEY: Our kid used to work for Yorkshire Electricity Board.

(*Beat.*) I used to wear his donkey jacket.

KATH: Are you right in the head Yebsley?

YEBSLEY: Yeah. Why?

KATH: Soss. I'm Kath. You from Hull?

YEBSLEY: Yeah. Anlaby Road.

KATH: I thought you was all, sort of, you know, like, Irish terrorists in there.

SINGE: We're like a box of sweets. Allsorts.

YEBSLEY: Yeah.

KATH: Being in Hull's bad enough. Being in prison in Hull must be hell.

SINGE: I love Hull, me. Rovers. Bob Carvers. Get to the coast in half hour. What more d'yer want?

KATH: I'm gonna live in London aren't I.

YEBSLEY: I got mates in London.

KATH: Yeah?

YEBSLEY: Yeah.

KATH: I've got to go to college.

YEBSLEY: See you later, yeah.

KATH: Dunno. I've got a gig tonight.

YEBSLEY: You in a band?

KATH: Yeah. I sing.

SINGE: Do you know 'Folsom Prison Blues' by Johnny Cash?

KATH: Me dad likes Johnny Cash.

YEBSLEY: I'm teachin' mesen bass.

KATH: Our bassist is rubbish.

YEBSLEY: What, he can't play?

KATH: He can play – but he's thirty-six, and he can't drive.

YEBSLEY: Right.

KATH: And he likes Emerson Lake and Palmer. When d'yer gerrout?

(*YEBSLEY's face drops.*)

Why have you got long hair? Dun't suit you.

SINGE: He's a Muslim.

KATH: How do you mean?

YEBSLEY: In here they cut your hair unless it's for like, you know, religious reasons. So I said I'm a Muslim.

KATH: I've got to go. Miss my bus. Tarra Yebsley.

(*She goes in, and locks her windows.*)

SINGE: You in love?

YEBSLEY: Fuck off.

SINGE: Nice. Keep swearing like that, and yer could get yersen a job as a woman at Birds Eye.

YEBSLEY: She's fit though, yeah?

SINGE: Lovely. The first time I realised I was in love, I was at Boulevard, in threepenny stand. Me, in me red and white, head down, surrounded by black and white. Rivers of piss trickling down that rotten wooden terracing, your lot, paralytic to a man, farting, all of them singing about some lonely cowboy who, 'in any kind of weather', fucks his pony.

YEBSLEY: Watch it.

SINGE: And I was happy. I was glad to be there – in Hell. Why? Cos our lass was standing next to me. Rita Hayworth, Gina Lollabrigida, Elizabeth Taylor – they're all a lot better looking than our lass, in fact in terms of film stars, she's more yer 'Walter Matthau', but what she does have is a rare, unique, priceless quality which none of them Hollywood beauties could ever have.

YEBSLEY: What's that Singe?

SINGE: She's happy to live with me on Greatfield Estate.

YEBSLEY: What were you doing in threepenny stand? You're Rovers.

SINGE: Think about it!

YEBSLEY: (*Amazed.*) What?! She's Hull FC?

SINGE: Aye, it's not just her teeth that are black and white. But that's what love is. Forgivin' the unforgivable. We don't want you being in love. You're hard enough to live with as it is. Have yer tekken yer pills today son?

YEBSLEY: Chemical lobotomy in't it. I gorr a coupla tabs of acid off Lewis. D'yer wanna corner?

(*Shows the tab.*)

SINGE: Fuck off. Never could see the attraction of drugs meself. A good night out for my generation was a couple of pints of mild, a bag o' chips, and a quick knee trembler down Barmy drain.

YEBSLEY: Yeah, yeah. Eh? How come you owe Mad Hatchet Jack fifty quid?

SINGE: He put a fiver on a ten to one shot at Wincanton which won but then got disqualified. So I wunt pay out.

YEBSLEY: A fiver? Kinell! Where's he get a fiver from?

SINGE: Where am I gonna get fifty quid from?

(*Enter CHRISTOPHER. He is a man of about thirty. He is dressed in new prison issue clothes, still creased. He looks lost. He is carrying a chair.*)

CHRISTOPHER: Hello.

SINGE: How do.

YEBSLEY: Where have yer come from?

CHRISTOPHER: I haven't been given a cell yet.

YEBSLEY: Yer new?

CHRISTOPHER: I arrived last night, about seven o'clock and I was in the middle bit –

SINGE: – Under the Centre.

CHRISTOPHER: – yeah. They were taking me to B wing, but then someone threw a bucket at an officer and it kicked off.

YEBSLEY: Where was yer last night?

CHRISTOPHER: C wing, I think.

YEBSLEY: What's going off ovver there?

CHRISTOPHER: I'm sorry?

SINGE: (*To YEBSLEY.*) Speak proper fucking English can't yer. (*To CHRISTOPHER.*) Sorry son, he's dead Hessle Road. (*To YEBSLEY.*) Can't yer tell when yer dealing with an educated man. (*To CHRISTOPHER.*) My friend Mr Yebsley wanted to know what it is that is occurring at the merment ovver on C wing.

CHRISTOPHER: They're tearing the place apart. I wanted to get out the way. Peaceful up here.

SINGE: Kaw! You got the short straw din't yer. Delivered fresh to Hull one hour before a riot.

CHRISTOPHER: Could be worse. I could be in China in the middle of the earthquake.

SINGE: Having an earthquake are they?

CHRISTOPHER: Yeah. Five hundred thousand dead.

SINGE: Or as Hull Daily Mail would say – 'Earthquake rocks China, no Hull people involved'.

CHRISTOPHER: It was last month.

SINGE: I an't heard owt about it.

YEBSLEY: Nope.

SINGE: Any road, you're alright on my roof as long as you behave.

(*Pause. YEBS and SINGE wait for an answer.*)

YEBSLEY: What Cat are yer?

SINGE: What Category prisoner are yer? A, B –

CHRISTOPHER: – Category A.

SINGE: But yer didn't do it. You're an innocent man?

CHRISTOPHER: Yes.

SINGE: If yer looking for sympathy, you'll find it in the dictionary between shit and syphilis.

CHRISTOPHER: You're innocent too?

SINGE: I was in the wrong place at the wrong time.

YEBSLEY: He was in a bank with a gun in his hand when the pigs burst in.

SINGE: To this day, I do not know how that gun got in my hand.

CHRISTOPHER: A real gun?

SINGE: It onny fired caps.

YEBSLEY: (*To CHRISTOPHER.*) They gorr away with six hundred thousand. They've stashed his share somewhere, burr he in't telling no-one. He's out in a couple of month. Going home to two hundred grand! eh Singe?!

SINGE: (*To CHRISTOPHER.*) I'm going home to nowt burr an ear bashing from our lass. There she is. Nance.
(*SINGE shows CHRISTOPHER a photograph.*)

CHRISTOPHER: Nancy?

SINGE: Aye, Nancy but 'Nance' saves valuable time.

CHRISTOPHER: Lovely smile.

SINGE: I love her.

(*SINGE shows him another photograph.*)

CHRISTOPHER: (*With something approaching distaste.*) And who's that?

SINGE: That's her in a bad mood. I'm only here, in Hull, cos I begged 'em to let me be near her and the kids. That's my little team. Andrew, ten, Janice, eight now – look at her, kaw!

CHRISTOPHER: She's a beautiful child.

SINGE: Got her mother's looks, her mother's brains, and my eczema. And that's David, six year old. He dun't hardly know who I am. That's me real sentence.

CHRISTOPHER: She's stuck by you then?

SINGE: Don't know why. You can't get two people more different.

CHRISTOPHER: Opposites attract.

SINGE: She's all Simon and Garfunkel and 'Bridge Over Troubled Water' and anything bloody sugary sentimental – her record collection could kill a diabetic. Me, I'm Johnny Cash, 'The Man In Black', yer know the drugs, the drink, the prison albums.

YEBSLEY: (*To CHRISTOPHER.*) Cat A then, eh?

CHRISTOPHER: I've been accused of killing my father.

SINGE: You're in good company here then.

YEBSLEY: We got forty murderers.

SINGE: Twennie manslaughterers an'all. Then there's assorted forgers, rapists and wounders and an 'undred and fifty decent hard working villains like me. Also, there's two men in for buggery. They purr 'em in the same cell for a while, burr after a couple of weeks they decided that that weren't much of a punishment.

YEBSLEY: I'm a political prisoner.

SINGE: There's a lot of politicals, IRA, the subversives, his lot.

CHRISTOPHER: Subversives?

YEBSLEY: Angry Brigade. You know, like Beider Meinhof gang, Black Panthers. Class warriors.

SINGE: The Angry Brigade told him how to build a bomb so he ordered sixty gallon, sixty fucking gallon, of liquid fertiliser to be delivered to his mam's thirteenth floor council flat down Arcon Drive, Anlaby. The agricultural supplier couldn't gerr all the barrels in the lift which is when someone called the filth.

CHRISTOPHER: What were you going to bomb?

YEBSLEY: A symbol of excess and conspicuous consumption in Hull.

SINGE: The delicatessen in Hammonds. But you don't know Hammonds do yer, so you wunt know why that's funny?

CHRISTOPHER: Never been to Hull.

SINGE: It's a wonderful place. East Hull any road.

(*Looks exchanged between YEBSLEY and SINGE.*)

CHRISTOPHER: What's that smell?

SINGE: West Hull.

YEBSLEY: Oi! Watch it!

SINGE: There's a few opposites in the world, Muslins and Christians, Chalk and Cheese, and then there's West Hull and East Hull. It's a city divided by a river.

CHRISTOPHER: What's the river called?

SINGE: River 'ull.

CHRISTOPHER: That's a bit fancy.

SINGE: Funny. You're alright son.

CHRISTOPHER: It's completely flat.

SINGE: No good if yer wanna tek yer driving test cos there's nowhere to do an hill start. The only slope of any significance is Park Street bridge. We're a very historical city. Sixteen forty-two there was a game of dominoes in the Olde White Hart, down Whitefriargate which gorr out of hand and turned into the English Civil War.

CHRISTOPHER: So Hull invented Constitutional Parliamentary democracy?

SINGE: Yer took the words right out of me mouth.

YEBSLEY: You bin to University?

CHRISTOPHER: Yes. Imperial College of Science, London.

SINGE: Now listen. I gorr an important question for yer son. You was in C wing last night?

YEBSLEY: Have they let out Mad Hatchet Jack?

CHRISTOPHER: How would I recognise him?

SINGE: He's called Jack, he's mad, and he's gorr an axe.

YEBSLEY: Full face spider web tattoo.

SINGE: Stutters on F. F f f f facking foreigners.

CHRISTOPHER: Yes, he's out.

SINGE/YEBSLEY: Oh fuck a duck! / Shit!

CHRISTOPHER: Last time I saw him he was making a spear out of a bit of two by two and a pair of scissors.

SINGE: Fucking buggering hell.

CHRISTOPHER: Is he dangerous?

SINGE: Is 'Mad Hatchet Jack' dangerous? What university did you go to?

YEBSLEY: He'd kill anyone yer like for two thousand quid.

SINGE: Burr if yer want 'em tortured first he'll do it for five hundred.

YEBSLEY: He's in for murder, malicious wounding and he's got three counts of rape an'all.

SINGE: Onny two of the victims was women.

YEBSLEY: He's the only trouble there is in here.

SINGE: You see in prison it's a case of you scratch my back, I'll scratch yours. But with Mad Hatchet Jack it's more like 'you scratch my back, and I'll fuck you up the arse'.

YEBSLEY: Singe here owes him money.

SINGE: And he's very Old Testament.

CHRISTOPHER: Yeah?

SINGE: Jack's found God, the Old Testament God. Why turn the other cheek when yer can have yer fun smashing someone's face in. Whatever you do, don't touch him.

YEBSLEY: Fuck no! Do not touch!

SINGE: His body is his temple.

CHRISTOPHER: What's the riot about then?

SINGE: (*Pointing at YEBSLEY.*) Him.

YEBSLEY: Don't blame me! I was in seg!

SINGE: You started all this.

YEBSLEY: Nowt to do wi' me I was in seg.

CHRISTOPHER: What is 'seg'?

SINGE: He got a week in the segregation unit for trying to escape.

YEBSLEY: That's why I'm in patches.

SINGE: (*To YEBSLEY.*) It all kicked off cos the Subversives and the Irish heard that you'd been beaten up. You! I can't believe you don't know that. Come here! What does that banner say on C wing roof?

YEBSLEY: (*Reading.*) Four warders beat up one prisoner. We demand full public enquiry.

SINGE: You are the 'one prisoner'.

YEBSLEY: I said I'd been beaten up. Burr I was lying.

SINGE: So if four warders did not give you a broken nose, what did happen?

YEBSLEY: The wing governor confiscated me book. So I punched him.

SINGE: What the fuck do you think will happen when the Irish find out you don't have a broken nose? Come on then, stand there.

YEBSLEY: What yer doing?

SINGE: I'm gonna brek yer nose for yer. It's for your own good.

(*SINGE raises his fists.*)

CHRISTOPHER: I've got a better idea.

(*CHRISTOPHER stands and starts undoing his trousers.*)

SINGE: What yer gonna do? Wack him over the head with yer knob?

(*CHRISTOPHER reveals a large elastoplast and bandage on his side.*)

CHRISTOPHER: Appendix. Couple of weeks ago.

(*He tears off the elastoplast.*)

Come here.

(*He puts the elastoplast over YEBSLEY's nose.*)

SINGE: I'm impressed wi' you son. Say ta. He hardly knows yer Yebsley and he's already given yer a second hand elastoplast.

YEBSLEY: Ta.

CHRISTOPHER: Yebsley. That's an unusual name.

YEBSLEY: Our kid used to work for Yorkshire Electricity
  Board.

SINGE: He used to wear his donkey jacket.

YEBSLEY: Panatella?

CHRISTOPHER: That's kind of you, thanks.
  (*To YEBSLEY.*) Why do you want to escape Yebsley?

YEBSLEY: Eh?

SINGE: It's norr a daft question. I don't wanna escape. I've
  onny got two months to go.

YEBSLEY: I'm twennie five, I've got eight more years to do. I'll
  be an old man when they let me out.

SINGE: I wish I was thirty fucking three.

YEBSLEY: You bin to University. How would you escape?

CHRISTOPHER: I'd walk straight out the door.

YEBSLEY: Oh yeah.

CHRISTOPHER: Every day a hundred, I guess maybe two
  hundred people walk straight in this prison, and at the end
  of the day, they walk straight out again.

YEBSLEY: It's not straight in and straight out. There's gates,
  doors, checks, passes. There's twenty-five CCTV cameras
  inside and seven outside.

SINGE: He's counted them.

CHRISTOPHER: Even with all those cameras, and doors, and
  rivers to ford, and mountains to climb, and seas to swim
  – every day a hundred people escape this prison.

YEBSLEY: But they're not prisoners.

CHRISTOPHER: Exactly! Over time you –

YEBSLEY: – Me?

CHRISTOPHER: Yes. You develop a relationship with the Art
  Teacher.

YEBSLEY: I don't do Art.

SINGE: Shurrup and fucking listen!

CHRISTOPHER: You fall in love with her. She falls in love with
  you. In the art class you kiss in the paint cupboard, quick
  frantic embraces – a lust made more driven and desperate
  because it cannot be consumated.

SINGE: – Good story this. Gissa panatella!
  (*YEBSLEY complies.*)

CHRISTOPHER: Thank you. Where was I.

SINGE: Quick frantic embraces in a cupboard. Actually, would you mind going ovver that bit again.

CHRISTOPHER: She'll do anything for you. Every now and then you achieve a surreptitious caress.

SINGE: I don't know worr it means, but I wunt mind having a go.

CHRISTOPHER: You study her. Her voice. Her face. Her legs. Her smell. The way she talks. The way she smiles, stands, scratches, sniffs, sighs, yawns, laughs. Alone in your cell, you practice talking like her. You teach yourself how to walk in high heels.

SINGE: Ha, ha.

CHRISTOPHER: She brings in her measurements. Inside leg, hips, waist, bust. You give her yours. You make a pair of breasts.

YEBSLEY: Yer what?

CHRISTOPHER: You make a pair of breasts.

SINGE: If it was that easy, we'd all be doing it.

CHRISTOPHER: The day of the escape is set, a long way off, a year ahead. She grows her hair, long, down over her eyes, covering the eye lashes, the ears.

SINGE: Adam's Apple. That's always a dead give away.

CHRISTOPHER: When it's long she has it all cut off and has a wig made from the cut hair, and she starts to grow it long again. You grow your nails.

SINGE: I say it again. Adam's apple.

CHRISTOPHER: When her hair is long again, they're ready.

SINGE: Adam's Apple.

CHRISTOPHER: The week before the escape, she has a car crash. Suffers whiplash. She has to wear one of those big collars round her neck.

(*CHRISTOPHER looks at SINGE. SINGE looks at YEBS.*)

SINGE: Thank you.

CHRISTOPHER: She's also bruised about the face, or says she is –

SINGE: – from the crash.

CHRISTOPHER: Yeah. So she wears very heavy make up for that week. Ostensibly to cover the bruising.

SINGE: Clever.

CHRISTOPHER: On the day of the escape you shave your head, your legs, the backs of your hands. She wears a two piece suit. Skirt and jacket. Shows a lot of leg. The clothes are a bit too big for her, but big enough for you. Shoes, a bit too big for her but big enough for you. Coming into the prison she wears the wig over her own long hair. She brings in make up, nail varnish; she wears distinctive dangly ear rings; carries a unique brief case. At the end of the art class, in the paint cupboard, she undresses. You undress.
(*Beat.*) You put on her clothes, and –

SINGE: – Hang on, hang on, haven't you missed summat out!

CHRISTOPHER: No.

SINGE: Oh God! It's been a year!

CHRISTOPHER: You put on the wig. She paints your nails. She does your lipstick. The heavy make up. You put on the whiplash collar. Then…

YEBSLEY: What?

CHRISTOPHER: Then you punch her in the face. You smash her nose. With a knife you cut her arm. You draw blood. You tie her up. Unpleasantly tight. You gag her with duck tape. You punch her again. You break the skin.

SINGE: 'kinnel.

CHRISTOPHER: Then you kiss her. On the lips. Lovingly.

YEBSLEY: That'd smudge my lipstick.

CHRISTOPHER: She fixes it for you. You leave. You walk out the prison, the same way she walked in.

YEBSLEY: Do I take her car?

CHRISTOPHER: Of course you take her car. 'You' are now 'she'.

YEBSLEY: Wouldn't work. They'd miss her.

SINGE: NO! 'She' an't gone missing, yer tit! She's gone home as normal. And you wun't be missed until 'Bang up' at nine o'clock.
(*Silence. YEBSLEY walks down stage and contemplates the plan.*)

YEBSLEY: That is fucking brilliant that is. One problem.

CHRISTOPHER: What?

YEBSLEY: Our Art teacher's a bloke.

(*To black.*)

SCENE TWO

(*More rioting music. New York Dolls. Same day, an hour later. Eight am. Lights up on DECLAN with an Irish tricolour and an armful of buff folders. He is staring out at the Humber. Only SINGE, YEBSLEY and DECLAN are on the roof. DECLAN is a middle aged Irishman.*)

DECLAN: Look at all them dockers on their way to work. Every last one of them on a bicycle. It's like the fucking tour de France…without the haste. I've heard say that the only manual work them dockers ever do is with a knife and fork. This is a fucking postcard! I bet ever since God himself was in short trousers this Humber estuary of his has never looked so fucking lovely. And look at all them beautiful docks. Brendan Behan, have yer heard of him, he's a Fenian man and an intellectual like meself. He tried to blow up a dock in Liverpool once in the name of Home Rule. Now, don't get me wrong, but how the fucking hell do you blow a dock up. It's already a fucking big hole in the ground. I'm glad he didn't take up republican politics with a serious intent. A proven idiot like that is best kept out of the way writing shite for the fucking theatre. Where's that butty of yours?

SINGE: Yebsley!

(*YEBSLEY comes out from behind the broom cupboard. His nose still wearing the plaster.*)

DECLAN: Oh look at yer. It's true then, we heard the screws give yer a right good mulin'.

YEBSLEY: Yeah.

DECLAN: And exactly where did they hit yer?

(*Beat.*)

YEBSLEY: Brok me nose.

DECLAN: That's unusual that is. Them screws have an imperative about not marking the face.

YEBSLEY: Are your lads gonna break out? I'm up for it. Count me in.

261

SINGE: Count me out.

DECLAN: They're doing an awful lot of thinking about it, at the moment, and I'll let yer all know what they come up with when they come up with it.

SINGE: Yer gorr about as much chance as a turkey on Christmas eve.

DECLAN: I will now deconstruct what yer just said. A turkey still alive the day before Christmas probably does have a good chance of escaping getting itself eaten on the big day, because there's an imperative to kill the birds well in advance in order to get them into the shops, and since there's generally no shops open on Christmas day, there's no imperative to slaughter on Christmas Eve, so this turkey of yours has been overlooked for a fucking good reason, and may well inevitably get through the season with it's life intact.

SINGE: Thank God for the Open University.

DECLAN: Jacques Derrida has given me a new way of looking at the whole fucking world.
(*Unfurling the Irish tricolour.*) Now then, Singe, I was wondering if yer wouldn't mind putting this bit of Ireland up on that lump of chimney over there.

SINGE: No. Fuck off. This is my roof. I'm norr having owt to do with the IRA, that flag, or this riot. I'm out in two month. Three years remission.

DECLAN: Home fer Christmas and of course, yer've got all that money to dig up somewhere an'all.

SINGE: I an't got no money to go to.

YEBSLEY: Is Jack out?

DECLAN: Ah, now that's was a very silly thing we done.

SINGE: Fucking brilliant!

YEBSLEY: Who the fuck let him out?

DECLAN: They found a way of ripping the doors off which was particularly entertaining, especially since half of the gang was intoxificated. You open the door, jam a big fucking plank in the gap, and slam the door as hard as yer can, and they just explode out the hinges with a fearful tearing and general destruction. We went down the whole the fucking

twos having a laugh and didn't realise we'd done the mad
bastard until he stepped over the threshold bollock naked,
with a hard on, sucking a lolly.

YEBSLEY: What happened then?

DECLAN: We all ran for our fucking lives. He beat the shit outa
that young proddy lad who makes the hooch and is now as
drunk as a nun after a double communion.

SINGE: Great.

DECLAN: You owe him money don't yer?

SINGE: Aye.

DECLAN: Then the next time I see yers might be at yer wake.

SINGE: Didn't yer bloody think?!

DECLAN: Only a man who never does anything at all, never
makes mistakes.

(*Enter CHRISTOPHER. DECLAN nods. CHRISTOPHER nods.*)

CHRISTOPHER: They've smashed the toilets up.

SINGE: Wankers.

YEBSLEY: What are them files Dex?

DECLAN: The lads broke into Admin and purloined all
the personal files. We thought there was a democratic
imperative to share them out. Harold Orlando Saint John
Calvert.

SINGE: Me dad was a crane driver.

(*SINGE takes his file.*)

DECLAN: Alan Bowden.

YEBSLEY: Yeah.

DECLAN: Personal and Confidential, all top secret fucking stuff
about yer mental state and that. Of the ones I've read,
yours is the funniest by a country mile. Ha! Yer think yer
a fucking black man!? Fucking Mary Mother of Christ I've
heard some –

YEBSLEY: – Genetically, yeah, I'm black.

DECLAN: Yer fucking mentally –

SINGE: – Declan! Lay off! That's enough. Alright?

DECLAN: Aye.

(*DECLAN hands over the file to YEBSLEY. During the next
YEBSLEY sits and reads his file with great commitment.*)

CHRISTOPHER: Do you think it's right reading other people's personal files?

DECLAN: I'll go away and have a sleepless night on it. Now I'm gonna shake your hand as a symbol of greeting young man, and that way we stand a better fucking chance of getting off on the right footing, even if you are a fucking Englishman. Declan MacCullagh. What cat are yer?
(*They shake.*)

CHRISTOPHER: Category A.

DECLAN: Are yous a political? By that I mean is yer driving imperative a set of principles and higher goals with the long term intent to improve the lot of humanity like me, or are yer just another lazy, feckless, morally bankrupted lump o' nothing, like me good friend Singe here?

SINGE: They say he killed his old man.

DECLAN: Oooh.

SINGE: But he din't do it of course.

YEBSLEY: Declan's IRA.

DECLAN: (*To CHRISTOPHER.*) Don't narrow yer eyes at me sunshine. If you were born me, you'd be like me, and you'd agree with every fucking despicable thing I ever done, cos it would be you who'd done it.

CHRISTOPHER: And what have you done Declan?

DECLAN: Six murders, one manslaughter, thirteen bomb attacks, possessing firearms, resisting arrest, plotting to cause an explosion, and having a black and white licence for a colour telly – which ironically enough is the only charge for which I'm totally fucking innocent. Did they bother themselves giving yous a name, or did they just slap you on the arse and go off to the pub?

CHRISTOPHER: Christopher. Hoffman.

DECLAN: We don't have no file for you though. That'll be cos of yer general all round newness I shouldn't wonder.
(*To CHRISTOPHER.*) Now you will remember that hand shake won't you? I don't want you going telling no-one that Declan of the Irish, wasn't a civil man with you on first meeting. I'm like this with everyone on account of me being, in a small way, an ambassador for me country.

CHRISTOPHER: It's a beautiful country. Ireland.

DECLAN: I didn't know you'd already done a visit. In that case I'll cut the fucking eulogy. If yer've been there yer'll know that it's one great big fucking outdoor asylum.

CHRISTOPHER: Paul Hill's in here isn't he? Guildford Four.

DECLAN: And what's it to you if he is or he isn't?

SINGE: Aye. Nice lad, Paul.

YEBSLEY: He's a mate.

SINGE: Before you get the fuck off my roof Dex. You know there's a meeting at Haydock today?

DECLAN: Aye, well we don't have a fucking television no more on account of Mr Michael Coyle. I had Michael down as a genuine Irish intellectual in the footsteps of George Bernard Shaw, Michael Collins, Yeats, James Joyce, Keats, Oscar Wilde, and Johnny fucking Giles. It was an imperative, he was gonna be the first Prime Minister of all Ireland. But then this morning he smashes up a perfectly good twenty-four inch colour telly just cos he likes the sound of breaking glass. It's enough to mek a Fenian man like meself vote for Ian fucking Paisley.

SINGE: I've gorr a telly. I'll tek yer bets. And I'll set the telly up on this wing at the end of the ones.

DECLAN: I can sense the imperative of desperation here?

SINGE: I owe Jack fifty quid.

DECLAN: You're a fucking dead man Singe.

SINGE: I'll take singles, doubles and crossbets. No multiples, no yankies. And it's on telly, ITV seven. I'm doing you a favour. In return I don't want no flags or owt on my roof. I'm spending the whole riot up here where the gov can see us.

DECLAN: I'll tell the lads. I think yous might get a bit of business.

(*DECLAN turns to go.*)

CHRISTOPHER: You did Guildford and Woolwich, didn't you. Paul Hill is innocent. Why don't you tell the police, Declan? And then Paul can go free. And Gerald Conlon and Patrick Armstrong and Carole Richardson. And Gerry's dad, Giuseppe, he's not well you know.

DECLAN: That's the kind of knowledge that could get you into a bit of trouble.

CHRISTOPHER: He didn't do it. The IRA knows he didn't do it.

DECLAN: There's a bigger picture you're refusing to look at. And that's the age old struggle of the Irishman to run his own fucking country.

CHRISTOPHER: You'll want the Americans to give Manhattan Island back to the Wappinger Indian tribe next.

(*DECLAN leaves. Sounds of rioting off. Singing. Fuck the Shah of Iran. YEBSLEY reads his file.*)

CHRISTOPHER: Fuck the Shah of Iran?

YEBSLEY: We mek furniture for Iran's prisons, here, in the workshops.

CHRISTOPHER: (*To SINGE.*) Why aren't you reading your file?

SINGE: I've seen it afore. Me and the governor, went through it page by page.

YEBSLEY: (*Reading from his file.*) What's a paranoid schizophrenic?

SINGE: It means yer really two people and both of you are fucking mad.

(*To YEBSLEY.*) Give me that.

(*SINGE snatches YEBSLEY's file from him.*)

478 Alan Bowden. N. T. B. R.

YEBSLEY: What's that mean? N. T. B. R.

SINGE: It's an acrylic.

(*YEBSLEY snatches the file of him and sits and reads it.*)

CHRISTOPHER: Not To Be…given Rice.

SINGE: There's no G.

YEBSLEY: What the fuck does it mean!!

SINGE: Is this that pretty psychologist you had a crush on?

YEBSLEY: Dunno.

SINGE: (*Reading.*) 'Alan was resistant, even aggressive at first to the 16 PF personality questionnaire but in the weeks following took a keen interest in Psychology as an academic subject, asking me many questions, and was always polite and helpful.' Yup. It's her.

YEBSLEY: She fancied me!

SINGE: Did she fucking 'eckers like!

YEBSLEY: She was crazy about me. I'd put money on it.

SINGE: Ten P. (*Reading.*) 'Alan has lost contact with reality, and has poor insight, particularly in relation to normal social functioning.'

YEBSLEY: (*To SINGE.*) What does that mean?

CHRISTOPHER: It means you owe him ten pence.

SINGE: (*Reading.*) 'Alan's sense of self is disorganised and he has an immature and gullible personality. Suicidal thoughts may –

(*YEBSLEY snatches the file back.*)

YEBSLEY: Gimme that.

SINGE: Kill yersen?! Never. Not you Yebs, eh? What's she say about you and suicide?

CHRISTOPHER: He might not want to read it out.

(*YEBSLEY reads.*)

SINGE: Each others secrets is the only fucking entertainment we get.

YEBSLEY: (*Reading.*) Alan should be placed on the 'in danger' register and his Largactyl programme should be managed so that lapses into hypomania are avoided. Additionally, he has become socially dependent on prisoner 336 –

SINGE: – that's me!

YEBSLEY: – whose low IQ –

SINGE: – I had flu the day I took them tests.

YEBSLEY: – and expedient approach to morality offers Alan nothing other than further value confusion.'

SINGE: Oh I see, everything's my fault. Fucking hell! I can get this at home!

YEBSLEY: There is, however, no suggestion of psychosis –

SINGE: – that's good news.

YEBSLEY: '– but he can become defensive, and aggressive when challenged' – fucking bollocks! That's not fucking true!

'He is often hyperactive and and occasionally hypomanic. Without largactyl, his revolutionary rhetoric matched with a volatile and rootless personality make Alan, in my judgement, a continuing threat to society.' Hence N.T.B.R.

SINGE: Not To...B...bother ringing. No.

CHRISTOPHER: Never…Try…Buggering…Racoons.

YEBSLEY: I'm not fucking suicidal!

(*YEBSLEY rips a tile off the roof and chucks it down. Off there is violent shouting of a mob and a cheer. They all go over and have a look at what is going on. This means they have to go down stage stage left and look leftwards.*)

SINGE: Eh up! The screws are mekking a charge.

YEBSLEY: Fuck off Slipper! You c –

SINGE: (*Putting a hand over his mouth.*) Not on my roof. Swearing!

CHRISTOPHER: Amazing. The prison officers have got no equipment at all. Builders hats, and dustbin lids.

SINGE: When this riot's ovver they'll do you all one by one. Kick the fucking shit out of yer. And none of yer'll have a single mark on yer faces.

(*Sounds of skirmish.*)

YEBSLEY: That didn't last long.

SINGE: Great. Back to stalemate.

CHRISTOPHER: How did this all start?

SINGE: Him.

CHRISTOPHER: What the complaint? Conditions?

SINGE: No way. Yer gerr a beautiful, big cell, your own cell. Money, yer can earn money, can't do that nowhere else. Yer can decorate yer cell. Pets, books, he's gorr his guitar.

YEBSLEY: Bass.

SINGE: First time in his life he's had his own room. Hey! I've done time in Winson Green and Armley, kaw! You wanna try gerrin to sleep when the bloke above yer's fucking the mattress.

YEBSLEY: Hull's Britain's Alcatraz innit.

CHRISTOPHER: They had to close Alcatraz.

SINGE: (*With a look to YEBSLEY.*) Too many no hopers.

YEBSLEY: I'm not a no hoper. I'm a political prisoner.

(*SINGE snorts with derision.*)

Fucking am Singe.

CHRISTOPHER: Che Guevara?

YEBSLEY: Yeah? So?

CHRISTOPHER: What do you know about Che Guevara?

YEBSLEY: Cuban.

CHRISTOPHER: Argentinian.

YEBSLEY: Yeah, yeah I know but he ended up in Cuba didn't he.

CHRISTOPHER: Do you know what he did in Cuba?

YEBSLEY: Who are you? What the fuck is this?!

CHRISTOPHER: I'm sorry.

SINGE: What did he do in Cuba?

(*YEBSLEY goes up stage to behind the chimney.*)

CHRISTOPHER: He organised firing squads. Labour camps.

SINGE: I thought he was, like, er…you know –

CHRISTOPHER: Today those camps are full of Castro's enemies – homosexuals, writers, dissidents, escapees.

SINGE: Did you know that Yebs?

YEBSLEY: I've gone fucking deaf, an't I.

CHRISTOPHER: Guevara died in Bolivia leading a guerilla war in which he'd failed to recruit one single Bolivian peasant. His ideology was hate, not love.

YEBSLEY: Fuck off.

CHRISTOPHER: 'Unbending hatred for the enemy, which pushes a human being beyond his natural limitations, making him into an effective, violent, selective and cold blooded killing machine.'

SINGE: Che Guevara said that?

YEBSLEY: You got that in your head?

CHRISTOPHER: I have a good memory.

YEBSLEY: Yeah, well when the revolution comes, proper like, there's gonna have to be some bastards up against the wall.

CHRISTOPHER: And you would do the shooting would you?

YEBSLEY: If they were rich.

CHRISTOPHER: The death penalty? Alright with you?

YEBSLEY: Yeah.

SINGE: Got a fully functioning topping shop in here you know. Here, just there, this side of D wing.

YEBSLEY: Last person hung in Hull was a woman.

SINGE: Ethel Majors. Murdered her husband.

CHRISTOPHER: Why did she kill him?

YEBSLEY: He come from Grimsby.

SINGE: If you marry someone from Grimsby it's only a matter of time before you start thinking about murder.

YEBSLEY: Her ghost still walks the twos on B wing.

SINGE: What's the point of keeping someone like Mad Hatchet Jack alive?

YEBSLEY: Or nonces. It's a waste of taxpayers' money.

SINGE: 'kinnel! You! Taxpayer? The day my arse an't gorr an hole!

YEBSLEY: Jack's a fucking head case. He's killed at least three people.

CHRISTOPHER: If you had the chance, would you kill him?

YEBSLEY: Yeah. I'd be doing it for the people an'all. Psychopathic murderers like Mad Hatchet Jack are an enemy to the working classes just as much as yer capitalist is.

CHRISTOPHER: He has a soul.

YEBSLEY: Are you a fucking liberal?

CHRISTOPHER: If it is considered that killing is wrong, then killing someone for having killed must also be wrong.

SINGE: He's a fucking liberal. Or religious. You religious?

CHRISTOPHER: I thought everyone found God in prison.

SINGE: He's not in here pal. Try Armley. I do have a soft spot for Jesus Christ though. Tried to model me life on his in a small way.

CHRISTOPHER: I didn't know he was a bank robber. What would it take for you to believe in God?

SINGE: A miracle.

YEBSLEY: Johnny Cash sings 'Bridge Over Troubled Water'.

SINGE: With the Angel Gabriel on backing vocals. But that in't never gonna happen is it.

(*To black.*)

SCENE THREE

(*Scene change music. 'Smash it Up Part II' by The Damned. Lunchtime. It has clouded over. YEBSLEY has his bass guitar and battery powered amp on the roof. He's playing 'Smoke on the Water' Deep Purple. It's slow, ponderous and dull. KATH is unimpressed and eats her sandwich as she listens.*)

KATH: That's shit.

YEBSLEY: It's Deep Purple.

CHRISTOPHER: He's not that bad.

YEBSLEY: What bands do you like then?

KATH: New York Dolls?

YEBSLEY: Never head of them. Have you got any gigs coming up yourself?

KATH: Yeah. Duke of Cumberland, Halfway, and we gorr a gig supporting The Rats at Dewsbury Town Hall.

YEBSLEY: Dewsbury? Kaw!

KATH: It's not LA Yebsley. It's Dewsbury.

CHRISTOPHER: D.

YEBSLEY: Eh?

CHRISTOPHER: Los Angeles. LA Dewsbury. D.

YEBSLEY: I know Trevor Bolder's grandmother. (*Beat.*) She taught Mick Ronson how to play piano.

KATH: Did she teach you?

YEBSLEY: No. I just know her.

KATH: Is it your bass?

YEBSLEY: Yeah.

(*To KATH.*) What's the name of your band?

KATH: (*With distaste.*) Heliotrope Convention.

YEBSLEY: What's it mean?

KATH: Dunno.

CHRISTOPHER: It means a big public meeting of purple flowers in a conference centre.

YEBSLEY: Quite like it.

KATH: It's hippy shit. I'm gonna start me own band. The Pilots.

YEBSLEY: (*Not enthusiastic.*) Not bad. Worr about The Night Shift; or The Gutter Snipes.

SINGE: The Bank Robbers.

YEBSLEY: The Robbers.

CHRISTOPHER: The Bank. The The.

YEBSLEY: You're fucking weird.

KATH: See you Yebsley. I only come home for me lunch. Tarra.

YEBSLEY: See yer!

(*CHRISTOPHER stands.*)

CHRISTOPHER: Is there such a thing as a lunch break in a riot? What do we do for food?

SINGE: Go back to the Centre, over the barrier, head up towards B wing and the kitchens are there opposite the classrooms. Bring us up summat if there's owt going. (*CHRISTOPHER leaves.*)

YEBSLEY: Who the fuck does he think he is?

SINGE: Nice lad. Educated. Are yer gonna tek that stupid T shirt off then? Walking about with a fucking fascist mass murderer on yer chest.

YEBSLEY: No.

(*Silence. Might help if YEBSLEY is down stage of SINGE and during the next there is no eye contact.*)

SINGE: Nance? Nancy!?

YEBSLEY: Yeah.

SINGE: Did Janice go to school?

YEBSLEY: Yeah.

SINGE: She still gorra temperature?

YEBSLEY: No.

SINGE: It's cleared up has it?

YEBSLEY: Yeah.

SINGE: Grand. Poor bain. What was it?

(*Beat.*)

What was it Nance?

YEBSLEY: Mumps.

SINGE: Mumps! Kaw! I thought she'd had mumps. Fucking hell she has mumps every couple of month.

YEBSLEY: When yer gonna fix that kitchen cupboard of mine?

SINGE: I can't fix it without the right bit. Don't wanna bodge it. I'll do it this afti.

YEBSLEY: Yer said that last week.

SINGE: Aye, well the sun come out dint it. We could go to With again today if yer want?

YEBSLEY: Me mother's coming round.

SINGE: Oh bugger! She come round last week.

YEBSLEY: She's me fucking mother!

(*Silence. YEBSLEY stands and walks away effectively ending the exchange.*)

SINGE: Eh! Yebsley, don't fuck off. Ta. Enjoyed that. Now, empty yer pockets?

YEBSLEY: You what?

SINGE: Empty yer pockets. I've gorra raise fifty quid.

(*YEBSLEY takes some coins out of his pockets. Lots of ten pence pieces.*)

YEBSLEY: One pound twennie.

(*He hands it over to* SINGE. SINGE *counts it and then chucks the coins in the potty.*)

Oh I gerr it. That's brilliant that is.

SINGE: Thank you.

YEBSLEY: I feel fucking weird.

SINGE: What's that all about then?

YEBSLEY: Coming off me Largactil. Feel like shit.

(*Sound of smashing of tiles and shouting off.*)

JACK: (*Off.*) You're facking nofin! You facking screws. One on one – you're facking nofin!

SINGE: Oh fuck! Quick! It's Jack!

(*SINGE and YEBSLEY hide in the broom cupboard. The pets are left downstage.*)

JACK: (*Off.*) I'm gonna kill myself a screw every facking day!

(*Enter MAD HATCHET JACK. He is naked from the waist up. He is drunk, and carrying a lemonade bottle in which there is one shot of hooch left. He also carries a three foot length of two by two with the head of a pair of scissors fashioned on to one end to make a spear. He looks around the roof. He is obviously psychologically different, more wired, from the first time we met him.*)

Singe! I know you're hiding up here you facking worm, you, you, facking piece of...facking worm shit. Yeah, are a facking worm shit collector, you are, Singe, you're a facking...toy train...you are a facking...broken train...a broken facking toy train...well you will be in a minute... you'll be a facking broken toy train you will be and you're dad can't mend it not even with facking glue and all his facking engineering shit. Hide and facking seek is it?!... alright I'm counting...I'll count to twenty... I got me eyes shut.

(*He closes his eyes and counts.*)

One elephant, two elephants, three elephants, f f f f f f
facking four elephants, f f f f f f facking five elephants,
six facking big facking elephants, seven elephants, eight
facking elephants, nine facking elephants, ten facking
elefackingphants, eleven facking big hairsy arsed facking
elephants, you wunt wanna go near 'em, seen the size
of those facking bastards, fack me there's eleven of 'em,
twelve! Facking hell, f f f f f facking firteen elephants, f f f
f facking fourteen elephants, facking hell where did they
all facking come from, f f f f f facking fifteen elephants, all
of them related to each other, incest, facking each other,
all of them, sixteen disgusting facking smelly elephants,
seventeen of the bastards, eighteen of them all pissing in
the lake and drinking their own piss, eighteen elephants,
facking elephant shit everywhere, nineteen elephants and
one of them's got a little bird on it's head, it can't facking
see the bird, but it can feel it, it's driving it facking mad
with its pecking, pecking, pecking, like a facking itch,
and when he facking catches the bird he's gonna do a big
facking poo on it's head, twenty elephants. Coming ready
or not!

(*JACK walks directly to the broom cupboard and starts kicking the
steel door. He forces it open (it opens outwards) and YEBSLEY
runs out, JACK turns as if to go for YEBS, and then SINGE tries
to run out but JACK pins him to the wall of the broom cupboard
using the spear. This is achieved without any physical contact.*)

SINGE: No! Please Jack!

JACK: I'm gonna facking kill you now!

SINGE: Can't you wait while end of the day. I'll have your
money then.

JACK: 'There is deaf in the pot'; Kings, chapter f f f f f facking
four, verse f f f f f facking forty. There is deaf in the pot!
(*JACK wields the spear as if to stab SINGE through the neck. Enter
CHRISTOPHER with bread and a tin of salmon.*)

CHRISTOPHER: 'But he said, then bring meal.'
(*CHRISTOPHER shows he's brought food.*)
'And he cast it into the pot. And he said, pour out for the
people, that they may eat. And there was no harm in the

pot.' Kings, chapter four, verse forty-one. Shall we eat.
Bread. Fish paste. What I don't have is a tin opener. What's
that?

JACK: A spear, a facking spear, my facking spear!

CHRISTOPHER: What's it for?

JACK: Killing and facking maiming!

CHRISTOPHER: If we take the end bit off, maybe we can use
it for opening the tin. You must be Jack. I've heard a lot
about you. None of it good.

JACK: What, you what, you facking what?

CHRISTOPHER: That's only one half of the scissors. What did
you do with the other half?

(*JACK goes into his pocket and gives CHRISTOPHER the other half
of the scissors. SINGE moves away down stage right.*)

CHRISTOPHER: Sit down. When did you last sleep?

JACK: I haven't slept f f f f f in two days.

CHRISTOPHER: Yeah, you look terrible. Do you want –

JACK: (*Snatching.*) Give me that facking bread.

(*CHRISTOPHER gives him some bread. JACK sits and tears at
the bread. JACK picks the gold fish out of the bowl and eats it.
CHRISTOPHER uses the scissors to open the tin.*)

CHRISTOPHER: You're a religious man then Jack?

JACK: 'I have seen God f f f f f –'

CHRISTOPHER: – 'face to face and my life is preserved.'
Genesis thirty-two / thirty.

JACK: Yeah.

CHRISTOPHER: So have I! Aren't we lucky?

(*JACK drinks. A whole half bottle of hooch and during the next
shows signs of falling asleep.*)

JACK: Where's my money Singe?

SINGE: I'll have it by the end of the day. I'm the only bookie
with a working telly.

JACK: F f f f f

SINGE: – fifty –

JACK: – quid's a lot of facking money!

SINGE: The Irish boys'll be betting with me this afternoon.
Haydock Park.

JACK: (*Sleepy.*) They smashed my gym up.

CHRISTOPHER: You're worn out Jack. You must've been charging around for a couple of days now. Relax.

JACK: My facking gym, them facking Irish arseholes, they facked my facking gym, slung the weights out the windows, all my weights.

SINGE: That's yer program in a morning in't it. Three hours in the gym.

JACK: I can't do my facking weights now, f f f f f facking free hours a day, in the gym, my life, my life, my facking life.

CHRISTOPHER: (*Offered to JACK.*) Singe. Fish paste sandwich?

SINGE: Yeah, ta.

(*SINGE approaches, takes a sandwich and sits on the roof and eats.*)

CHRISTOPHER: Yebsley?

YEBSLEY: I'm vegetarian.

SINGE: It's onny tinned.

YEBSLEY: I'll have some bread.

(*CHRISTOPHER gives YEBSLEY some bread. They all eat. Enter DECLAN.*)

DECLAN: (*Seeing JACK.*) Ah fuck!

SINGE: Declan! It's right in't it that your lads are gonna bet with me, this afti, Haydock.

DECLAN: Aye, that's the truth, aye. We don't have a telly yer see Jack. Jack?

(*JACK has fallen asleep.*)

CHRISTOPHER: (*To DECLAN.*) Here, some bread.

DECLAN: (*Fearful all the time of JACK. Takes bread.*) Thank yers. Lovely.

Look at that. Like a fucking baby.

YEBSLEY: What about the break out?

DECLAN: Tonight, maybe. At the present time the lads are all amusing themselves drilling a hole through the gymnasium floor into the Governor's office. The plan is to put a gas pipe down there and pump in some of that gas, and then blow the fucking office to God and the Devil. We're the IRA remember, a day without a big fucking bang is a day wasted.

CHRISTOPHER: (*To YEBSLEY.*) Now's your chance.

YEBSLEY: What?

CHRISTOPHER: You can kill him. Jack. The death penalty.
Execute him. You could spear him or just lift the chair and
tip him over the edge.
(*CHRISTOPHER hands YEBSLEY the scissors. YEBSLEY
approaches JACK.*)

SINGE: Yebs!

DECLAN: Eh, young fellah. What's going off here!?

YEBSLEY: I'm gonna kill him.

SINGE: No you're not. You know the rules of this roof!

CHRISTOPHER: Che Guevara wouldn't hesitate. Che would do
it. Or rather he'd get someone else to do it.

YEBSLEY: Fuck off.

CHRISTOPHER: Che could do it because he believed in hate.

YEBSLEY: Who the fuck are you?

CHRISTOPHER: You can't do it can you?

DECLAN: It's not a bad idea. It is an opportunity knocking.
Yer could tip the big lump outa his chair over the side and
they'll say he just fell off the fucking roof.
(*YEBSLEY puts the scissors down and goes to behind the chair,
and takes hold of it.*)

DECLAN: Just tip him over. Like a fucking wheelbarrow. In one
swift manoeuver.
(*YEBSLEY tests to see how easy it would be, and thinks.*)

CHRISTOPHER: Don't think about it. Do it. Your credo is hate
remember.

SINGE: Forget the whole thing will yer Yebs!
(*SINGE grabs YEBSLEY. YEBSLEY throws SINGE off.*)

YEBSLEY: I'm gonna fucking do it.

SINGE: (*To CHRISTOPHER.*) You leave our Yebsley alone. He's
not a bad kid. He's a bit you know.

YEBSLEY: What?

SINGE: Easily led.

YEBSLEY: Fuck off.

SINGE: Well you are.
(*YEBSLEY starts to tilt the chair and JACK towards the edge like
tipping a load out of a wheelbarrow.*)

SINGE: Stop it Yebs! Are you mad?

YEBSLEY: Yeah! According to my file I am fucking mad, yeah.

(*YEBSLEY tries again, pushing the chair nearer the edge. He looks set to push him over the edge.*)

I can't do it. I can't do it.

(*YEBSLEY stops himself. Has a bit of a cry. Goes upstage and sits on his own.*)

SINGE: Let's lock him up. Stick him in that broom cupboard. He'll never get out of there, they've concreted the floor and that's a steel door.

CHRISTOPHER: Good idea.

SINGE: Don't touch him. Just carry the whole chair in there.

(*They carry JACK into the broom cupboard.*)

DECLAN: What d'yer think of this Yebsley? Your butty Singe here has turned us all into screws.

(*To CHRISTOPHER.*) And you, young fellah. What was all that about. If you want the fucking headcase killed, yer shoulda killed him yourself.

SINGE: Yebs! Giss them keys again.

(*YEBSLEY complies and JACK is locked into the cupboard with the padlock.*)

CHRISTOPHER: I'm against the death penalty.

DECLAN: Aye, I'd be against the death penalty if I'd killed me fucking father. How long do the English give nowadays for patricide?

CHRISTOPHER: Life.

DECLAN: You're lucky. Coulda bin a lot longer. The trick is not to get too gloomy about it son. If it helps, in my experience, the first few minutes are the worst. Now I know this sounds a bit Irish but there is something longer than life, and that's a thing called Never to be Released. N.T.B.R.

(*YEBSLEY stands and approaches.*)

(*Beat.*) It's all gone quiet. I can hear the wind whistling in me fucking ears. What have I said?

SINGE: Never to be released. N. T. B. R.

DECLAN: It's a terrible gloomy acronym.

YEBSLEY: (*Desperate.*) Never to be released. Singe?

SINGE: It's alright son. It's just Dex here, having a bit of a laugh.

(*During the next YEBSLEY flips and rips slates and coping stones off the roof and starts slinging them off the roof at the police and prison officers gathered beyond the walls.*)

YEBSLEY: Come on then you fucking bastards! Come on! Fuck you! Here! You want some?! Catch that! Never to be Released!! I'll fucking show yer. NEVER TO BE RELEASED!! Suicidal!! Fucking Suicidal!! I'll show you how fucking suicidal I am. Is this mad enough for you!? Yer want madder than this do you?!

SINGE: Calm down Yebsley! For fuck's sake.

CHRISTOPHER: Come away from the edge Yebsley.

YEBSLEY: Fuck off you. Who are you? Eh. You've been sent in an't yer. Yer a prison officer, eh. A sleeper. A plant.

CHRISTOPHER: No.

YEBSLEY: We know nothing about you? Who the fuck are yer!?

CHRISTOPHER: I'm not important. I just want you to come away from the edge.

YEBSLEY: Stop telling me what to fucking do! Who are you? My fucking dad?! Are you my fucking dad!?

CHRISTOPHER: No. I'm a good friend.

YEBSLEY: I don't have good friends, I'm gullible, I have suicidal tendencies. Don't come any nearer! I'll take you with me. I fucking would. Never to be released. Never! Do you know what 'never' means. It means fucking never!

CHRISTOPHER: Come away from the edge Yebsley.

YEBSLEY: No. I'm gonna jump.

(*He turns as if to jump.*)

KATH: Yebsley!

YEBSLEY: What?

(*YEBSLEY turns and looks up to the flats.*)

KATH: I've just had a phone call!

YEBSLEY: What!

KATH: We've sacked the bassist!

YEBSLEY: Yer what?!
KATH: We need a new bassist!
    (*To black.*)
    (*Interval.*)

Act Two

SCENE ONE

(*Lights down. The Ramones play loud. 'Blitzkrieg Bop'. As the lights come up the sound of the song is sourced from KATH's flat. Thursday September 2 1976. The roof. Mid-day. Not sunny and consequently somewhat colder. SINGE is making cheese sandwiches using processed cheese, a catering size tub of margarine, and a packet of Jacobs Cream Crackers. A full box of Mars bars sits on a chair. He is trying to listen to a transistor radio – the BBC news, Radio 4. YEBSLEY is standing down stage looking up at KATH's, and rolling a joint. CHRISTOPHER is upstage using the binoculars to view Hull. 'Blitzkrieg Bop' finishes abruptly and the French windows are closed.*)

YEBSLEY: She's shut her door.

SINGE: Bit parky innit.

(*YEBSLEY sits and lights the joint.*)

I'm norr 'aving you doing drugs on my roof.

YEBSLEY: It's onny a joint.

(*YEBSLEY lights it and takes a long slow toke, and takes it way back. SINGE reads an old Hull Daily Mail.*)

CHRISTOPHER: What are those strange houses there? Those funny little houses with –

SINGE: – You mean them luxury detached bungalows set in their own grounds. Garden at the front. Garden at the back. Gardens all round. Piped in television.

YEBSLEY: Prefabs.

SINGE: Hopewell Road. Built to last ten years – thirty year ago. What no-one knew about prefabs is that they breed. In the night. They're ambisextuous.

YEBSLEY: What's that mean?

SINGE: They're like cucumbers. They can fuck themselves. You stick up a run of five prefabs on a bit of waste land, and in the morning, there'll be six of them. Morning after that there'll be seven.

YEBSLEY: Yer wun't catch me living in a prefab.

SINGE: Hull folk are terrible prejudiced against prefab dwellers. We think they're aliens from outer space.

CHRISTOPHER: Why do you think that?

YEBSLEY/SINGE: Cos they are.

YEBSLEY: They're really fucking weird.

SINGE: They don't age, yer see. They come from a planet where at birth you're already fifty-six years old and like gardening.

CHRISTOPHER: Emergency housing wasn't it? After the war?

SINGE: We'd never heard of 'urban redevelopment' in Hull so we gorr a foreign company in to do it for us. The Luftwaffe. I blame Herman Goering for all my career choices. When I grew up there was a bomb site every ten yards and yer could always find summat to snaffle and sell on.

(*CHRISTOPHER goes up on to the broken roof upstage right.*)

YEBSLEY: Yer gorr enough for Jack?

SINGE: Twenty quid short.

(*SINGE reads the Daily Mail.*)

There's a sale at Comet?

(*Beat.*) Nance! I said, there's a sale at Comet.

YEBSLEY: Yeah?

SINGE: Do you wanna go?

YEBSLEY: No.

SINGE: Oh go on love. We don't have to buy owt. We could just have a look around. Gerr us out the house.

YEBSLEY: I'm gonna watch the Grand Prix on telly.

SINGE: You don't like motor racing.

YEBSLEY: It's grown on me.

SINGE: Nice electric cooker here.

YEBSLEY: We're on gas.

SINGE: Are we?

YEBSLEY: Shows how much cooking you do.

SINGE: What is it? North Sea Gas?

YEBSLEY: How the fuck would I know.

SINGE: Oh don't put your face on love. Our David wants to go to the baths.

YEBSLEY: What? East Hull baths?

SINGE: Yeah.

YEBSLEY: I'm not having that.

SINGE: Why not?

YEBSLEY: He can't swim. He can go when he learns how to swim.

SINGE: How's he gonna learn if you don't let him go?

YEBSLEY: Stop going on at me.

SINGE: I'm not having a go at you. But you've got your face on for some reason.

YEBSLEY: I'm up to here with you! 'Slams door.'

SINGE: I'm sorry Nance. (*Beat.*) I said I'm sorry Nance.

YEBSLEY: I've gone. I went out the house. Din't you hear me – I said 'slams door'.

SINGE: She wouldn't do that. She's not like that.

YEBSLEY: Aye, well, she just has.

(*Silence. Takes a drag on the joint. Sounds of riot.*)

SINGE: Eh, up. Here we go!

YEBSLEY: How long can we go on for? You know before they call the army in.

SINGE: One more day, mebbe two. The fun's ovver now. We got no toilets.

YEBSLEY: Plenty of food.

SINGE: Not proper food. Not hot, cooked food.

YEBSLEY: I think they'll storm us today.

SINGE: What's the point? They've got us right where they want us. Up shit creek with a severe shortage of paddles. This is a siege. We can't win. And your lot, the subversives, and the Irish are gonna get the shit kicked out of you summat fucking terrible. Oh yeah, the screws'll have their fun. If I lose my remission cos of this I might even join in.

YEBSLEY: They'll really do me won't they.

SINGE: Yer did start it. Not the brightest thing yer've ever done. Whacking the wing governor over the head with an hardback copy of Learn Yersen Sociology weren't the brightest thing yer've ever done.

YEBSLEY: Still got a coupla tabs of acid. How about if we give Jack one for a laugh?

SINGE: Fuck off, he's mad enough as it is.

YEBSLEY: Giss one of them crackers. Ha, ha! Stick a coupla tabs in there, he'll never notice.

(*YEBSLEY takes a cracker and opens it and slots in a tab of acid under the cheese. He then goes and knocks on the broom cupboard door. SINGE drags him away.*)

SINGE: 'kinnel! Are yer mad?! Let the fucking animal sleep.

YEBSLEY: Just a bit of a laugh. I'll put it down here. Alright.

(*YEBSLEY puts the cracker down.*)

SINGE: I can hear him breathing. With a bit of luck this'll all be ovver afore he wakes up.

CHRISTOPHER: What are you going to do after prison Singe? You're out in two months –

SINGE: Be a miracle now, that.

YEBSLEY: He's got two hundred thousand pounds buried somewhere.

SINGE: Tek no notice son. I'm a chippy now. Joiner.

CHRISTOPHER: I saw the workshops. Quite a serious operation.

SINGE: It's all mechanised that. Purr a log in one end, press a button, and a coffee table comes out t'other.

YEBSLEY: He's a craftsman.

SINGE: Onny proper schooling I've ever had. Inside.

YEBSLEY: They learned him to read.

SINGE: Eh! That's enough.

CHRISTOPHER: I'm quite good with wood.

SINGE: You?

CHRISTOPHER: I can put a set of shelves up. My step father was a chippy.

SINGE: I'll miss breaking and entering though. The camaraderie, the job satisfaction, yer get to see how people live. Kaw! The state of some people's houses. They should be ashamed of themselves.

(*KATH comes out onto the balcony. SINGE fiddles with the radio to get the news.*)

KATH: Hiya Yebs!

YEBSLEY: Hiya. Y'alright?!

KATH: Yeah. Not bad.

YEBSLEY: Not at college today.

KATH: Twagged off an't I.

YEBSLEY: Yeah?

KATH: Yeah.

YEBSLEY: Who was that you was playing earlier on?

KATH: Did yer like it?

YEBSLEY: It were fucking brilliant.

KATH: I'll play it again shall I.

YEBSLEY: Yeah.

> (*KATH goes in. SINGE fiddles with the radio, trying to find the news. He is distracted by CHRISTOPHER.*)

CHRISTOPHER: Is it easy to break into a house?

SINGE: Does Dolly Parton sleep on her back? It's like shooting fish in a barrel. I'd go round Kirkella of an evening, eight/ nine o'clock, dark but not night time. People are stupid. They go out for the night but leave a light on in the hall

CHRISTOPHER: – to make you think there's someone in.

SINGE: Aye. That light tells you one of two things. Either, they've gone out for the night, OR they've decided to spend all night sitting in the hall.

> (*'Blitzkrieg Bop' plays. KATH comes out on to the balcony.*)
> Oi! Turn that racket off I'm trying to get the twelve o'clock news!

KATH: D'yer think you can play bass like that?

SINGE: I can play bass like that.

KATH: It's gonna purr an end to all that, like, introspective, middle class, capitalist, like, you know, guitar solos. Like Eric Clapton and that.

CHRISTOPHER: I like Eric Clapton.

YEBSLEY: Come on then! Who is it?

KATH: The Ramones.

YEBSLEY: (*With awe.*) The Ramones.

KATH: They're Punk.

YEBSLEY: Punk eh?

CHRISTOPHER: (*In mock awe.*) The Ramones! The New Messiahs.

KATH: Yer what? Say that again.

CHRISTOPHER: I was being ironic.

KATH: Where did you get that from? The New Messiahs.

YEBSLEY: D'yer mek that up?

CHRISTOPHER: Hey! Take it, it's yours.

KATH: The New Messiahs. Great name for a band eh?

SINGE: (*With the radio to his ear.*) Eh, shutup. Turn the Remains off!

(*KATH closes the French window.*)

RADIO FX: A massive earthquake in Northern China centred on the industrial city of Tangshan has killed six hundred thousand. Reports from travellers and western journalists suggest that the quake happened in late July but news of it has been suppressed by the Chinese authorities. This is the worst death toll for an earthquake in recent times. A hosepipe ban in Matlock –

(*SINGE turns the radio off.*)

SINGE: 'Kinnel! Six hundred thousand dead.

KATH: Oh God, that's terrible.

SINGE: Six hundred thousand dead. 'Kinnel!

KATH: There can't be a God if he lets stuff like that happen.

CHRISTOPHER: Alternatively…let's hope there is a God. Then they'll all be in heaven.

SINGE: Eh?

CHRISTOPHER: This earthquake is only a tragedy if there is no heaven, if there is no God, and Jesus Christ was a fake. It's a problem of knowledge, Epistemology.

SINGE: He pissed a lot of people off. That's why they crucified him. What I'd like to know is how you knew about this earthquake yesterday? Christopher. Young fellah me lad…

CHRISTOPHER: It's only yesterday.

SINGE: This is the fost news of it. Breaking news. You're in prison and yer've got better contacts than the BBC?

(*CHRISTOPHER walks away from YEBSLEY and looks out on to the street below.*)

CHRISTOPHER: (*Shouted to a kid.*) D'yer wanna Mars bar!?

SINGE: Eh!? You're avoiding the question.

YEBSLEY: You're a plant aren't you. A fucking plant. MI5!

CHRISTOPHER: What?!

SINGE: Leave him be.

(*CHRISTOPHER throws the kid a Mars bar.*)

Yer've done it now.

CHRISTOPHER: Done what?

SINGE: This is Hull mate, yer don't chuck a kid a Mars bar
and gerr away with it. In thirty seconds time there'll be a
thousand kids down there shouting for Mars bars.

KATH: Yer on fire. Did yer know that?

(*They all look across to C wing.*)

SINGE: Oh fuck.

YEBSLEY: That's C wing.

(*A faint cry of a baby is heard.*)

SINGE: That'll be Dex's lot. Fucking nutters.

KATH: I'd better be going.

YEBSLEY: Play us some more Ramones Kath, eh!

(*Baby cries.*)

KATH: I'm busy. Later.

YEBSLEY: Yeah. See yer Kath. Have a nice day.

SINGE: Tarra love.

(*KATH goes in and closes up her flat.*)
They're an amazing civilising influence aren't they.
Women. In all my puff I don't think I would ever expect
you, Yebsley, to say to anyone 'have a nice day'.

(*SINGE and CHRISTOPHER are both watching YEBSLEY.*)

CHRISTOPHER: She's crazy about yer.

YEBSLEY: Yer think so?

SINGE: The way she lights a ciggy.

CHRISTOPHER: All the nose blowing.

SINGE: The way she casually ses 'tarra' and closes the door as
if you mean nowt to her at all.

YEBSLEY: Yeah?

SINGE: Definitely.

CHRISTOPHER: Concur.

YEBSLEY: I heard a bain crying. Did you?

SINGE: Aye. Behave yersen from now on and yer might gerr
a coupla year knocked off. And who knows what, you
know…

CHRISTOPHER: I'll cut your hair for you if yer like. Punks have
short hair.

SINGE: She dun't like yer hair long.

YEBSLEY: Can you cut hair?

CHRISTOPHER: Can't be that difficult can it. I'll go and find some scissors.

(*The sound of a group of children in the street shouting up. 'Giss some sweets mister!'*)

SINGE: Told yer. We won't get no peace all day now.

CHRISTOPHER: Ha! I don't believe it. There's hundreds of them!

(*CHRISTOPHER exits.*)

YEBSLEY: There's summat fucking weird about him.

SINGE: I like him.

(*A baby cries, really cries rather loudly. It's coming from KATH's flat. YEBSLEY stands and goes downstage to listen. SINGE follows a yard or two behind, focussed on YEBSLEY and not the baby.*)

YEBSLEY: She's gorra fucking baby!

End of Act Two Scene One

SCENE TWO

(*Judy is a Punk' plays. Lights up. It's colder. SINGE is wrapped in a blanket. SINGE is looking East down the river towards Paull with the binoculars. YEBSLEY is in a chair. He has just had his hair cut by CHRISTOPHER, who stands behind him holding scissors, and occasionally trimming the odd bit. There is a pile of hair on the floor.*)

YEBSLEY: Thing is, yer see, I'm black, yeah? I'm a Negro.

CHRISTOPHER: You don't look like a black man to me Yebsley.

SINGE: I'm not saying owt.

YEBSLEY: I don't look black, but I am. Genetically innit. One of my ancestors way back when, had it off with with someone from the Ivory Coast.

SINGE: I've always said that was a long way to go just for a fuck. Furthest I've ever had to travel to service me needs was North Ferriby.

YEBSLEY: Slave days wannit. He had this thing with this African woman and she got pregnant, and the bain was infected with Sickle Cell Anemia trait, that's what they call it, another name is Haemoglobin SS, but I don't like to use that name cos of the SS bit, and then that kid, who was a boy, slept with a girl who was also had Sickle Cell trait and they had a kid who was born with full Sickle Cell Anaemia,

like me. Don't worry, you can't catch it off me, but I'll give
it to my kids if I have any, but it's not my fault is it, they
can't blame me, nothing I can do about it.

CHRISTOPHER: (*Fiddling with his hair.*) Do you want some more
off the sides?

YEBSLEY: So I connect, like, totally with what it means to be
black, and oppressed, and with the Panthers yeah, and the
Nation of Islam, and Malcolm X and all that.

CHRISTOPHER: And you're a Muslim?

YEBSLEY: Yeah, I'm like, total, er…a follower of Muhammad.

CHRISTOPHER: And Che Guevara. And Malcolm X.

YEBSLEY: Yeah.

CHRISTOPHER: What do you know about Muhammad?

SINGE: Eh up, here we go!

YEBSLEY: What about Muhammad?!

CHRISTOPHER: Peace be upon him. Where was he born?

YEBSLEY: You're winding me up aren't yer! Singe!?

SINGE: Leave him be son.

CHRISTOPHER: I'm just trying to get you to question your
heroes.

YEBSLEY: Muhammad –

CHRISTOPHER: – peace be upon him –

(*YEBSLEY squares up to him, serious.*)

YEBSLEY: – He was a prophet, wan't he, chosen by God,
and a –

CHRISTOPHER: – a warrior?

YEBSLEY: Yeah, actually, yeah.

SINGE: – Alright, alright, alright! Enough! What the fuck
is going on here! This is the roof of Hull prison not the
Oxford debating society. Right, knock it on the head.
(*To YEBSLEY.*) You, say 'thank you', for the haircut.

YEBSLEY: Ta.

SINGE: And you. Just shut the fuck up.

CHRISTOPHER: OK. I'm hungry. What have we got?

YEBSLEY: Do you want a cracker? Cheese.

CHRISTOPHER: Yes please.

(*YEBSLEY takes the cracker out of his pocket and gives it to
CHRISTOPHER who eats it quickly.*)

YEBSLEY: Alright? Good yeah?

CHRISTOPHER: It's a cracker with cheese. I'm not going to write a review.

YEBSLEY: You're fucking weird.

(*Enter DECLAN tentatively, warily. During the next he approaches JACK's prison.*)

DECLAN: Have yer got that mad beast locked up there?

SINGE: Aye.

YEBSLEY: Is there gonna be a break out? Eh!? Count us in, yeah?!

DECLAN: There is a plan in formation, and we'll let yous know about it when it's good and ready.

YEBSLEY: He's asleep.

(*YEBSLEY bangs on the door.*)

SINGE: Don't fucking wake him!

YEBSLEY: I think we should starve the bastard to death.

CHRISTOPHER: I thought we could do some extreme medical experiments on him, you know like the Nazis did with their prisoners. Of course we're going to feed him! What are we – animals?

YEBSLEY: He's hardly bloody human.

SINGE: He's gorr a wife. She runs a f f f f facking fish farm in Kent.

DECLAN: Ah, a wife. I've pulled up a few fucking trees in me time, oh yes, but I never did find meself a little woman of me own. Someone always there in the corner, someone yer could rely on, fer a bit o' warm dinner, some entertaining gentle verbal abuse, nothing too threatening, just a regular ticking off, aye, and er…a bit of sex after mass of a Sunday.

SINGE: Why din't you marry Declan?

DECLAN: Cos with the Belfast Provisionals there's an imperative of secrecy about the whole day to day business of murdering the English and really no separation whatsoever between work and play, so if yer wanted a wife yer had to choose from within the movement as it were. And I don't know what it is about them Belfast RA boys but they had some fucking terrible ugly sisters.

SINGE: (*Snorts with derision.*) Typical Irish. Never use one word where ten will do.

(*During the next CHRISTOPHER puts a slice of bread on a piece of newspaper and prepares to slide it under the door. They watch. The newspaper is pulled rapidly under the gap in the door. This makes DECLAN and YEBSLEY jump.*)

DECLAN: It's a fucking unusual arrangement for us cons to be running a prison of us own.

YEBSLEY: Fucking hell. He's still alive.

SINGE: And awake.

DECLAN: With a fucking appetite!

YEBSLEY: (*To CHRISTOPHER.*) What yer gonna do for him next? Read him an Open University course.

CHRISTOPHER: Not a bad idea. Are you alright Jack? ARE YOU ALRIGHT JACK?

JACK: (*From within.*) I'm f f f f –

SINGE: – he's cold.

JACK: – facking freezin!

CHRISTOPHER: There's a blanket here.

(*CHRISTOPHER slides a blanket under the door. JACK pulls it through.*)

DECLAN: (*To CHRISTOPHER.*) There's something fundamentally good about you Christopher which I have to say I find attractive, but not in an erotic way, yer understand, just something spiritual about yer behaviour which I have to admit I'm a sucker for, having been surrounded all me life by thieving, killing and gangsterism, and that's just me sisters. I'm not a bad person meself, and deep down I've always felt that within me, despite it all, there's a big fat nun trying to get out.

CHRISTOPHER: Now, if we're going to run a prison do you not think that we should give him all the benefits and luxuries you've been asking for for ourselves. Televison?

SINGE: He's not having my telly.

CHRISTOPHER: Recreational drugs?

YEBSLEY: Fuck off.

CHRISTOPHER: A sexual partner?

DECLAN: Not today.

SINGE: No, it's twenty-four hour bang up for him.

DECLAN: It's educational isn't it, being on the other side of the fucking moral divide.

SINGE: What's going off ovver there? There was a fire a minute ago.

DECLAN: Aye, that's part of the plan we're working on.

SINGE: You and your lot couldn't organise a piss up in a brewery.

DECLAN: Let me deconstruct what yer just said there. I've been inside a few breweries and none of them in my experience would even have fucking glasses for a hundred. Then there's yer toilet facilities. Yer wouldn't want the bride's mother squatting down in a corner of the despatch department pissing into a pile of fucking sawdust and –

YEBSLEY: What's the –

DECLAN: – and it could be dangerous, I mean, the thought of a hundred strangers, all of them fucking legless, wandering about among the vats and machines and that, ah, you'd never get a licence from the local magistrate. Mary mother of God! At the end of the day, organising a piss up in a brewery is a fucking impossible task and well beyond the intelligence of ordinary men.

YEBSLEY: What's the break out plan?

DECLAN: It's beautiful in it's simplicity. First off, we set fire to the whole fucking prison –

SINGE: – brilliant.

DECLAN: – then we get everyone to scream the place down like they're all dying and that, then the fire brigade'll feel an imperative to drive onto the site to save our sorry fucking lives. By brute force we commandeer their vehicles and then with a big lump of fire engine we bust through that Hedon Road gate there, turn right, and drive to fuckin Dublin.

SINGE: In a fire engine?

DECLAN: We might have to change horses, as they used to say in the old days, before they had cars, when all they had was horses.

YEBSLEY: I'm in. Count me in, yeah.

SINGE: When's this gonna happen?

DECLAN: Five o'clock today.

SINGE: How long do you think it'll tek yer to drive through Hull in the rush hour?

DECLAN: We're gonna put the siren on.

CHRISTOPHER: Setting fire to the prison? Tell me more.

DECLAN: We've been experimenting with the fires. What yer do is yer stack a load of them steel filing cabinets what we've purloined from Administration, yer stick them round the inside of the windows, making a kind of wall, then you light a little bonfire within that protective circle. It meks it look like the whole fucking wing's alight when in fact the fire's are quite ably contained.

YEBSLEY: I'm up for it. Alright Dex?

DECLAN: It's not you we're interested in. We need some brute force. We need a couple of foot soldiers to scare the shit out of the fire brigade, maybe kill one or two of them so they run off and leave us the engine, and the keys. I don't think you'd scare anybody much is what I'm saying. Not with a haircut like that. Especially them fire brigade lads who can be quite butch themselves, you know.

SINGE: You want Jack don't yer. That's why yer've come over here onto my roof, and done all the smooth talking. He in't mine to give! I'm not lerrin him out, for the good of everyone, and my budgie.

YEBSLEY: I could kill a screw.

SINGE: He dun't want yer! He wants Jack.

DECLAN: (*DECLAN bangs on the door.*) Jack! It's me it is, Declan, one of the RA boys. D'yer fancy killing a screw, and mebbes a fireman or two, we're escaping and we only got seven seats in the bus, as it were, metaphorically speaking.

JACK: You've destroyed my facking prison!

DECLAN: Ach! They'll build yers another one!

SINGE: (*To DECLAN.*) I'm not lerrin him out. He'll kill me. I owe him money. I got the key.

DECLAN: How much did yer make on the horses yesterday?

SINGE: Norr enough. I'm twenty quid short of fifty quid.

DECLAN: Ah, well if it's only money that's a worry to yer, I'll
   talk to the lads. Be back in a tick. With some folding stuff.
   (*DECLAN exits.*)
CHRISTOPHER: Cold. I'm going to find some more blankets.
   Yebsley?
YEBSLEY: What?
CHRISTOPHER: Blanket?
SINGE: Don't ask him, just go. Owt waterproof an'all. It's
   looking a bit black ower Bill's mother's.
   (*CHRISTOPHER exits through the roof hole.*)
YEBSLEY: Are yer gonna stay up here even if it rains?
SINGE: Aye.
YEBSLEY: Yer've lost yer remission for sure Singe. Come and
   break out with us. With Dexie.
SINGE: Declan's break out plan is terrible. However,
   Christopher's Art Teacher plan that's a good un.
   Strategically thought out.
YEBSLEY: Yer what?
SINGE: Dressing up as the Art Teacher. That's strategic. Teks a
   couple a year if I remember. It weren't a rushed thing, not
   merely 'tactical'.
YEBSLEY: What's the difference between tactical and strategic?
SINGE: Tactical is…right…if you pay Raquel Welch to rewire
   yer house, tactically, that's a bloody brilliant idea. For two
   hundred quid yer get one day with Raquel Welch crawling
   round yer house in a fur bikini. However, strategically, in
   the long term, disaster, house burns down, yer lose the wife
   and kids.
YEBSLEY: But without a break out the riot's been pointless
   innit.
   (*Silence during which YEBSLEY slopes off and sulks some.*)
SINGE: Nance?
YEBSLEY: What?
SINGE: They're building bungalows on our kid's allotment. Just
   started. Digging foundations I think.
YEBSLEY: So what?
SINGE: Me brother's at Paull!
YEBSLEY: Oh I'm with yer. Bloody hell.

SINGE: Yeah.

YEBSLEY: How long do they tek to dig foundations?

SINGE: Dunno. A week. A month. Two month. What the fuck do I know work?

YEBSLEY: You an't done that cupboard door yet?

SINGE: Yeah, I'll do it later. It's on me list.

(*Beat.*) Gissa cuddle.

(*Pause.*)

Oh come on squirrel.

YEBSLEY: No.

SINGE: Go on. Been a while.

YEBSLEY: No. I'm not in the mood.

SINGE: What is it love?

YEBSLEY: Time of the month.

SINGE: Oh well. What about Saturday? Saturday night. We could get a baby sitter, go to Dockers. Jed'll bona fide us in like last time.

YEBSLEY: I don't wanna go to fucking Dockers.

SINGE: Where do you wanna go? Money no object.

YEBSLEY: Wun't mind eating out. Lantern.

SINGE: 'kinnel.

YEBSLEY: You said anywhere.

SINGE: Alright, alright. You know I don't like eating in public. I get embarrassed. I start to sweat, throw the bread on the floor, talk bollocks – really loud, apologise when I don't need to, pile the dirty plates up in the middle of the table, I drum on the table with the knife and fork, lick me plate, I'm a fucking idiot!! –

YEBSLEY: – That's what I want to do! Eat out.

SINGE: Alright, alright. Lantern it is. I'll put me suit on.

YEBSLEY: We get a taxi. I'm not gerrin the bus.

SINGE: Anything you want Nance!

YEBSLEY: Right then, you're on.

(*Enter CHRISTOPHER with blankets. SINGE leaps up and goes to look out at Paull now cheery.*)

SINGE: Smashing!

CHRISTOPHER: Good news?

YEBSLEY: He's on a promise.

CHRISTOPHER: They've turned the water off.

YEBSLEY: Fuck. I need a bath.

SINGE: Bath now is it? 'Kinnel, you were gonna kill yersen yesterday.

CHRISTOPHER: Sarcasm's not helpful.

SINGE: I'm a bank robber, not the Samaritans.

CHRISTOPHER: I'm sceptical about the Samaritans. If they really cared, they'd ring you.

YEBSLEY: Singe? Why do they want Jack but not me?

SINGE: Jack's a nuclear weapon. You're not gonna scare no-one are yer. Angry Brigade by name, but not very scary by nature.

(*YEBSLEY sulks off to a corner.*)

I'm sorry. But it's true.

(*CHRISTOPHER joins YEBSLEY and gives him a cigarette.*)

CHRISTOPHER: I would never have thought that this country, I mean England, would produce young men willing to bomb and blow up other Englishmen.

YEBSLEY: Guy Fawkes.

CHRISTOPHER: That was religion. Obviously we'll never see that kind of mediaeval madness again.

YEBSLEY: I'd do it again. It's an international revolution innit. There's Baader Meinhoff and Red Army Faction in Germany, Red Brigade in Italy, IRA, PLO...

CHRISTOPHER: Bit of a difference between those nationalist terrorist movements and your bunch of Cambridge graduates.

YEBSLEY: They wan't all Cambridge.

SINGE: Your lot never killed no-one neither.

YEBSLEY: We tried.

CHRISTOPHER: Proud of it.

YEBSLEY: You killed your father.

CHRISTOPHER: Not proven. I bet if I do a bit of digging I'll find your father lurking.

YEBSLEY: Me dad's dead.

CHRISTOPHER: Sorry.

YEBSLEY: Worked at Radiators. Got black lung disease. Pneumoconiosis. It's same as what miners get. It in't always that serious, but if you're unlucky it can be. Me mam always said of me dad 'if it weren't for bad luck, he wun't have no luck at all'.

CHRISTOPHER: It's a BB King song that.

SINGE: BB King got it off Yebsley's mam.

YEBSLEY: It's the biggest word I know. Pneumoconiosis. When I first saw it written down, I never thought I'd be able to say it even. Yer just break it down. Pneumo. Coni. Osis. Pneumoconiosis. Easy. I used to walk round Hammonds. Looking at like the posh women who had nowt to do all day but go shopping, and I used to think, 'my dad's fucking dead and all you do is shop' and I wanted to blow them all to hell.

CHRISTOPHER: With all due respect, Yebsley, how did you get involved in an elite clique of University educated terrorists?

SINGE: You was roadieing want yer?

YEBSLEY: The Vertebrates –

CHRISTOPHER: Good name for a band.

YEBSLEY: Yeah. Cos it kinda means The People dunnit, like, all living things have a spine don't they?

CHRISTOPHER: Invertebrates don't, but let's not worry about that. And anyway invertebrates are much less likely to buy records.

YEBSLEY: (*Stands.*) You think you're fucking clever don't yer!?

CHRISTOPHER: I'm sorry Alan.

(*YEBSLEY moves off to a corner of the roof.*)

I'm tingling.

SINGE: You alright son?

CHRISTOPHER: Feel strange. That's all. Hungry.

(*CHRISTOPHER goes over to YEBSLEY and offers him a packet of cigarettes.*)

SINGE: Tell him about that girl you met. Deborah.

YEBSLEY: Denise. She was the girlfriend of one of the Angries.

SINGE: They had guns yer know.

YEBSLEY: Denise took me along to a meeting cos I could supply them with whatever they wanted.

SINGE: Drugs.

YEBSLEY: It was this squat in Stoke Newington. They did their meetings proper like, you know, minutes and that. Denise was laughing her head off at summat, dunno what. I wan't laughing. I was watching 'em all. They were tryna pick a target, you know, like you would try and make up a name for a band, you know, just riffing. All their targets was like rich or you know, government people. An' then it fucking struck me, all these rich like tories they had on their list were people just like their dads, cos their dads was all magistrates, and businessmen and that. An' then I spoke. And they all listened. I suggested blowing up people on the Underground, cos no-one's innocent are they, you know not if they, like, work in a bank, or I dunno, somewhere like a big shop.

CHRISTOPHER: And they all looked at you as if you were insane.

YEBSLEY: But that kind of thing works dunnit. Look at the PLO. They killed all them Israeli athletes at the Olympics. They were on telly for four days, and they did kill them, and now everyone knows that the Palestinians are serious about what they want.

CHRISTOPHER: But they wouldn't let you bomb the tube?

YEBSLEY: No. They liked me though.

CHRISTOPHER: They liked you because you're the real thing. Working class, northern.

SINGE: Daft.

YEBSLEY: They went on about me Hull accent. I din't even know I had a fucking accent.

CHRISTOPHER: For them it's a tragedy being born middle class in Basingstoke.

YEBSLEY: I had to kill this bloke, William Batty, he was Mr Big at Fords, Dagenham.

CHRISTOPHER: They didn't want to do that themselves. They got you to do it.

YEBSLEY: Yeah. Three sticks of gelly, in his kitchen. It didn't kill him.

SINGE: But it ruined his kitchen.

(*CHRISTOPHER drops to his knees.*)

CHRISTOPHER: I'm getting wet. Is it raining?

SINGE: No, it's not raining.

CHRISTOPHER: I'm soaking wet.

YEBSLEY: Must be too much cheese in that cracker.

SINGE: 'kinnel. Are you alright son?

CHRISTOPHER: Did you get a snog? From Denise.

SINGE: No, he din't.

YEBSLEY: So I was gonna build me own bomb after that. A big one.

SINGE: Thank fuck they caught yer. I like Hammonds.

CHRISTOPHER: Has Denise ever visited?

YEBSLEY: What? Me? Here? Fuck off.

CHRISTOPHER: Are you a virgin?

(*YEBSLEY stands and squares up to CHRISTOPHER.*)

YEBSLEY: You what?

CHRISTOPHER: Are you a virgin?

SINGE: Oi! That's enough.

CHRISTOPHER: It's a fair question.

(*SINGE comes over with a blanket.*)

SINGE: Let it lie will yer! Yer shun't have come off yer largactyl. And that tab of acid in the cracker can't have helped.

CHRISTOPHER: The acid was in my cracker.

SINGE: Oh fuck.

CHRISTOPHER: It's alright. Was it one tab or two?

SINGE: I dunno.

YEBSLEY: Two.

CHRISTOPHER: Great.

YEBSLEY: You tingling?

CHRISTOPHER: Yeah.

YEBSLEY: Have you done acid before?

CHRISTOPHER: Not in a cream cracker.

YEBSLEY: But you've had trips, yeah.

SINGE: We've all had trips.

CHRISTOPHER: Yeah. Usually good.

YEBSLEY: Good.

CHRISTOPHER: But not always.

YEBSLEY: Ooops!

(*CHRISTOPHER sinks to his knees.*)
What can you see?

SINGE: You can't fly. Alright? You're on a roof.

CHRISTOPHER: Look at the sea!

(*CHRISTOPHER walks towards the edge. SINGE holds him fearful that he'll jump off.*)

SINGE: That's the Humber.

CHRISTOPHER: The water's so clear! Blue! Green! Amber! I can see fish. It's beautiful.

SINGE: (*To YEBSLEY.*) Fucking hell. I'll have one of what he's had!

(*Turns to look at the cemetery. Stage left.*)

CHRISTOPHER: Give me your keys! We must let Jack out. He has to see how clear the water is.

SINGE: No. Gerroff!

(*CHRISTOPHER starts going through SINGE's pockets and the keys are dropped on the floor.*)

CHRISTOPHER: (*Suddenly.*) Why have those people been killed? Singe! Who killed those people?

SINGE: Yer what?

CHRISTOPHER: Hundreds of them. A massacre.

SINGE: (*To YEBSLEY.*) Look what you've fucking done!

CHRISTOPHER: Those bodies. The dead, over there.

SINGE: No-one's been killed Christopher.

CHRISTOPHER: Who killed them?

YEBSLEY: It's the cemetery.

SINGE: Fucking hell.

YEBSLEY: Point him t'other way.

(*SINGE tries to turn him. During the next SINGE and YEBSLEY manhandle him off the roof into the wing.*)

CHRISTOPHER: No! Look at them. Old men, women, lying in mud, drowning in mud, crawling naked. Ha, look he's got a suit on, ha! His best suit. Herringbone. Look, look! A baby. On her own. In the mud. A baby. Who left that baby all alone in the mud!? I need to help her. She'll drown, look –

SINGE: – We've got to get him off the roof.

YEBSLEY: Alright, alright. Come on Chris. We'll go inside now, yeah.

CHRISTOPHER: – that child is drowning in mud!

SINGE: It'll be alright! There's not so much to see. Come on son.

YEBSLEY: You can have a lie down.

CHRISTOPHER: NO!!

(*SINGE and YEBSLEY freeze, there's an import in CHRISTOPHER's voice.*)

I have to tell you! Both of you, my friend Yebsley, Singe, I am Christ, Jesus of Nazareth, Yeshua,

SINGE: Oh fuck. Come on let's gerr him inside.

CHRISTOPHER: After China, the earthquake, I argued with my Father, with God, I have come to save you. You Yebsley, you, in particular. To show my father it can be done! To give you hope Yebsley! My plan, my escape plan, a gift, to give you hope –

(*They shepherd him off the roof. It darkens somewhat. It starts to rain, slowly at first. Enter DECLAN carrying a rolled up newspaper.*)

DECLAN: Singe! Singe!!

(*He looks around. KATH comes out on to the balcony.*)

KATH: Eh! You!

DECLAN: Hello love. What is it?

KATH: Have you seen Yebsley?

DECLAN: You mean, the young mentally ill fellah?!

KATH: Yebsley.

DECLAN: What shall I say if I sees him?

KATH: Nothing.

DECLAN: Nothing at all. That's difficult for me, I'm a bit of a talker you see. I'll tell him you was asking after him and that.

KATH: Thank you. It's gonna rain.

DECLAN: You'll not be wrong there.

(*KATH goes in. DECLAN finds the ring of keys which have fallen on the floor. He goes to the broom cupboard.*)

Jack. Jack! Eh, big fellah! Are yer awake?

(*A stream of urine comes trickling between his legs.*)

Ah, Jesus! Yer pissing on me boots, ah well, I suppose
that's good news that your well, and everything's working
perfectly. I'm gonna let you out Jack. D'you hear me! I'm
gonna let you out. But there's an imperative around the
conditions for your release, alright, are yer listening to me
big fellah? It's me Declan, of the Irish. Dex.

JACK: I don't want to be let out. I like it in here. I can get some
f f f f f facking finking done.

DECLAN: What the hell are you thinking about Jack?

JACK: Facking Life.

DECLAN: I got a little something for you here, Jack, from the
boys. Kind of a present for you. I think you'll like it.
(*Takes a big knife out of the newspaper.*)

JACK: What is it?

DECLAN: A fucking big knife. The screws are going to storm
the prison and we thought you might want to take the
opportunity to you know, like, er…kill a few of them. Does
that idea appeal to you Jack?

JACK: Yes.

DECLAN: Grand. So, I'm gonna open this door alright, and
I'll keep out of your way. I'll leave the knife on the floor
for yous. I'll step back out the way like. I'll make a special
effort not to intrude on your personal space like.
(*DECLAN opens the door gingerly, and quickly puts some space
between himself and JACK by moving down stage left. JACK
emerges. He picks up the knife. Inspects it.*)
Yer see we've set fire to the wing. That'll tempt the fire
brigade in, cos they've got an imperative to save our lives
don't yer see. Then you kill a few of them with that big
fuck off knife there and they'll all run off and leave us with
a big lump of fire engine, and then we batter our way out
of this fucking godforsaken place. Aye.

JACK: There is a sound of abundance of rain. Kings chapter
eighteen, verse f f f f facking forty-four.

DECLAN: Aye, it's starting.

JACK: Where's Singe?

DECLAN: Don't know Jack. Come on then. Follow me.

JACK: He owes me money.

DECLAN: I wouldn't worry about a little thing like that when yer got the chance of escaping this place.

(*JACK finds the budgie. He takes it out of the cage.*)

Oh Jack, please. It's an innocent little budgie, can't think for itself, not really responsible for anything. And there's no meat on it worth talking about.

(*JACK bites the head off and chucks the body on the ground. He spits the head out.*)

JACK: Life for life, eye for eye, tooth for tooth, hand for hand, foot for foot, burning for burning, wound for wound, stripe for stripe.

DECLAN: Aye, it's a grand book that first one. None of that messing about with er…you know, forgiveness, and love and that. Aye, the New Testament and the Old Testament is like the modern day difference between the Guardian and the Daily Mail.

(*Enter SINGE. He stops dead seeing JACK with knife.*)

SINGE: Edna. Oh bugger.

JACK: Where's my facking money Singe?

SINGE: I'm twennie quid short. I can give yer thirty odd.

(*JACK laughs.*)

DECLAN: Forget the money Jack. Come on! If yous comes with me, yous can be outa here in half an hour.

JACK: C wing's on f f f f f – ablaze. My church is this end of C wing.

DECLAN: No Jack, you're getting the wrong end of the stick there. Them fire's all nicely contained, we're making it look like the whole bloody wing's on fire. The church is not in any of our schemes. We're trying to draw the fire engine in, then you kill a few of them, they all run off, and then we get inside the fire engine and we're away. It's a kind of Trojan Horse strategy if you like, but in reverse, painted red, with Denis written on the front, and a big fucking diesel engine attached, and no Trojan soldiers any fucking where.

SINGE: He doesn't want to kill firemen. Do you Jack?

JACK: I was gonna be a f f f …trainee.

DECLAN: You don't have to kill them, you could just frighten
    them a bit.

(*Enter YEBSLEY. He is immediately wary of JACK.*)

YEBSLEY: 'kinnel. Who let him out?

JACK: (*Mainly addressed to Declan.*) Hull is my f f f facking
    favourite prison. A facking lovely prison this was, mice
    in the canteen that's all, a f f f f few facking mice that's
    all. You facking…you facking…why d'yer do this to my
    facking favourite lovely prison…my weights…eh?…my
    lovely weights…my lovely heavy weights…facking gone…
    you stupid cant…Albany prison, facking Wales innit, I
    bin in there, facking terrible! He said I was mentally ill!
    Cheeky Cunt! I said I might be facking mentally ill, but
    at least I'm not facking Welsh. The Scrubs, too near the
    facking missus. Armley, didn't respect me, no respect, no
    facking respect – I had to bite someone's f f f facking face
    off, still no respect, no facking respect, can you credit it.
    Lincoln – the vicar was a facking queer. God spoke to me,
    he said the same fing over and over again for three facking
    days – 'Jack! Kill the arse bandit. Jack! kill the arse bandit.
    Jack! Kill the arse bandit. Jack! Kill the arse bandit! Jack!
    Kill the facking filthy arse bandit! Come on Jack! Kill the
    arse bandit! Jack! Facking hell, what yer doing son, kill the
    arse bandit, you have my permission, kill the facking arse
    bandit!'. So I did, I had to, I want getting no facking sleep.
    Look at it! It was a facking lovely prison this. I got the sun
    in the mornings. Seagulls! Seagulls are alright, I facking
    hate pigeons. You cunt!

(*There's the noise of CHRISTOPHER trashing the chapel.*)

SINGE: Where's miladdo?

JACK: What the facking hell's that now! You! Talk!

YEBSLEY: That's er…the new blok…Christopher. He's in
    the chapel. He's trashing the joint. I gorr out cos o' what
    the Irish said, you know, like it was out of bounds. He's
    completely fucking flipped. Chucking the bibles out the
    window, smashing up the whatsaname, and all the altar
    and that –

(*There is the sound of breaking glass as* CHRISTOPHER *trashes one of the chapel windows.*)

Fuck. He's started on the windows now.

JACK: That's facking God's house that is.

SINGE: He's new.

YEBSLEY: He dun't mean it.

SINGE: It's nothing personal to you Jack.

JACK: I'll facking kill him.

YEBSLEY: He's having a bad trip. Acid. He's only smashing the chapel up.

SINGE: Shutup Yebsley.

YEBSLEY: Oh shit.

JACK: He's facking dead.

DECLAN: Come on Jack, we better go now.

JACK: I don't want to escape as it happens.

DECLAN: Eh?

SINGE: Yer happy here aren't yer?

JACK: Yeah.

SINGE: He's gorr everything he wants inside Declan. He's gorr his gym and he's gorr his church.

JACK: Yeah. And it's very difficult getting a job with this tattoo.

DECLAN: Yer could stick an elastoplast over the worst of it.

SINGE: He dun't wanna go. Come on Dex. It in't difficult to understand why.

YEBSLEY: I'll come with you Dex. Please. Yeah?

SINGE: You're not going nowhere. Anyhow, it don't look like that fire engine of yours is gonna come in anyhow. The wing's been on fire for quarter of an hour and not even a siren.

(CHRISTOPHER *is heard approaching, laughing.*)

DECLAN: They godda come in. They can't let us all burn to death.

SINGE: The only reason they'd wanna save you is so that they can enjoy kicking the shit out of you.

(*It is now raining hard. Enter* CHRISTOPHER *wearing vestments.*)

CHRISTOPHER: I've just been in the chapel and my father told me I've got to build an ark because it's going to rain forever more. I said 'fuck off Dad!'

JACK: Curse God and die! Curse God and Die!

CHRISTOPHER: Job. Chapter something verse something. Ha, I don't know. Jack. My friend.

(*CHRISTOPHER goes straight towards JACK with arms out stretched.*)

SINGE: Chris! Don't touch him!

YEBSLEY: 'kinnel.

(*CHRISTOPHER stops.*)

CHRISTOPHER: They don't want me to touch you Jack.

SINGE: No son, please, forget it, don't touch him.

YEBSLEY: Jesus.

CHRISTOPHER: I can see inside your body.

SINGE: He's alright Jack, he's just tripping.

YEBSLEY: He's had a couple of tabs of acid. He dun't mean out by it.

CHRISTOPHER: Lungs, heart, spleen, diaphragm, red corpuscles. Look at them, racing around in there, racing, pumping round, ha –

(*CHRISTOPHER hugs JACK. Couple of beats. JACK stabs him and CHRISTOPHER dies.*)

SINGE: Jesus.

YEBSLEY: Oh fuck.

DECLAN: Mary Mother of God.

YEBSLEY: You killed him.

JACK: Course I facking did. Right. I'm off. Singe. Sort this out will yer! If anyone asks. You did it.

(*As soon as JACK is at a safe distance, SINGE kneels down beside CHRISTOPHER.*)

SINGE: (*To DECLAN.*) Go on then. You've got what you want. If you make it to Dublin, have a pint of Guinness on me, and I hope it chokes you.

DECLAN: Ah, now Singe, me old butty, that's no way to –

SINGE: – Gerr off my fucking roof!

(*DECLAN goes. SINGE kneels down beside CHRISTOPHER desperately attending to him as if there is a chance that he might live.*)

Come on Chris! Come on! You're alright! You're gonna be alright. Come on!!

YEBSLEY: He's dead.

(*SINGE gives up.*)

SINGE: I liked him.

YEBSLEY: What we gonna do with him?

SINGE: Better tell someone. Call an ambulance.

YEBSLEY: (*Assertively.*) No. He's dead. We'll just stash the body.

SINGE: That's not decent.

YEBSLEY: You're too decent for yer own good, you. I'm not gonna let you fuck up now. You're out in two month, or –

SINGE: Fat chance of that now.

(*During the next SINGE implodes, he sits on the roof floor in the pool of blood and cries.*)

I can't do it. I can't do another three year. I don't know what I'm gonna do Yebs! I can't do any more.

YEBSLEY: This is all my fault.

SINGE: Eh?

YEBSLEY: The riot. I started it din't I.

(*YEBSLEY starts dragging CHRISTOPHER's body into the broom cupboard.*)

SINGE: What yer doing?

YEBSLEY: Gonna stash him in here. Lock him in. It'll be all locked up like before the riot started. The screws'll not think of looking in here, ever, why would they. It might be a month, two month, a year afore they find him, by which time you'll be out.

SINGE: Someone'll have seen.

YEBSLEY: All them cameras are pointing over to C wing. For the fires.

SINGE: It's not right.

YEBSLEY: Giss the keys.

(*YEBSLEY more takes the keys from SINGE than has them given to him and locks the broom cupboard.*)

There. Yer gonna keep yer remission.

SINGE: Tek a miracle.

YEBSLEY: Come on, it's raining, let's gerr inside.

SINGE: No. I'm staying up here.

YEBSLEY: Yer'll catch yer death.

(*YEBSLEY goes down to the edge of the roof, looking up at the flats. He gives it a couple of beats. He turns and heads down into A wing through the hole in the roof. He is just out of sight when* –)

KATH: Yebsley!

(*YEBSLEY sticks his head out of the roof hole.*)

YEBSLEY: (*Pause. Surly.*) What?

KATH: Just wanted to say hello.

YEBSLEY: Hello. Happy now?!

KATH: What's gorr into you?

YEBSLEY: You've gorr a bain.

KATH: I've gorr a niece. Me sister's gorr a baby.

YEBSLEY: You're not married then?!

KATH: Do I look married?

YEBSLEY: I thought you was married! Will yer come visit me. Please!

KATH: Yeah. Alright. Be a bit mad, but yeah, alright.

YEBSLEY: Bring some punk in. I can have records, on headphones.

KATH: Yeah. Can you have paintings on your walls?

YEBSLEY: Yeah. I could do wi' some posters going up.

KATH: No, paintings. You could hang some of my paintings.

YEBSLEY: You're a painter?

KATH: Yeah.

YEBSLEY: I thought you was at college?

KATH: I'm at Art College aren't I.

YEBSLEY: Fucking hell. Are you gonna be a proper painter then?

KATH: Huh. Probably end up teaching.

YEBSLEY: Teaching what?

KATH: Art!

(*SINGE's head lifts. YEBSLEY gives him a look.*)

YEBSLEY: You're gonna be an art teacher?

KATH: Yeah.

YEBSLEY: Will you visit me?

KATH: I thought you'd never ask.

YEBSLEY: They might send me to Leeds, I dunno, Brixton.

KATH: London?

YEBSLEY: Yeah. London, mebbe. Yer could get a job teaching
    Art, couldn't you, in a prison mebbe.

KATH: Yeah, mebbe, be a laugh.

    (*KATH goes in.*)

SINGE: I'm never wrong.

YEBSLEY: Ta, Singe.

    (*YEBSLEY gives SINGE an extra blanket and metaphorically
    tucks him up. YEBSLEY exits the roof. SINGE sits in his chair,
    in the rain wraps a blanket around him. He lights a cigarette.
    The lights dim, the rain beats down, the worst yet SINGE's head
    goes down. He's asleep. Johnny Cash sings 'Bridge Over Troubled
    Water' from American 4 (at least the first two verses including
    the talk over bit or as much of the song as possible). It's like the
    voice of God. SINGE does not hear it. At one point in the song
    there is a flash of light from within the broom cupboard.*)

SCENE THREE

(*The lights come up. SINGE is asleep. The rain has stopped. It is bright
day. Enter the GOVERNOR from stage left. He is in uniform. He looks
around the roof. Inspects SINGE.*)

OFFICER: (*Off.*) Y'alright there sir?!

GOVERNOR: Yes thank, you. It's only Calvert. He's no trouble.
    (*Waking him.*) Come on Calvert! Singe! Morning. Come on.
    You'll catch your death.

SINGE: (*Wakes up.*) What day is it?

GOVERNOR: Friday. It's all over. There's a bus waiting for you.

SINGE: Where am I going?

GOVERNOR: Ten pin bowling. Where do you want to go?
    Leeds? Manchester? Dartmoor?

SINGE: 15 Tanfield Grove.

GOVERNOR: Look Singe, why don't you get yourself down the
    hospital block. Looks like you might have a bit of fever.

SINGE: I'm not leaving this roof.

GOVERNOR: It's over.

SINGE: I weren't involved. Not in owt. I'll go if you tell me I aren't gonna lose me remission.

GOVERNOR: Why didn't you go to B wing when it all kicked off, like everyone else?

SINGE: I tried. They wun't let me through. I an't been off this roof once. Worr happened. Did they make a break out?

GOVERNOR: They agreed to give themselves up to Hull Officers only. And they wanted the Chairman of the Board of Visitors to be there. He's there now.

SINGE: I wan't involved.

GOVERNOR: Course you weren't involved. You're out in three months.

SINGE: Two.

GOVERNOR: Two is it? I'll miss you.

SINGE: There was a nice lad. Unusual. Christopher summat. What's that actor? In that film. The Graduate. Short arse. Big nose.

GOVERNOR: Anne Bancroft.

SINGE: No! Fucking hell. Jewish name!

GOVERNOR: Dustin Hoffman.

SINGE: Christopher Hoffman. Jack stabbed him. He's dead.

GOVERNOR: Fuck.

SINGE: The body is in there. Here.

(*SINGE gives the GOVERNOR the key. The GOVERNOR opens the broom cupboard. It's empty.*)

GOVERNOR: In here?

(*SINGE gets up and looks in the cupboard.*)

SINGE: Fucking hell. Jack killed him. And me and Yebs put his body out the way in here. I'm the only one with a key.

(*The GOVERNOR looks at a clipboard he carries.*)

GOVERNOR: Hoffman? Hoffman? Hock. Hoggard. No.

SINGE: He was new. They couldn't find a file on him. He was delivered Tuesday. Cat A. So he said.

GOVERNOR: We had no new stock delivered Tuesday. You've got a fever Singe.

Where's Bowden?

SINGE: He's a good lad is Yebs. He's young. Bit confused. Weren't you ever young and confused?

GOVERNOR: No. I always new I was gay. Unusual name. Yebsley. I've never understood that nickname of his.

(*SINGE drifts off and takes another look down the river to Paull.*)

SINGE: His brother used to work for Yorkshire Electricity Board.

(*Beat.*) And Alan used to wear his jacket.

GOVERNOR: What are you looking at?

SINGE: Eh?

GOVERNOR: You're looking for something?

SINGE: Oh nowt much.

GOVERNOR: 336! Calvert!

(*They exit stage left along the roof.*)
(*To black.*)

Richard Bean
Plays One

THE MENTALISTS

UNDER THE WHALEBACK

THE GOD BOTHERERS

with an Introduction by Paul Miller

ISBN 1 84002 569 7 • £14.99

'The Mentalists confirms Richard Bean as a writer of beguiling originality with a gift for both laugh-out-loud dialogue and a sympathetic understanding of the darker recesses of the human heart'
Charles Spencer, *The Daily Telegraph* on *The Mentalists*

'An instant modern classic'
Kate Bassett, *The Independent on Sunday*
on *Under the Whaleback*

'Richard Bean must have had a hell of a life'
Michael Billington, *The Guardian* on *The God Botherers*

www.oberonbooks.com

Richard Bean
Plays Two

TOAST

MR ENGLAND

SMACK FAMILY ROBINSON

HONEYMOON SUITE

with an Introduction by Jack Bradley

ISBN 1 84002 662 7 • £14.99

'Toast is as funny, touching, and brilliant an account of men at work as any we have had since David Storey's *The Changing Room*'
The Spectator on *Toast*

'Cunningly effective'
The Times on *Mr England*

'A brilliant, black satire that plays on an Ortonesque reversal of values. Bean distributes deftly crafted, razor-sharp lines among a cast of characters who would sooner snort them than deliver them'
The Guardian on *Smack Family Robinson*

'Suddenly with four new plays opening within 12 months, Richard Bean has become the playwright of the moment and now, in *Honeymoon Suite*, his most prestigious play to date, he has written what seems like the perfect play'
The Financial Times on *Honeymoon Suite*

www.oberonbooks.com